T0133827

Reconfiguring the Firewall

Reconfiguring the Firewall

Recruiting Women to Information Technology across Cultures and Continents

edited by
Carol J. Burger, Elizabeth G. Creamer, and Peggy S. Meszaros

A K Peters, Ltd.
Wellesley, Massachusetts

Editorial, Sales, and Customer Service Office

A K Peters, Ltd.
888 Worcester Street, Suite 230
Wellesley, MA 02482
www.akpeters.com

Library of Congress Cataloging-in-Publication Data

Reconfiguring the firewall : recruiting women to information technology across cultures and continents / edited by Carol J. Burger, Elizabeth G. Creamer, Peggy S. Meszaros.
    p. cm.
    Includes bibliographical references and index.
    ISBN-13: 978-1-56881-314-1 (alk. paper)
    ISBN-10: 1-56881-314-7 (alk. paper)
    1. Computers and women. 2. Women in computer science. 3. Women computer industry employees--Recruiting. 4. Information technology--Study and teaching--United States. I. Burger, Carol J. II. Creamer, Elizabeth G. III. Meszaros, Peggy S. (Peggy Sisk), 1938- IV. Title: Recruiting women to information technology.
    QA76.9.W65R33 2007
    004.082--dc22
                                  2006038895

Cover image © 2007 JupiterImages Corporation

Printed in Canada
11 10 09 08 07   10 9 8 7 6 5 4 3 2 1

Contents

Acknowledgments   vii

Part I: Introduction

Sizing Up the Information Technology Firewall   3
Carol J. Burger, Elizabeth G. Creamer, and Peggy S. Meszaros

1. Predicting Women's Interest in and Choice of a Career in
   Information Technology: A Statistical Model   15
   Elizabeth G. Creamer, Soyoung Lee, and Peggy S. Meszaros

Part II: The Secondary School Level

Revisiting Culture, Time, and Information Processing Factors in
Connecting to Girls' Interest and Choice of an Information
Technology Career at the Secondary Level   41
Peggy S. Meszaros and Jane Butler Kahle

2. Changing the High School Culture to Promote Interest in
   Information Technology Careers among High-Achieving Girls   51
   Ann Howe, Sarah Berenson, and Mladen Vouk

3. Examining Time as a Factor in Young Women's Information
   Technology Career Decisions   65
   Sarah Berenson, Laurie Williams, Joan Michael, and Mladen Vouk

4. Information Processing and Information Technology Career
   Interest and Choice among High School Students   77
   Peggy S. Meszaros, Soyoung Lee, and Anne Laughlin

Part III: The Post-Secondary Level

Considering Individual, Social, and Cultural Factors in the
Construction of Women's Interest and Persistence in Information
Technology at the Post-Secondary Level   99
Elizabeth G. Creamer and Lesley H. Parker

5. A Cultural Perspective on Gender Diversity in Computing   109
   Lenore Blum, Carol Frieze, Orit Hazzan, and M. Bernardine Dias

6. Sociopolitical Factors and Female Students' Choice of
    Information Technology Careers: A South African Perspective   135
    Cecille Marsh

7. Women's Entry to Graduate Study in Computer Science and
    Computer Engineering in the United States   147
    J. McGrath Cohoon and Holly Lord

8. Women's Interest in Information Technology: The Fun Factor   161
    Bettina Bair and Miranda Marcus

Part IV: Information Technology Careers

Women and Information Technology Careers   179
Carol J. Burger and William Aspray

9. Women on the Edge of Change: Employees in United States
    Information Technology Companies   191
    Sarah Kuhn and Paula Rayman

10. Multiple Pathways toward Gender Equity in the United States
    Information Technology Workforce   211
    Paula G. Leventman

11. Barriers to Women in Science: A Cautionary Tale for the
    Information Technology Community   239
    Lesley Warner and Judith Wooller

Part V: Conclusion

Refocusing Our Lens to Reconfigure the Firewall   253
*Peggy S. Meszaros, Elizabeth G. Creamer, Carol J. Burger,
and Anne Laughlin*

Appendix A   261

Appendix B   263

Appendix C   267

Contributors   269

Index   273

Acknowledgments

The editors wish to express thanks and appreciation for the support and encouragement of Ruta Sevo and Jolene Jesse, former and current, respectively, Program Directors of the Research on Gender in Science and Engineering at the National Science Foundation, and our thanks to Caroline Wardle, Program Officer in Computer and Network Systems. We also wish to acknowledge the financial support by the National Science Foundation for the project that led us to envision this volume and helped support the conference from which these chapters came. We also wish to thank Cisco Systems, Inc., Texas Instruments, Inc., and Microsoft Corporation for their contributions to the conference Crossing Cultures, Changing Lives: Integrating Research on Girls' Choices of IT Careers that was held July 31–August 3, 2005.

This volume reflects the equal and interdisciplinary collaboration among the three editors. From the nascent idea for an investigation about how girls make career decisions that can lead to jobs in computer-based fields, to seeing the need for an international gathering about the topic, and finally, to the development and production of this book, we have worked together in a way that has made the outcome greater than the sum of its parts.

The Women and Information Technology team at Virginia Tech has had the good fortune to work with two able and conscientious doctoral students, Anne Laughlin and Soyoung Lee. They have helped us in innumerable ways over the five years since the inception of this project, through the planning and organization of the conference, to the project completion as presented in this volume. In addition to her role as coauthor of one of the chapters, Anne Laughlin played a particularly influential part in preparing the final manuscript for publication. Anne reviewed all of the chapters and edited them to eliminate duplication while linking their key findings to the thread that flows through the volume. She made substantive contributions to the concluding chapter and developed the index. We are grateful for her timely and insightful contributions.

We thank the conference participants who helped frame the research and action items we have included and those who completed manuscripts for this book. We especially acknowledge the help of Bill Aspray, Jane Butler Kahle, and Lesley Parker, who reviewed abstracts, acted as discussion leaders at the conference, reviewed and commented upon chapter submissions, and coauthored the introductions to the parts of the book.

This material is based upon work supported by the National Science Foundation under Grant No. HRD-0120458. Any opinions, findings, and conclusions or recommedations expressed in this material are those of the author(s) and do not necessarily reflect the views of the National Science Foundation.

Carol J. Burger, Elizabeth G. Creamer, and Peggy S. Meszaros

Part I

Introduction

Sizing up the Information Technology Firewall

Carol J. Burger, Elizabeth G. Creamer, and Peggy S. Meszaros

Carla, a sophomore in high school, can't remember when she first used a computer; there was always one at home and at school to use. She enjoys using the computer to communicate with her friends, find information for schoolwork, and play games. She doesn't think computers are just for boys and doesn't think of herself as a "nerd." Her mom says that Carla is the member of the family they call on to "fix the computer" when something goes wrong. Carla's mom thinks it's important for Carla to have a good career. When asked about career plans, both Carla and her mom think she should go into the same business as her father and brother—they are bill collectors.

Why would a young woman who has the interest and ability to use computers not think about pursuing a computer-based career, such as one in information technology (IT)? What was missing from the advice she was getting that resulted in her not seeking out more information about IT careers? When we began contemplating these questions, we wondered if girls who consider careers that are not traditional for women face different developmental demands as they process conflicting information, wrestle with stereotypes, and, at times, encounter negative feedback. We further wondered how girls' interests vary across cultures and regions. As we rethink these questions in light of new scholarship that specifically targets the career decision-making processes, areas of future research are uncovered and practical implications appear.

In the process of uncovering research about the factors that influence and support IT career choices for women, we found some interesting cultural differences in girls' perceptions of career paths open to them. We found evidence that the "women in IT" question has received worldwide attention through a number of international conferences. The GASAT (Gender and Science and Technology Association) conference encourages the presentation of research about all aspects of gender differentiation in science and technology education and employment, while the European Gender and ICT Symposium has merged with the Christina Conference on Women's Studies and now has a broader cultural focus. There are also regional and local conferences that feature research about women and information technology, such as AusWIT, the Australian Women in IT Conference, and the WINIT International and Interdisciplinary Conference on Gender, Technology, and the ICT Workplace at the Information Systems Institute at the University of Salford, UK.

The three coeditors of this volume first began talking about an international conference in 2002. We envisioned a relatively small conference structured for the maximum amount of interaction between and among participants and presenters, and where the travel expenses of some of the presenters would be supported in order to ensure that participants could come from around the world. With support from the National Science Foundation (NSF), Microsoft, Texas Instruments, and Cisco, we developed and produced a conference in Oxford in the United Kingdom in July 2005. We invited three well-known discussants for the three sections of the conference. Drs. Jane Butler Kahle, Miami University; Lesley Parker, Curtin University, Perth, Australia; and William Aspray, Indiana University, are scholars who are well known and respected for their research about women and STEM (science, technology, engineering, and mathematics) careers.

The conference attracted 50 participants from all over the world. Participants at the conference included researchers who had been funded by Ruta Sevo in the Program for Gender Equity, and Caroline Wardle of what was then called the IT Workforce Grants at NSF. They came from Australia, Africa, Asia, North America, and Europe. The international group of scholars who gathered in Oxford discussed a wide range of issues that reflect the rapid transitions that are occurring within IT. Friendly differences quickly became apparent as conference participants raised questions about a number of assumptions that have framed research about women and IT. Participants raised such provocative questions as:

- Does the academic convention of emphasizing gender differences and downplaying areas where there are no significant gender differences in research papers unintentionally serve to perpetuate gender stereotypes about the place for women in the IT world?
- Is the pipeline metaphor still useful given that women enter computing jobs in numerous ways?
- Does the assumption that there are no longer significant gender differences in access to computers minimize pressing issues of access that continue in non-Western countries, particularly Africa?

Goals and Audience for this Book

The primary goals of this book are to synthesize key research findings and conference discussions that cross the secondary, post-secondary, and professional settings in different countries; disseminate results of global research conducted about women's participation in information technology and education; and establish an agenda of critical areas for future research about women and IT. The chapters in this book also touch on retention issues at all levels.

The audiences for this work include K–12 educators, college faculty and advisors who implement activities and programs designed to increase interest in IT, those who fund these programs, academic researchers, and IT industry professionals committed to a diverse workforce. These practitioners and scholars will find the studies in this volume illuminating and prescriptive as they design new, more effective intervention programs and plan future research.

What Is IT?

Information and communication technology is a field where change is so rapid that it is difficult for practitioners, researchers, funding agencies, and policymakers to promote agendas that keep pace with it. Nowhere is this more evident than in the disagreement among researchers and practitioners about the utility of the term "information technology" to embrace fields of study as diverse as computer engineering, information systems, network engineering, and computer science. The term information technology (IT) or, as it is known outside of the US, information and communications technology (ICT), embraces both computer and communications hardware and the software used to automate and augment clerical, administrative, and management tasks in organizations. It is a term that includes all forms of technology used to create, store, exchange, and utilize information in its various forms including business data, conversations, still images, motion pictures, and multimedia presentations. The interweaving of IT, telecommunications, and data networking gave rise to ICT; Western Europeans favor the term ICT, in part, because it may be more attractive to women who favor career options in a field that is more "people oriented" than hardware oriented. Our use of IT is explicit because we are concentrating on the study of computer-related fields rather than on the adoption or use of technological inventions and products.

At the beginning of the IT revolution, most of the innovation was produced by computer scientists and computer engineers. In the mid-1980s when US women's graduation rates from computer science (CS) departments rose to 37%, there was great hope that the burgeoning IT field would be a place where women could participate equally with their male peers. However, in the later part of the twentieth century, the rate of women entering CS declined and has remained virtually flat for the past 20 years. For example, US women received 32.5% of the bachelor's degrees in CS in 1981; 29.6% in 1991; and 27.6% in 2001 (NSF, 1994; NSF, 2004). The percentage decline was not more startling because the number of males who chose CS as a major also declined over this period; this mitigated the percentage decline of females in the major even while the total number of female CS majors was in a steep decline. Meanwhile, the college graduation rates for women in the life sciences and mathematics reached parity with men, but the promise of equity in a physical science, engineering, or technology (SET)[1] field did not materialize. Over time, the participation of women and minorities in the technology explosion has been uneven and limited even as the number of IT job openings increased.

Since 1980, science and engineering jobs have been created four times faster than other US jobs. The Americans who fill them, however, are aging and stagnant in number, leaving others to fill the gap. The National Science Board (2004) predicts that between now and 2012, the US will need to train nearly 2 million more scientists and engineers. While women represent 46.6% of the US workforce, only about 35% of the US IT workforce is female (Information Technology Association of America, 2003). More disturbingly, women hold only 10% of the top US IT positions, and fewer women are rising up the IT leadership ladder than in the past (Gibson, 1997; D'Agostino, 2003). The impact on society of the relative absence of women in IT careers is that women's perspectives and concerns are not reflected in the design, development, implementation, and assessment of emerging technologies. There are also economic implications for women if they are not prepared for a career in one of the fastest growing and financially rewarding career opportunities. To fill the gap in IT workers, women must consider IT as a viable career path. What is required to recruit women into IT careers in any significant numbers? Our purpose is to uncover the factors that influence females' interest and choice of IT as a career field, and how this varies across race and culture; this purpose is at the heart of the previous question and forms the basis for this volume.

Access to technology is still the number one issue for people in developing countries. Sophia Huyer (2003) of the Institute for Women's Studies and Gender Studies at the University of Toronto, Canada, reported on the relative numbers of women with access to IT education and training in light of the gendered roles and sociocultural customs these women face. Huyer, Hafkin, Ertl, and Dryburgh (2005) analyzed the worldwide gender digital divide, focusing on developing regions of Africa, Latin America, and Asia. Information from the 33 countries they examined showed that, even when controlling for infiltration of technology (computers and Internet access as well as cell phones and fax machines) into a particular society, women were still less likely to have access to IT than their male counterparts. The gender gap among IT workers is radically altered when governments, such as those in India, Singapore, and some parts of Africa, promote IT jobs as a key element of economic development.

The disparity in numbers of women studying and working in scientific and technical fields has been discussed and studied from the perspective of two frameworks: as a result of individual barriers, such as innate gender differences in ability or socialization factors, or as a result of institutional barriers, such as the scientific culture and male-oriented pedagogy and curricula. Most researchers now reject the idea that there is a genetic difference in mathematical or scientific ability between males and females, but they continue to seek to determine the interplay among individual differences, cultural socialization, and institutional policies—both written and unwritten—that lead women to dismiss IT and other SET fields as viable career options. As research about women's interest in SET fields has grown increasingly more sophisticated over the last twenty years, research has moved to the use of comprehensive models that encompass both individual and structural qualities.

Challenges in Recruiting Women to IT

Some researchers have struggled to understand why even proactive efforts to recruit women to degree programs in computer-based fields often are not successful (e.g., Cohoon, Baylor, & Chen, 2003). Even when they have both skills and interest in computers, females of all ages consistently express less confidence in their technological skills (Gurer & Camp, 1998; Lee, 2003; Sax, Lindholm, Astin, Korn, & Mahoney, 2005) and often fail to make a connection between skills, interests, and career choice (O'Brien & Fassinger, 1993). A number of researchers have been baffled by the discovery that, unlike men, women with little access to or knowledge of computer applications are more likely to express interest in the field than those who have had broader exposure. Perhaps because stereotypical views are often explicitly or implicitly reinforced in many interactions about careers, we found in our own study that women's interest in IT diminished over time and as they had more interactions with others about the field (Creamer, Lee, & Meszaros, in this volume). While it is unlikely that unrealistic views about the nature of the field will translate to persistence, it is equally evident that considerably more attention is required to evaluate the types of information and strategies that are effective in recruiting young women to IT.

Increasing the number of women of all races and cultures who are interested in IT requires considerably more ingenuity than simply delivering information in an engaging way. Initiatives, like summer programs, are apt to be effective when they invite parental involvement and manage to communicate personal concern and interest in young women who are participating in the activity. While emphasizing that the field has the potential for lucrative positions seems to influence men, women are more likely to be interested in activities that portray the creative aspects of the field and its potential to address pressing social problems. Activities that engage students in reflecting about skills, interests, and values and how these match a number of career options are critical to making a well-informed career choice. Recruiting efforts can have a significant impact on the career interests of women when they extend over a long enough period of time so that a sense of community and trust is fostered.

Understanding Factors that Predict Women's Interest in IT

Our interdisciplinary team has used self-authorship theory as a research framework (Baxter Magolda, 1999). At the center of the Information Technology Career Interest and Choice (ITCIC) model we developed is a set of variables related to how students process new information to make career decisions (see Chapter 1 for a full discussion of this model). The ITCIC model indicates that many students lack the skills to evaluate information about unfamiliar careers and to offset negative or stereotypical information they hear about IT and related fields. Understanding this process has particularly strong implications for students from low socioeconomic status (SES) backgrounds, rural settings, and/or where they have no one in their immediate circle of trusted others who works in an IT field. One of the greatest challenges faced by educators in the IT field is to present career information in a way that encourages students to consider career options that are not modeled by people in their immediate environment.

Our model, as well as much additional research, underscores that parents are integral to the career choice process, even through the college years. It is important to provide materials directly targeted at educating parents about career options in IT. Involving parents in pre-college activities designed to expose students to information about a variety of IT careers is likely to have a direct impact on women's interest in IT. Parents, advisors, and parent groups like the PTA (Parent Teacher Association) can go a long way to advancing the consideration of a wide array of career options by helping parents learn how to promote mature decision-making. The ITCIC model demonstrates that secondary and post-secondary school women in our sample who expressed an interest in a career in a computer-related field share five characteristics:

- They are minorities (African Americans, Asian Americans, Hispanic Americans, Native Americans, and multiracial Americans).
- They perceive that their parents support this career choice.
- They use computers frequently and in various ways.
- They have positive views about the qualities of workers in the IT field.
- They have not sought out much career information about the field.

High school and college men in our sample who express an interest in IT share most of these characteristics. They, however, are less directly impacted by their parents' perceptions of appropriate career choices and are even less likely than their female counterparts to seek out teachers, counselors, or others for career advice. When it comes to career choice, neither women nor men appear to engage in a systematic approach to career data collection. This is particularly problematic for new and emerging fields like IT where close acquaintances and the media offer only the most minimal insight.

Organization of the Book

This book is organized in three distinct sections that present research about women's interest and persistence in IT majors in secondary schools, post-secondary schools, and careers in the IT profession. These sections represent multiple layers of the gender equity dilemma we face in IT within the US and internationally. We invited Drs. Jane Butler Kahle, Miami University, Oxford, Ohio; Lesley Parker, Curtin University, Perth, Australia; and William Aspray, Indiana University, Bloomington, all of whom are scholars who have researched and published in the area of women and IT education and careers, to act as advisors and to each partner with one of the editors to produce a section introduction. These introductory, integrative pieces synthesize the section chapters, add a broader, international perspective to the topic area (secondary, post-secondary, or professional), and deepen our understanding of the context and consequences of the findings.

The depth of the work presented in this volume springs from the inter-disciplinary teams who formed the research questions and conducted their research using a variety of methods. A team of authors from different disciplines—anthropology, human development, computer science, education, economics, biology, business, physical sciences—lends richness to the work and value to the conclusions. Chapters were reviewed by the editors and advisors and accepted for inclusion in this volume based on their theoretical contributions, the quality of the research, and cultural diversity. The chapters broaden our understanding of the barriers and transition points women encounter as they move through the educational system and into the working world both in the US and in international settings.

Over the course of the development of this volume, the editors, advisors, and chapter authors reached agreement about a few important points that cross cultures and educational levels. We first agreed that, while there are some similarities, findings about the role of gender in the recruitment and retention of women in other SET fields cannot be generalized to computer-based fields. Second, it is important to conduct research that considers differences among the attitudes and skills of workers in different information technology subfields. Finally, we agreed that the public's perception of the 1990s "dot-com bust" and outsourcing of computing jobs does not match the reality of the job market which will continue to expand in all countries—albeit at different rates and with some variation over time.

The Secondary School Level

The authors of chapters in the secondary school section identify key factors precluding females from choosing a pathway leading to an IT career. The themes of failure to connect to the helping or relational interests of females, perceptions of a hostile "geek" culture and extended time required both in study and work life, curricular accessibility in high school, and the difference in support for information processing and decision-making for males and females from teachers, counselors, and parents form the chapters in this section.

A clear theme emerging from our research and that of authors in this section about female secondary school students and career decisions was the importance of a career that captures "helping." This follows previous work investigating the reasons behind the preponderance of female majors in the social and life sciences. The drawing power of the helping professions was seen early in women's participation in nursing and teaching fields. The life sciences, like biology and environmental science, and the social sciences drew large numbers of undergraduate women because of their apparent and overt connection to the human condition. Secondary school students do not often see IT careers as part of the "helping" professions.

In their discussion about how a change in the culture surrounding computer-supported courses could promote girls' long-term interest in IT, Howe, Vouk, and Berenson reinforce the idea that it is the perception of the IT culture as male, competitive, and having little connection to the practicalities of everyday life that keeps female secondary school students from entering and remaining in computer classes beyond keyboarding and, perhaps, Web design. Other perceptions discouraging their sample of high-achieving females from selecting a career in IT were the failures of secondary school computer science classes to be perceived as both accessible and necessary as well as the lack of supportive teachers.

Berenson, Williams, Vouk, and Michael examined time as a factor in female career decisions and found that perceptions of extended time among their sample made the choice of an IT career unattractive. The long hours of post-secondary study required, combined with the long working hours necessary to advance in IT careers, discouraged their females from choosing the IT career path. The intensity of the computer "geek" culture did not give them the long-term flexibility they desired.

Meszaros, Lee, and Laughlin reviewed models of both male and female secondary school students' predictions of interest and choice of an IT career and found significant differences in their information processing and decision orientation. This finding suggests that a greater support role from parents, teachers, and counselors is needed for females. Specific suggestions for building trust and communicating support are given.

The Post-Secondary Level

The authors of the chapters in the post-secondary section of this volume engage the reader in reflection about different views on the effectiveness of female-targeted interventions. Both Bair and Marcus and Cohoon and Lord argue, in their respective chapters, that female and male undergraduate and graduate students are attracted to computing fields for the same reasons: that is, enjoyment of the activities that can be accomplished with computers. Cohoon and Lord argue, however, "Being gender blind does not attract women into computing." Their demonstration that recruiting by male faculty members and graduate students has a significant negative effect on the enrollment of women in graduate programs in computer science and computer engineering should lead to more research about more effective recruitment approaches.

Authors of two other chapters in this section take a very different view of the appropriateness of gender-centered activities and programs. Blum et al. maintain that "women do not need handholding or a 'female friendly' curriculum in order for them to enter and be successful in CS or related fields, nor is there need to change the fields to suit women. To the contrary, curricular changes based on presumed gender differences can be misguided, particularly if they do not provide the skills and depth needed to succeed and lead in the field. Such changes will only serve to reinforce, even perpetuate, stereotypes and promote further marginalization." For example, having a special preprogramming course for women may give weight to the stereotype of women as less than capable of programming and in need of remedial help. A better approach, used in the Carnegie Mellon University model, is to reach out to secondary school CS teachers to increase their awareness of the best practices needed to recruit and retain female students who will then be prepared for post-secondary CS courses.

The chapters by Blum, Frieze, Hazzan, and Dias and by Marsh argue that many outcomes attributed to gender differences are largely the result of cultural and environmental conditions. These chapters remind us that it is more accurate to say that the underrepresentation of women is not a universal problem but one that reflects certain countries and cultures. These are settings where IT is less likely to be characterized as a masculine field and where there is strong governmental support for women's participation in economic development.

Several authors challenge the traditional view that access to and use of computers and access to programming classes are essential to effective recruiting to computing majors. Blum et al. point out that the success of Carnegie Mellon University in recruiting women to computing majors was achieved, in part, by eliminating the admission requirement for prior experience with computer programming, a skill that is much more characteristic of male than female applicants. Similarly, Marsh, from Walter Sisulu University, South Africa, demonstrates how a proactive governmental policy can attract women with little prior access or exposure to computers or IT majors. By attracting more women into undergraduate and graduate IT fields, the government hopes to increase its technology workforce and aid in economic growth.

IT Careers

The long-range goal of all gender equity research in the IT fields is to increase the number of women who enter and succeed in IT careers. These can be academic, teaching at the post-secondary or secondary school level; in industry, as a primary IT worker developing hardware or software; or as a network manager or IT technical resource person in any number of private businesses or government agencies. At all levels and in any IT workplace, male IT workers outnumber females. To get a picture of how women and men enter IT, Leventman introduced the concept of multiple pathways into professional IT positions. The pathways, labeled Traditional, Transitional, and Self-directed, are examined and compared to each other in the areas of job satisfaction, career development, technical and supervisory responsibilities, mentoring, networking, and keeping skills current.

Leventman's findings overlap with those of Kuhn and Rayman, which together bring into question the usefulness of the pipeline metaphor for IT. They report that women in IT jobs often get there through circuitous pathways and opportunities. Kuhn and Rayman delved deeper into the "job satisfaction" area and found that many women and some men were concerned about their inability to balance work and family responsibilities, with work usually winning. Both research projects report that the workers are very satisfied with their work and feel that they "fit into" the IT culture. All IT workers are inquisitive and like solving the puzzles that their work presents. This "puzzle solving" theme is one heard by many interviewers. Both women and men define success in terms of "income, challenge, and recognition." What is not seen is the reason female students report for their interest in the biological sciences—that of "helping people." While this might be an important recruiting strategy, it does not appear to be in the top reasons women stay in or leave their IT jobs. Having enough time for a personal life seems to be more important to those who have stayed in the pipeline long enough to secure an IT position than helping others through their work. This could be the result of some self-selecting out of the IT pipeline because they don't see IT as a career that welcomes those who do want to help people or provide practical solutions for social problems.

Moving from the northeastern US to the antipodes, Warner and Wooller give us a better understanding about the historical timeline of legislation that resulted in equal opportunity/affirmative action laws and policies being enacted in Australia. The driving force for these changes in Australia and, as they show, in the European Union countries, was the realization that in order to be competitive in IT, countries had to support anyone—including females—who had an interest in IT.

As stated above, the goals of programs that deal with females in the education pipeline with additional projects targeted to inform parents, or those that come from informal sources—museum programs, mentoring or networking programs, or summer computer camps, for example—are usually altruistic. Countries and companies are more interested in the economic benefits and prestige that come from having an IT workforce that is inventive and productive. As we see in all of these chapters, the historically male culture of computer science and engineering sometimes subverts these goals. The satisfaction women feel as IT professionals may not overcome the stress of the workplace environment, the choices they must make about whether or not to have children, or the time they spend on the job or commuting to their jobs.

Some of the insight offered by this volume might be reflected in how Carla's decision-making process matured and her interest in IT grew as a result of actions taken by individuals using a new ecological lens to view the barriers surrounding an IT career. We will visit Carla again in the final chapter to see how research put into practice has helped her achieve success in an IT career.

References

Baxter Magolda, M. B. (1999). *Creating contexts for learning and self-authorship: Constructive developmental pedagogy.* Nashville, TN: Vanderbilt University Press.

Cohoon, J. M., Baylor, K. M., & Chen, L.-Y. (2003). Continuation to graduate school: A look at computing departments. Charlottesville, VA: Curry School of Education, University of Virginia.

D'Agostino, D. (2003. October 1). Where are all the women IT leaders? *Eweek.* Retrieved September 29, 2006, from www.eweek.com/article2/0,1759,1309599,00.asp

Gibson, S. (1997, October 6). The nonissue—gender in the IT field. *PC Week, 14*(42), p. 112.

Gurer, D., & Camp, T. (1998). *Investigating the incredible shrinking pipeline for women computer science.* Retrieved June 9, 2006, from http://women.acm.org/documents/finalreport.pdf

Huyer, S. (2003). *Gender, ICT, and Education.* Unpublished manuscript.

Huyer, S., Hafkin, N., Ertl, H., & Dryburgh, H. (2005). Women in the information society. In G. Sciadis (Ed.), *From the digital divide to digital opportunities: Measuring infostates for development* (pp. 135–196). Montreal: Orbicom.

Information Technology Association of America (2003). *Building the 21st century information technology workforce: Groups underrepresented in the IT workforce* [Task force report]. Retrieved October 10, 2005, from http://www.itaa.org/workforce/studies.recruit.htm

Lee, A. C. K. (2003). Undergraduate students' gender differences in IT skills and attitudes. *Journal of Computer Assisted Learning, 19*(4), 488–500.

National Science Board. (2004). *Science and engineering indicators 2004: Vol. 1* (Publication No. NSB 04-1). Arlington, VA: National Science Foundation

National Science Foundation. (1994). *Women, minorities, and persons with disabilities in science and engineering: 1994* (NSF Publication No. 94-333). Arlington, VA: Author.

National Science Foundation. (2004). *Women, minorities, and persons with disabilities in science and engineering: 2004* (NSF Publication No. 04-317). Arlington, VA: Author.

O'Brien, K. M., & Fassinger, R. E. (1993). A causal model of the career orientation and career choice of adolescent women. *Journal of Counseling Psychology, 40*(4), 456–469.

Sax, L. J., Lindholm, J. A., Astin, A. W., Korn, W. S., & Mahoney, K. M. (2005. May). Paper presented at the annual meeting of the Association for Institutional Research, San Diego, CA.

Notes

1. While mathematics is foundational for all of the science, engineering, and technology fields, women have reached parity in mathematics college degrees. Therefore, we have chosen to concentrate on SET rather than on STEM.

Chapter 1

Predicting Women's Interest in and Choice of a Career in Information Technology

A Statistical Model

Elizabeth G. Creamer, Soyoung Lee, and Peggy S. Meszaros

Abstract

This chapter explains a theoretically driven and empirically supported model that identifies key factors that predict high school and college women's interest in and choice of a career in information technology. At the center of the model is the developmental construct of self-authorship and a set of variables related to the process individuals use to make personal and educational decisions. It is our conclusion that reliance on guidance from a narrow circle of trusted others that includes family members, but rarely teachers and counselors, is one reason that women continue to express an interest in sex-typical careers. Findings have direct implications for recruiting and advising practice.

Introduction

Research since the early 1970s indicates that a different set of variables is required in models that predict women's and men's career interests and choice (O'Brien & Fassinger, 1993). There are, for example, significant gender differences in how men and women become interested in, enter, and remain in the computing field (Almstrum, 2003). A number of factors are associated with women's career interests that are not significant for men, including self-efficacy (Bandura, 1982), consideration of the needs of others (Taylor & Betz, 1983), attachment to parents (Armsden & Greenberg, 1987; O'Brien, Friedman, Tipton, & Linn, 2000; Rainey & Borders, 1997) and the value awarded to marriage and a family (Fassinger, 1990). There is a much weaker connection for women than there is for men between interests, enjoyment, and career choice (O'Brien & Fassinger).

The purpose of this chapter is to explain a theoretically driven statistical model that identifies key factors that predict high school and college women's interest and choice in a career in IT. Chapter 4 in this volume, by Meszaros, Lee, and Laughlin, examines the impact of most of the same factors for a subset of the population, high school women and men. By IT, we mean a full range of professional careers that are computer driven, including those that involve Web design and development, and hardware and software engineering, but exclude data processing. Although the model has been documented statistically through path analysis of 373 female respondents, we set out to explain it a nontechnical way in order to reach a wide audience. Our target audience includes not only academics engaged in research about gender and IT, but also educators who design and implement programs targeted at recruiting and retaining women in IT majors and careers. To clarify our discussions about female students' characteristics in our model, we also used comparison data from 404 male respondents.

At the center of our theoretical model is the developmental construct of self-authorship (Baxter Magolda, 1992, 1999) and a set of variables related to the process individuals use to make personal and educational decisions. In the model, this process is represented by four variables: decision orientation, receptivity, information sources, and information credibility. These variables relate to the role of information from others in career interests. Analysis of data from 170 interviews with high school, community college, and college women between 2002 and 2005 alerted us to the salience of this set of variables.

Figure 1 depicts the full conceptual model. Key findings from analysis of both our qualitative and quantitative data have led us to conclude that for both male and female high school and college students, the expression of interest in a career in the IT field is often made with little concrete information from sources outside of the immediate circle of trusted friends and fam-

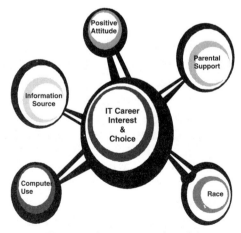

Figure 1. The conceptual model.

ily members. In general, women who expressed an interest in IT as a potential career choice perceived that their parents supported the choice, but the choice was not significantly impacted by information from other sources. Surprisingly, the fewer contacts our respondents made to talk about career options, the more likely they were to express an interest in an IT career. Because this indicates that individuals are making career choices with little self-reflection and circumscribed information, this finding does not bode well for the likelihood of long-term persistence in the field. Findings support the conclusion that one of the biggest challenges facing educators who want to promote women's interest in SET fields (science, engineering, and technology) is to develop a portfolio of developmentally appropriate strategies that engage young women in thoughtful reflection about career options that are good matches for their values, skills, and interests.

Summary of Key Findings

In addition to the exogenous variables that are controlled for in our model (birth year, educational level, and mother's and father's educational level), there are five key variables that impact women's IT career interest and choice in a direct and indirect way. Variables with a statistically significant direct impact are (a) race, (b) parental support, (c) computer use, (d) positive attitudes about the attributes of IT workers, and (e) information sources. Variables that have an indirect impact on women's interest and choice of a career in IT are (a) parents' education levels, and (b) decision orientation.

In the section below is a description of a fictional character, Kiaya. Kiaya is a composite figure who integrates the central findings from the qualitative and quantitative findings of our long-term research project.

Kiaya: The Next Generation IT Worker

Kiaya is an African American college sophomore who completed high school in a suburb of a large metropolitan city. Kiaya was raised in a two-parent, middle class home. Both of her parents completed a college degree and both are employed full-time in a professional position. Kiaya had access to a home computer from a young age. She uses a computer daily for a variety of purposes.

Kiaya has positive views, rather than stereotypical views, about the attributes of IT workers, thinking that they are smart, creative, and hard working. She is moderately confident she can solve computer problems when she encounters them. She knows people employed in the IT field and who enjoy working with computers. She is not particularly concerned that IT is a male dominated field.

Kiaya's parents, particularly her mother, are key to understanding the process she uses to make important life decisions, including the choice of a career. They believe that the IT field is an appropriate choice for their daughter and have encouraged her to talk with others who are acquainted with the field. They have promoted Kiaya's confidence in her own judgment by modeling effective decision-making. They have encouraged her to seek input from informed outsiders when making an important life choice, while at the same time repeatedly underscoring the importance of making choices that match her values, interests, and skills. In these ways, Kiaya's parents have promoted her development of self-authorship.

Our fictional composite, Kiaya, presents the key characteristics that we have found through empirical research to be associated with high school and college women's interest in a career in IT.

First, they are more likely to be a minority than Caucasian.

Second, they have parents who support the importance of a career and encourage career exploration. Their mothers have completed a higher level of education than those who express little or no interest in a career in IT. Participants who expressed an interest in IT had parents who felt that IT offers job options that are a suitable match with their daughter's interests and skills.

Third, participants who expressed an interest in a career in IT used computers in their home from an early age. They use computers on a daily basis and for a variety of purposes, including social exchanges through email or instant messaging. They feel reasonably confident that they can solve problems they encounter on the computer. Some have had the opportunity to be employed in a setting where computers are used for problem solving.

Fourth, participants who expressed an interest in a career in IT have positive views about the attributes of workers in computer-related fields, believing that they are smart, hardworking, and creative. They do not endorse stereotypical views that workers in these fields are "geeks," "loners," or "antisocial." The fact that IT is a male-dominated field is not considered a significant deterrent to interest in the field.

Fifth, Kiaya is an ideal character, compared to many of our participants, in that she has had the advantage of parents who have promoted the development of mature decision-making skills and encouraged her to genuinely reflect on the input of informed outsiders without disregarding her own personal values, skills, and interests. Kiaya has played an active role in seeking out career information and has given thought to the input of others both within and outside of her immediate family, including from teachers, counselors, advisors, and professionals in her fields of interest. Her parents' style of parenting has promoted the confidence Kiaya feels about making decisions. Kiaya is further along in the journey toward the development of self-authorship than most of our participants.

In the remainder of the chapter, we will summarize our theoretical framework and details of our research methods. A list of questionnaire items in each variable, plus statistical information about the reliability of the variables in the model, appears in the appendices. The central portion of the chapter is organized around key variables in the model. In the section about each variable, there is a summary of the relevant literature, a description of key findings from our research, and a brief discussion of the comparison to men in our sample. Each section ends with reflections about the implications for practice. We reacquaint you with Kiaya in each section by repeating the relevant portion of our composite character.

Theoretical Framework

We employ the developmental construct of self-authorship as a theoretical lens to understand the cognitive processes students use to make decisions, including career decisions (Baxter Magolda, 2002). Defined as "the ability to collect, interpret, and analyze information and reflect on one's own beliefs in order to form judgments" (Baxter Magolda, 1998, p. 143), self-authorship is grounded in the work of Perry (1970) and Kegan (1982). Self-authorship is linked to decision-making because it influences how individuals make meaning of the advice they receive from others and the extent to which the reasoning they employ reflects an internally grounded sense of self (Baxter Magolda, 1998, 1999, 2001).

Individuals at different stages of cognitive development have different ways of approaching decisions. Individuals early in the journey to self-authorship—a stage Baxter Magolda refers to as external formulas—are likely to make decisions that reflect unquestioned faith in the views of trusted others. They trust others to know what career choices best fit them. Those who have advanced to the middle point of the development of self-authorship—what Baxter Magolda calls transitional knowers—have lost the comfort of unquestioned trust in authorities, but have yet to develop other criteria to judge input and make decisions. They are skeptical of authorities, but have no systematic set of criteria to approach decisions or to evaluate knowledge. It is only after achieving a full measure of self-authorship that an individual can be genuinely open to the input of others, without allowing the exchange to erode a sense of self. A self-authored career decision is one that is made with the internal compass of a clear sense of self, an openness to the input of others, and a sense of the match between the demands of a field and personal interests, values, and skills.

Developmental theorists provide a framework that is at odds with the assumption that high school and college students automatically accept the word of learned authorities. They offer developmental reasons for why many college students may not be in a position to genuinely engage diverse viewpoints from unfamiliar others, including from advisors and teachers. First and second year students of a traditional-age are likely to be absolute knowers (Baxter Magolda & King, 2004). They are engaged in dependent relationships where decisions are made to please trusted others, like parents and friends. It is probably difficult for this group to accept advice that conflicts with the guidance provided by trusted others. College juniors and seniors are most likely to be transitional knowers (Baxter Magolda, 1999) but still have no systematic way of approaching personal decisions and few criteria to judge the advice of others. Trust and care for the person offering advice may become the principal criteria for making a life decision (Creamer, Lee, & Laughlin, 2006) because until the later stages of epistemological development individuals have few criteria other than the nature of the relationship to judge advice or the advice giver (Hofer & Pintrich, 1997).

Methods

Research Participants and Data Collection

The overall data collection and analysis procedures consist of three phases: the first survey and interview data collection, the follow-ups and revisions, and the second survey and interview data collection testing our theoretical model and subsequently revised survey questionnaires and interview protocols.

First phase of data collection (2002). For the first-year data collection, letters seeking cooperative agreements to participate in this project were sent to high schools, community colleges, and colleges in Virginia. We received written letters of agreement from ten high schools, two community colleges, and four colleges in rural and urban locations in Virginia and distributed the survey questionnaires about participants' computer-related attitudes, career influencers, and career decisions to these schools during spring 2002. A total of 467 participants returned completed usable questionnaires for a 62% response rate (467 of 750). The first-year survey participants consisted of (a) 346 females (74.1%) and 121 males (25.9%); (b) 177 high school students (37.9%), 118 community college students (25.3%), and 172 college students (36.8%); and (c) 322 whites (69.0%), 139 minorities

(29.7%), and six unidentified races (1.3%). We also completed one-on-one 30 minute telephone interviews with a total of 119 female students (46 high school, 40 college, and 33 community college women) and 25 parents of the high school interview participants during fall 2002.

Second phase of data collection (2003). The main purpose of the second phase of data collection was to refine the data collection instruments. We revised the survey questionnaire based on the analysis of the first-year survey and interview data. We developed more comprehensive items about self-authorship, parental support, information credibility, and IT career interest and choice and reformatted the survey questionnaire to be more user-friendly. Also, we added questions to the interview protocol about the role of parents and the decision-making processes related to IT career interest and choice. During spring 2003, we distributed the revised survey questionnaire to those who participated in the first-year survey data collections. Among 467 first-year survey participants, we distributed the survey questionnaire to 423 students who had provided their mailing addresses while completing the first year survey. We received a total of 124 completed survey questionnaires from 63 high school (50.8%), 31 community college (25.0%), and 30 college students (24.2%). Since 51 survey questionnaires were not delivered, our final survey response rate for the second phase was 33.3% (124 of 372). Other detailed demographic characteristics of the second year survey participants are as follows: survey participants consisted of 103 females (83.1%) and 21 males (16.9%). Also, 92 whites (74.2%) and 30 minorities (24.2%) participated in this second year study, and two students' racial information was unidentified (1.3%). The follow-up telephone interviews were conducted with 13 female high school students and 12 parents, and each interview took from 30 minutes to one hour.

Third phase of data collection (2004–2005). The third phase of this research project was intended to test reliability and validity of the revised survey questionnaire and to confirm our theoretical model of women's IT career interest and choice. The third version of the survey questionnaire was distributed to four high schools in Virginia and one college in Pennsylvania. To recruit high schools, we contacted the original high schools participating in the first phase of the data collection. Four of the original ten high schools agreed to participate. During fall 2004, we mailed a total of 845 survey questionnaires and received 556 usable surveys returned from these four high schools (66%).

To gather survey and interview data from college students, we worked with personnel from the School of Information Sciences and Technology (IST) Advising Center at Pennsylvania State University (PSU). During spring

2005, 221 out of 350 college students completed our questionnaire and 40 of these students signed up to participate in face-to-face interviews. We conducted hour-long face-to-face interviews with 19 female and 19 male IST students during spring 2005. Our final questionnaire response rate for this phase was 65% (777 out of 1195). Tables A1 through A4 in Appendix A provide the detailed demographic characteristics of respondents to the third-year questionnaire.

Measurements

Questionnaire. A 119-item paper-and-pencil Career Interest and Choice Questionnaire was developed over the course of three revisions between 2002 and 2005. The final instrument includes eight 4-point Likert-type scales designed to measure levels of parental support, information orientation features (decision orientation, receptivity, information sources, and information credibility), attitude toward IT workers, computer use, and IT career interest and choice among high school and college students. Item options are disagree (1), slightly disagree (2), slightly agree (3), and agree (4). All measures were coded such that the higher the value, the more positive the interpretation. Also, items asking about general demographic information were included in this questionnaire, such as birth years, parents' educational levels, race, school years, family structures and characteristics, and employment status.

To address content and construct validities of each scale, all the survey scales were constructed based on the relevant literature and our team members' expertise. We also conducted face validity tests. In particular, to address the information orientation features' content (decision orientation, receptivity, information sources, and information credibility) and construct validities, the original items were developed in collaboration with Dr. Marcia Baxter Magolda.

Interview protocols. Semistructured interview protocols were used for telephone and face-to-face interviews in our research project. The original telephone interview protocol was designed in 2001 in collaboration with Dr. Baxter Magolda and refined for the second and third interviews. We included a question asking participants to identify some important decisions they had made in their lives and then to select one to talk about during the interviews. A question about the role of parents was also added to the revised protocol because it emerged as central to decision-making in the analysis of the first year survey and interview data. Example questions are as follows: (a) Please tell me about some important life decision you have made in the last few years. We're going to be talking about your choice of major and career later in the interview, so I'd like you to select some decision other than that. (b) What process have you gone through or are going through to make a decision about your major and career interests? (c) Were there events or incidents in your earlier life or people who played a role in your decision? (d) Were there people who had a significant influence on your decision? Who were these people, and what role did they play in the process you went through to make the decision? And (e) what role did your mother and father, if you interacted with them regularly at the time, play in the process you went through to make the decision? All the interviews were audio taped. We prepared a verbatim transcript of each interview.

Data Analysis

Quantitative data. The first step in the development of the statistical model involved confirming elements of the theoretical model that played a significant role in predicting interest and choice of IT as a career pursuit. Factor analysis was used to confirm which combination of questionnaire items produced the most reliable measure of each of seven independent and one dependent variable. Each of our scales' internal consistencies is reasonable (Cronbach's alpha = 0.603–0.842), establishing high reliabilities of the survey measurements.

The questionnaire items in each of the scales that appear in the final models are summarized in Appendix B.

The mean and standard deviation for each scale appear in Table 1. Correlations among the scales are displayed in Table 2.

Using the independent t-test, we next examined group differences in eight key scales in our research—parental support, information orientation features (decision orientation, receptivity, information sources, and infor-

Table 1. Mean and standard deviation of each scale (n = 777).

Variables	M	SD
Parental support	28.65	5.19
Decision orientation	37.44	4.73
Receptivity	15.60	3.01
Information credibility	28.41	5.49
Information sources	16.07	5.82
Attitudes toward IT workers	22.47	3.33
Computer use	15.05	4.08
IT career interest & choice	21.14	4.40

Table 2. Correlations among scales in the model predicting women's interest in and choice of IT (n = 777).

Variables	1	2	3	4	5	6	7	8	9	10
1. Gender	1									
2. Race	.141***	1								
3. Parental support	-.025	-.098**	1							
4. Decision orientation	-.083*	-.027	0.49	1						
5. Receptivity	-.100**	.095**	.430**	-.056	1					
6. Information credibility	-.067	.040	.351***	-.022	.430***	1				
7. Information sources	-.100**	.046	.351***	.156***	.293***	.474***	1			
8. Attitudes toward IT workers	-.168***	-.201***	.073*	.094*	.163***	.114***	.087*	1		
9. Computer use	.194***	.183***	.183***	.068	.135***	.162***	.195***	.025	1	
10. IT career interest & choice	.211***	.082*	.228***	.058	.132***	.165***	.099**	.156***	.462***	1

* $p < 0.05$, ** $p < 0.01$, *** $p < 0.001$

mation credibility), attitude toward IT workers, computer use, and IT career interest and choice—by gender, race, age, participants' level of education, and parents' levels of education. Differences by gender are statistically significant for all but two of the variables in the model, supporting the decision to present separate statistical models for men and women.

Females showed more positive attitudes toward IT workers, relied less on external formulas, were more receptive to others advice, and communicated with more people than males. However, male students used computers more often and were more interested in IT careers than female students. Table 3 shows the detailed results of the independent t-test analysis, comparing group differences by gender in each of the scales in the model.

We conducted a path analysis to test our theoretical model, running a separate model for women and men. Path analysis is a unidirectional causal flow model (Maruyama, 1998), which explains relationships between observed variables by arrows (Raykov & Marcoulides, 2000). Path analysis is very useful for researchers to articulate theoretical models underlying their logic. It is also beneficial to show direct and indirect causal effects of each independent variable on dependent variables (Maruyama; Raykov & Marcoulides). Each factor or scale in the model contains several items from the questionnaire.

Table 3. Group differences in model variables by gender (n = 777).

Variables	M		SD		t
	Females (n = 373)	Males (n = 404)	Females (n = 373)	Males (n = 404)	
Attitudes toward IT workers	23.06	21.93	3.18	3.38	4.69***
Parental support	28.79	28.52	5.18	5.19	0.71
Decision orientation	37.85	37.06	4.58	4.84	2.32*
Receptivity	15.91	15.31	2.98	3.01	2.81**
Information sources	16.67	15.51	5.68	5.90	2.80**
Information credibility	28.79	28.06	5.47	5.49	1.87
Computer use	14.23	15.81	3.89	4.11	-5.51***
IT career interest & choice	20.17	22.03	4.48	4.14	-6.01***

* p < 0.05, ** p < 0.01, *** p < 0.001

Note. Code: females = 1 & males = 2 so that negative t values mean that male students have higher mean scores than female students.

Interview data. We used both a deductive and inductive method to create the coding scheme for the transcripts. The deductive element consisted of codes developed in previous research. The inductive element refers to codes that emerged during the process of analyzing transcripts. We used an iterative process, coding and recoding the transcripts separately until agreement about the codes and their definitions was reached. After agreeing on the coding scheme, we returned to the transcripts, coding them separately once again and meeting on several occasions to establish a level of agreement about the coding of the transcripts. As a final step in coding, we entered the data in the qualitative software, ATLAS TI. After that, we dealt with both the original coded transcripts and a printout that summarized responses to all of the key variables in the study.

Variables that Influence Women's Interest in and Choice of an IT Career

The following section of the chapter describes key findings, including gender differences, for each of the key variables in the model. Each section is organized in a similar fashion. A brief summary of literature related to the variable or scale is followed by a reference to the composite figure, Kiaya, we created. This is followed by a summary of the key statistical findings about the role of this variable in IT interest and choice and how this varies by gender, if at all. The section on each variable closes with a brief discussion of the implications for practice.

Variable 1: Race

Several studies have examined racial discrepancies in computer and technology use, access, attitudes, and skills (Flowers, Pasearella, & Pierson, 2000; Flowers & Zhang, 2003; Hackbarth, 2004; Lowry, 2004). While research has contributed to our understanding of existing racial differences in information technology use that begin in childhood (Volman & van Eck, 2001) and continue through the college years (Flowers et al.; Flowers & Zhang), few studies have examined the relationship between race and IT career interest and choice. Differences exist in technology use and skills by race among college students (Flowers et al.; Flowers & Zhang). A lack of computer competence is more clearly concentrated among minorities, especially younger females "of color" (Hackbarth). However, some 4th grade girls in talented and gifted classes, who had greater opportunities for internet, access both at home and at school, showed increasing interests in computers over time. Year-to-year changes in affection for computers did not systematically vary due to race or ethnicity among the 4th graders (Hackbarth). As an extension of prior research, our model shows that racial differences also exist in terms of career interest and choice in IT. However, in our model, minority females showed more interest in IT careers than Caucasian females did.

There is a direct and significant relationship between race and IT career interest and choice in the statistical model. Both our female and male respondents who are minorities (African Americans, Asian Americans, Hispanic Americans, Native Americans, and multiracial Americans) were significantly more likely to express an interest IT than our respondents who self-identified as Caucasian.

Variable 2: Parental Support

Our findings support a fairly substantial body of empirical research that documents the instrumental role of parents in career decision-making for high school and college women (Altman, 1997; Fisher & Griggs, 1994; Ketterson & Blustein, 1997; Way & Rossmann, 1996). Parents have a more significant impact on career choice than do counselors, teachers, friends, other relatives, and people working in the field (Kotrlik & Harrison, 1989). Parental attachment is positively associated with vocational exploration among college women (Ketterson & Blustein). Parents who discuss issues openly and promote independent thinking in their children encourage more active career exploration (Ketterson & Blustein).

A qualitative study by Schultheiss, Kress, Manzi and Glasscock (2001) examined family influences on both vocational exploration and career decision-making. The majority of participants felt that their mothers, fathers, and siblings had played a positive role in their career exploration by indirect means such as providing emotional and informational support and by more tangible means such as providing educational materials. Furthermore, 36% of our participants indicated that their mother was the most influential person in their career exploration process, while 21% indicated this was true of their father.

A fairly large set of research studies provide support for the role of mothers in women's vocational choice (Felsman & Blustein, 1999; Ryan, Solberg, & Brown, 1996) and career orientation (O'Brien & Fassinger, 1993). Adolescent girls were more likely than boys to report that their mothers provided positive feedback, supported their autonomy, and were open to discussions about career decisions (Paa & McWhirter, 2000). Rainey and Borders (1997) determined that the career orientation of adolescent females is influenced by a complex interplay of their abilities, agentic characteristics, gender role attitudes, and relationship with their mothers.

As our composite figure, Kiaya, illustrates, parents were influential in her career interests not so much because they identified and supported a specific career choice, but because they modeled ways for Kiaya to develop relatively sophisticated decision-making skills for someone of her age.

In the statistical model, the scale for parental support includes nine questionnaire items relating to perceptions that parents support the importance of a career and encourage career exploration, as well as agreement with the belief that parents have an idea of what would be an appropriate career choice. Parental support has a direct and positive impact on women's, but not men's, interest and choice of a career in IT. High school and college women who express an interest in an IT career believe that their parents support this career choice. Male respondents perceived parental support for their career choices too, but this did not have a significant impact on their interest and choice of IT.

Consistent with what has been reported in the research literature, parental support has a significant positive impact on both men's and women's career information-seeking behavior. Parents influenced how likely both male and female respondents reported they were to value others' input (the variable, receptivity), seek out career advice (the variable, information sources), and how they evaluated the credibility of different sources of career information (the variable, information credibility).

The level of education completed by each parent had a direct and positive impact on the support they provided for a career and career choice (the variable, parental support). For men, but not women, this variable also had a direct impact on computer use. High school and college women whose mother had completed a college degree were significantly more likely than those whose mother only had completed a high school degree to report parental support for a career and career exploration, as well as with another important variable in our model, computer use. There is no significant relationship between mother's educational level and any of the variables in the model for men.

The direct relationship for women between parental support and interest in an IT career supports the idea that sharing career information with parents or involving them, particularly mothers, in educational activities is likely to have a positive impact on IT career interest. Findings from our qualitative research underscore that the challenge facing educators is how to design activities, such as recruiting events targeted to women, in a way that promotes trust and the ability to genuinely consider the information supplied.

Variable 3: Computer Use

The connection between computer use and positive attitudes and interest has been amply supported by previous research (Dryburgh, 2000; Shashaani, 1997). It is no surprise, therefore, to learn that computer use had a direct and positive impact on women's interest in a career in a computer-related field. This held true for men as well. What is unusual about our findings, however, is that for women, an interest in an IT career is significantly related to amount of computer use, but not necessarily type of computer use.

While experience with computers games has been shown to be an important predictor of men's interest in computer-related fields (Volman & van Eck, 2001) this is not the case for our women respondents. Other research has shown, however, that experience with computer programming may be an important predictor of self-efficacy and success in a computer field for women. Learning a programming language is significantly associated with an increased sense of computer competence for women (Miura, 1987; Wilder, Mackie, & Cooper, 1985). High school programming experience has also been shown to be a significant predictor of women's success in computer science at the college level (Bunderson & Christensen, 1995). These factors probably have more to do with the prognosis for long-term success in an IT career than the measures we have developed.

Kiaya, our composite figure, has the good fortune to have ready access to a computer, both at home and in school. She uses a computer on a daily basis and for a variety of tasks.

The respondents to our questionnaire gauged how often they used different types of computer applications, ranging from simple communication through email and instant messaging to more sophisticated purposes, such as development or design of Web pages. Not surprisingly, college students used computers on a significantly more regular basis than did high school students. For both male and female respondents, the more positive the attitudes about the attributes of workers in computer fields, the more time respondents reported they spent using the computer and the greater their interest in IT as a possible career choice.

Our findings add to the volume of previous empirical literature that supports interventions that provide opportunities for hands-on use of many kinds of computer applications. It is very likely that experience and comfort with more sophisticated computer applications is associated with the ability to persist in a computer-related major or career, but is not, according to our findings, a prerequisite for preliminary interest in a computer-related major.

Variable 4: Positive Attitudes about the Attributes of IT Workers

It is surprising to learn that few systematic studies have been undertaken to examine the relationship between attitudes toward IT and IT workers and interest in IT as a possible career. Most research has been framed with a broader interest in the relationship between different attitudes (likeness, confidence, usefulness, gender stereotyping, and anxiety) and science. These studies suggest that a favorable or positive attitude toward computers and science influences higher level of acceptance of computer technology and enthusiasm about using specific technologies (Noble & O'Connor, 1986). Positive attitudes about computers and science are also related to certain behaviors. Positive attitudes about computers strongly influence computer utilization as a professional tool, the degree of access to computers, and the number of computer-related courses taken (Al-Khaldi & Al-Jabri, 1998).

Our composite character, Kiaya, has favorable views about the characteristics of people who work in the IT field, agreeing with the portrayal of IT workers as being smart, hardworking, and creative.

In our statistical model, positive attitudes about the attributes of people who work in computer-related positions had a direct positive impact on an interest in IT as a career choice for both women and men. High school students had significantly more positive attitudes about IT workers than did college students. Positive attitudes significantly influenced frequency of computer use and receptivity to career advice.

Significant gender differences are evident in our variables measuring attitudes about the attributes of IT workers. Women were significantly more likely than men to agree with the list of positive attributes and disagree with a list of negative or stereotypical qualities of IT workers. However, for both men and women, only positive attitudes had a significant direct impact on the dependent variable, IT career interest and choice. When all other factors were considered, agreement with the list of negative stereotypical qualities of IT workers had no significant impact on IT career choice or interest for either men or women.

The impact of positive views about the qualities of IT workers on interest in a career in IT, like beliefs about the nature of IT work, differs from previous research that suggests that men, in particular, are likely to agree with stereotypical views about IT workers and that these views deter women, but not men, from an interest in the field (Creamer, Burger, & Meszaros, 2004). We suspect that part of the explanation for the differences between our findings and previous research is related to the disappearance of significant gender differences in access to computers.

Findings from this variable endorse the implementation of activities that promote positive views about the nature of IT workers. This is a slightly different focus than that of programs that might explicitly set out to reduce stereotypical views about workers in the computer field. Opportunities to use computer applications that highlight creativity and problem solving, particularly related to pressing human problems, are likely to be particularly effective with women.

Variable 5: Information Orientation

Four variables related to openness to input about careers from others make up a latent variable, information orientation, that is at the center of our model. As we have suggested throughout this chapter, unlike the assumption that high school and college students are open to the direction of authorities, our qualitative and quantitative data converge to suggest that women may experience considerable difficulty genuinely engaging different points of views about appropriate career options. This inclination might appear agentic or self-directed if it were not for the fact that skepticism exhibited by women may limit the career choices they consider.

Our qualitative data led us to conclude that the failure to consider a broad range of information sources before making a career choice is not because career information is not available, as much as it is that many of our female participants seemed reluctant to genuinely consider the information or advice supplied by outsiders to the family, particularly when that advice came in conflict with the input they had received from trusted others (Creamer & Laughlin, 2005). Our interview participants readily acknowledged the importance of seeking input from others, but seemed reluctant to approach adults to talk about career options and to consider new or contradictory information once they heard it. This reliance on guidance from a narrow circle of trusted others that includes parents, but rarely teachers and counselors, may be one reason why many women may fail to consider a broad range of career options, including ones that familiar others have little knowledge about.

Kiaya has used a considerably different process to reach a decision about her interests than have most of our respondents.

Significant gender differences were found for all but one of the variables in information orientation. The exception was a variable we call information credibility. The names, definitions, and key findings for each of the four variables in the information orientation scale are summarized below.

Decision orientation. This variable is a proxy for the theoretical construct of self-authorship. This variable includes confidence in decision-making ability, clarity of career goals, and likelihood of being unduly influenced by the opinions of parents and close friends. We do not call this variable "self-authorship" because we have not been able to measure all three dimensions of self-authorship (the intrapersonal, interpersonal, and epistemological dimensions) adequately. We have not been able to achieve satisfactory levels of reliability to include questionnaire items pertaining to the epistemological dimension in our measure.

Women scored significantly higher on the variable, decision orientation, than did men, underscoring the influence of others on women's career choices. Women expressed significantly higher levels of confidence in their decision-making ability, but also were more likely to agree than were men that others influenced their decisions. This is not to say that they were significantly more confident than men in their career choice. The higher score is consistent with literature that suggests that women are more influenced than men are by the opinions of others (Seymour & Hewitt, 1997).

For women, there was a statistically significant path between the variables decision orientation, receptivity (likelihood of seeking and value of the input of others), and information sources (how often women consulted others about career options). The negative relationship between decision orientation, our proxy for self-authorship, and information credibility means that the lower the levels of self-authorship the more likely women were to seek and to value the input of others. This finding that is not entirely consistent with the research about self-authorship.

Receptivity. The variable, receptivity, was computed from four questionnaire items related to the extent that the respondent seeks and values the input of others when making a big or important decision. Female respondents were significantly more likely than male respondents to indicate that they found it helpful to consult others when making an important decision and that they sought the input of family and friends when making an important decision. Receptivity directly impacted how credible they found advice from different groups, which, in turn, directly impacted the behavior of seeking out others for information when making an important decision. This provides statistical documentation for the link between self-authorship—or our variable, decision orientation—and women's response to information during career decision-making.

Information credibility. This variable relates to how likely respondents reported they were to consider advice offered by ten groups of people that cluster in four factors (parents; teachers or counselors; other family members and friends; and others, such as an employer). The credibility awarded to different information sources was directly linked to how often different sources were consulted for career information. There were no significant differences by gender on this variable.

Information sources. This variable refers to how often respondents indicated they had spoken to groups of others about career options. These include parents, teachers, counselors or advisors, male or female friends, and others, including employers. There were pronounced gender differences in the impact of this variable on interest in IT.

Findings for the impact of the variable, information sources, and the dependent variable, IT career interest and choice were unexpected. This variable had a significant direct impact on women's IT career interest and choice, but the relationship is a surprising one because it is negative. Women indicating an interest in IT had consulted fewer individuals than those who did not express a similar interest. This supports the conclusion that women who express an interest in a career in IT may be doing so with parental support, but with little information from other sources.

Our model demonstrates the connection for women between level of self-authorship, as measured by our variable decision orientation, and each of the variables related to career information-seeking behavior. Respondents with lower measured level of self-authorship were more likely than other respondents to value the input of others and to find a variety of sources of career information to be credible. They were less likely, however, to actually seek out others for career information. It is possible that this gap between attitudes and behavior is explained by the fact that students may be endorsing a behavior advocated (e.g., consulting others) by adults that they are not yet developmentally ready to pursue.

Conclusion

Our model demonstrates that high school and college women who express an interest in a career in a computer-related field share five central characteristics:

- They are minorities, which include African Americans, Asian Americans, Hispanic Americans, Native Americans, and multiracial Americans.
- They perceive that their parents support this career choice.
- They use computers frequently and in various ways.
- They view the qualities of workers in the IT field positively.
- They have not discussed career options with a variety of people.

Table 4 summarizes key findings, organized by each of the key variables in the model.

Table 5 provides a summary of significant difference by gender on the key variables.

Findings support the conclusion that one of the biggest challenges facing educators who want to promote women's interest in careers in SET fields, including information technology, is to develop a portfolio of strategies that engage young women in thoughtful reflection about career options that match their skills and interest. Reliance on the broad dissemination of written information about nontraditional careers for women is not sufficient to

Table 4. Key findings for women by model variables.*

Variable	Finding
Age, education level	Younger students had more positive attitudes and used computers more frequently than older students.
Parental support	Parents directly influence women's interest in an IT career. They indirectly influence career choice through the career exploration they encourage
Parental education	More educated parents offered greater support for the importance of a career and promoted more frequent use of the computer than parents with lower levels of education.
Computer use	The more frequently computers are used, the greater the interest in an IT career.
Attitudes about the characteristics of IT workers	Agreement with statements that attribute positive qualities to IT workers.
Information-seeking behavior regarding careers	Women who express an interest in IT have consulted few sources about career information.

*All findings are statistically significant at the .01 or .05 level.

Table 5. Significant differences by gender in model variables.*

Variable	Finding
Age, gender, education level	Male respondents were significantly more likely than female respondents to express an interest in a career in IT career.
Parental support	There were no significant gender differences in respondents' perceptions of parental support.
Parental education	Mother's educational level played a significant role in women's career interests, but had no significant effect on men's career interests.
Computer use	Male respondents used computers significantly more frequently than did female respondents.
Attitudes about the characteristics of IT workers	Female respondents had significantly more positive views than male respondents about the attributes of IT workers.
Information-seeking behavior regarding careers	Female respondents were more likely than male respondents to seek input from others about career options.

*All findings are statistically significant at the .01 or .05 level.

promote the genuine consideration of suitable options that is necessary to make a well-informed career decision.

Directions for Future Research

As is typical for statistical procedures like multiple regression or path analysis, the majority of the variance in women's interest and choice of a career in IT remains outside of the ability of our conceptual model to explain. This was true for men as well. There are undoubtedly many structural variables, such as cultural factors that support racial differences, gender stereotypes, and gender-based occupational segregation, as well as interactions that occur in the classroom, that would add to the predictive power of the model were it possible to quantify them. Similarly, we have yet to investigate the relationship between performances in certain types of course and course taking patterns to an interest in a career in IT. We plan to pursue many of these issues in the next phases of our research project.

Implications for Practice

The focus in our model on information seeking and processing skills has a number of implications for practices targeted at recruiting women to the IT field. When findings from our qualitative research and from the questionnaire are considered together, there is strong evidence to suggest that increasing the number of women interested in IT requires considerably more ingenuity than simply delivering information in an engaging way.

Instead, our research suggests that these efforts are most likely to be effective when they incorporate parents and manage to communicate personal concern and interest in young women in the audience. This can be accomplished, not by emphasizing how lucrative positions in the field are, but by discussing the creative aspects of the field and developing strategies that encourage women to gauge the match between their values, skills, and interests and those of a variety of career options. Recruiting efforts are most likely to have a significant impact when they extend over a long enough period of time so that participants can begin to feel a sense of affinity and trust for those that direct the activities.

A constructive-developmental framework offers educators a way to understand that how students make meaning shapes their receptivity to career and academic advice. The learning partnerships model (Baxter Magolda, 2004) identifies principles and practices that educators can apply to promote complex decision-making and problem solving to foster self-authorship. Such interventions focus on creating safe environments where students have the opportunity to reflect on the process they have used to make an important decision and to explore the role that values and identity play in personal decisions with long-term consequences. An interdisciplinary context, such as offered by block scheduling of new students in interrelated general education courses, could create opportunities for students to explore the development of identity through biographies or life stories. When reflection and interaction are built in as a regular component, internships, service-learning experiences, study abroad, leadership development and activities, and many team-building experiences can create the context for the development of skills required for complex decisions making and a safe environment for the exploration of diverse viewpoints.

Acknowledgments

This research was supported by funds from the National Science Foundation under grant HRD-0120458.

References

Al-Khaldi, M. A., & Al-Jabri, L. M. (1998). The relationship of attitudes to computer utilization: New evidence from a developing nation. *Computers in Human Behavior, 14*(1), 23–42.

Almstrum, V. L. (2003). What is the attraction to computing? *Communications of the ACM, 46*(9), 51–55.

Altman, J. H. (1997). Career development in the context of family experience. In H. S. Farmer (Ed.), *Diversity and women's career development: From adolescence to adulthood* (pp. 229–242). Thousand Oaks, CA: Sage.

Armsden, G. C., & Greenberg, M. T. (1987). The inventory of parent and peer attachment: Individual differences and their relationship to psychological well-being in adolescence. *Journal of Youth and Adolescence, 16*(5), 427–454.

Bandura, A. (1982). Self-efficacy mechanism in human agency. *American Psychologists, 37*(2), 122–147.

Baxter Magolda, M. B. (1992). *Knowing and reasoning in college: Gender-related patterns in students' intellectual development.* San Francisco: Jossey-Bass.

Baxter Magolda, M. B. (1998). Developing self-authorship in young adult life. *Journal of College Student Development, 39*(2), 143–156.

Baxter Magolda, M. B. (1999). *Creating contexts for learning and self-authorship.* Nashville: Vanderbilt University Press.

Baxter Magolda, M. B. (2001). *Making their own way: Narratives for transforming higher education to promote self-development.* Sterling, VA: Stylus.

Baxter Magolda, M. B. (2002, April). *The central role of self in learning: Transforming higher education.* Paper presented at the annual meeting of the American Educational Research Association, New Orleans, LA.

Baxter Magolda, M. B. (2004). Learning partnerships model: A framework for promoting self-authorship. In M. B. Baxter Magolda & P. M. King (Eds.), *Learning Partnerships: Theory and Models of Practice for Self-authorship* (pp. 37–62). Sterling, VA: Stylus.

Baxter Magolda, M. B., & King, P. M. (Eds.). (2004). *Learning partnerships: Theory and models of practice to educate for self-authorship.* Sterling, VA: Stylus.

Bunderson, E. D., & Christensen, M. E. (1995). An analysis of retention problems for female students in university computer science programs. *Journal of Research on Computing in Education, 28*(1), 1–15.

Creamer, E. G., Burger, C. J., & Meszaros, P. S., (2004). Characteristics of high school and college women interested in information technology. *Journal of Women and Minorities in Science and Engineering, 10,* 67–78.

Creamer, E. G., & Laughlin, A. (2005). Self-authorship and women's career decision-making. *Journal of College Student Development, 46*(1), 13–27.

Creamer, E. G., Lee, S., & Laughlin, A. (2006). *Self-authorship as a framework for understanding life decision-making among college women in Korea.* Manuscript submitted for publication.

Dryburgh, H. (2000). Underrepresentation of girls and women in computer science: Classification of 1990s research. *Journal of Educational Computing Research, 23*(2), 181–202.

Fassinger, R. E. (1990). Causal models of career choice in two samples of college women. *Journal of Vocational Behavior, 36,* 225–248.

Felsman, D. E., & Blustein, D. L. (1999). The role of peer relatedness in late adolescent career development. *Journal of Vocational Behavior, 54*(2), 279–295.

Fisher, T. A., & Griggs, M. B. (1994, April). *Factors that influence the career development of African-American and Latino youth.* Paper presented at the Annual Meeting of the American Educational Research Association, New Orleans, LA.

Flowers, L. A., Pasearella, E. T., & Pierson, C. T. (2000). Information technology use and cognitive outcomes in the first year of college. *Journal of Higher Education, 71,* 637–667.

Flowers, L. A., & Zhang, Y. (2003). Racial differences in information technology use in college. *College Student Journal, 37*(2), 235–241.

Hackbarth, S. (2004). Changes in 4th-graders' computer literacy as a function of access, gender, and race. *Information Technology in Childhood Education Annual, 16*, 187–212.

Hofer, B. K., & Pintrich, P. R. (1997). The development of epistemological theories: Beliefs about knowledge and knowing and their relation to learning. *Review of Educational Research, 67*(1), 88–140.

Kegan, R. (1982). *The evolving self: Problem and process in human development.* Cambridge, MA: Harvard University Press.

Ketterson, T. U., & Blustein, D. L. (1997). Attachment relationships and the career exploration process. *Career Development Quarterly, 46*(2), 167–178.

Kotrlik, J. W., & Harrison, B. C. (1989). Career decision patterns of high school seniors in Louisiana. *Journal of Vocational Education Research, 14(2)*, 47–65.

Lowry, D. W. (2004). Understanding reproductive technologies as a surveillant assemblage: Revisions of power and technoscience. *Sociological Perspectives, 47*(4), 357–370.

Maruyama, G. M. (1998). *Basics of structural equation modeling.* Thousand Oaks, CA: Sage.

Miura, I. T. (1987). The relationship of computer self-efficacy expectations to computer interest and course enrollment in college. *Sex Roles, 16*(5/6), 303–311.

Noble, G., & O'Connor, S. (1986). Attitudes toward technology as predictors of online catalog use. *Research Notes*, 605–610.

O'Brien, K. M., & Fassinger, R. E. (1993). A causal model of the career orientation and career choice of adolescent women. *Journal of Counseling Psychology, 40*, 456–469.

O'Brien, K. M., Friedman, S. M., Tipton, L. C., & Linn, S. G. (2000). Attachment, separation, and women's vocational development: A longitudinal analysis. *Journal of Counseling Psychology, 47*(3), 301–315.

Paa, H. K., & McWhirter, E. H. (2000). Perceived influences on high school students' current career expectations. *Career Development Quarterly, 49*, 29–44.

Perry, W. G. (1970). *Forms of intellectual and ethical development in the college years: A scheme.* Troy, MO: Holt, Rinehart & Winston.

Rainey, L. M., & Borders, D. (1997). Influential factors in career orientation and career aspiration of early adolescent girls. *Journal of Counseling Psychology, 44*(2), 160–172.

Raykov, T., & Marcoulides, G. A. (2000). *A first course in structural equation modeling.* Mahwah, NJ: Lawrence Erlbaum Associates, Inc.

Ryan, N. E., Solberg, V. S., & Brown, S. D. (1996). Family dysfunction, parental attachment, and career search self-efficacy among community college students. *Journal of Counseling Psychology, 43*(1), 84–89.

Schultheiss, D. E. P., Kress, H. M., Manzi, A. J., & Glasscock, J. M. (2001). Relational influences in career development: A qualitative inquiry. *The Counseling Psychologist, 29*, 214–239.

Seymour, E., & Hewitt, N. M. (1997). *Talking about leaving: Why undergraduates leave the sciences.* Boulder, CO: Westview Press.

Shashaani, L. (1997). Gender differences in computer attitudes and use among college students. *Journal of Educational Computing Research, 16*(1), 37–51.

Taylor, K. M., & Betz, N. E. (1983). Applications of self-efficacy theory to understanding and treatment of career indecision. *Journal of Vocational Behavior, 22*, 63–81.

Volman, M., & van Eck, E. (2001). Gender equity and information technology in education: The second decade. *Review of Educational Research, 71*(4), 613–634.

Way, W. L., & Rossmann, M. M. (1996). *Lessons from life's first teacher: The role of the family in adolescent and adult readiness for school-to-work transition* (Report No. NCRVE-MDS-725). Berkeley, CA: National Center for Research in Vocational Education. (Eric Document Reproduction Service No. ED396113)

Wilder, G., Mackie, D., & Cooper, J. (1985). Gender and computers: Two surveys of computer-related attitudes. *Sex Roles, 13*(3/4), 215–228.

Part II

The Secondary School Level

Revisiting Culture, Time, and Information Processing Factors in Connecting to Girls' Interest and Choice of an Information Technology Career at the Secondary Level

Peggy S. Meszaros and Jane Butler Kahle

The chapters in this section present a sense of déjà vu as we relive the late 1970s in mathematics and the early 1980s in science. Even the language is similar; for example, Allison Kelly's (1987) term, "girl-friendly science," coined during her groundbreaking work in British schools, has been transformed to "girl-friendly technology" or "girl-friendly software or programs." Jacque Eccles's (1989) research in gender and mathematics that showed—through path analysis—that boys attributed success in mathematics to their own skills and intellects, while girls attributed their success to hard work is echoed in chapters in this section. And, once again, we are chasing after role models, girl friendly activities, and mathematics skills and achievement levels to understand why there are so few girls and women entering, or involved in, IT careers.

Today, as in previous years, the number of women entering IT careers is affected by their enrollments and success in secondary mathematics and physical science as well as the numbers and types of technology courses available in the secondary schools. This is an international problem noted by Jane Butler Kahle at the 2005 international IT conference. She was reminded by a colleague from Norway, where the percent of women studying engineering has not kept pace with other advances for women, that the number of young women who enter engineering programs in colleges and universities is limited by the number who take physics in secondary school.

As with math and science, researchers and educators are again turning to societal and cultural issues to understand and eventually alleviate the lack of girls and women in IT. For over two decades in the United States, we have known that girls have fewer experiences in science outside of school than boys (Kahle & Lakes, 1983). We also have known that girls desire to have more experiences, yet our educational system has not attempted in a systematic way to provide additional experiences for girls and underrepresented minority students. Rather, we continue to "blame" the parents and home situations. Today, we hear similar warnings about girls and technology: e.g., "the games are violent and directed at boys"; "parents send more boys, compared to girls, to computer camps"; "boys dominate classroom computers"; and so on.

Today in technology, as in the past in science and mathematics, studies of gender differences have focused on inward tendencies, relating findings to the characteristics of girls. If one interprets girls' underachievement in math and science and their lack of involvement in IT through the characteristic lens, differences are related to girls' maladaptive motivational patterns, and the burden of change is placed on the girls. On the other hand, if achievement and involvement differences are viewed through the response lens, girls' underachievement and lack of participation is not because of their characteristics but is rather a response to teaching environments that produce motivational patterns not conducive to learning (Boaler, 2002).

Key themes in chapters in this part revisit old problems but use the new lens of response. For instance, the problem of courses girls do not take at the high school level may be viewed as a high school culture problem of access and availability; the problem of lack of motivation may be viewed instead as a girls' careful consideration of efficient time spent working with teams as well as the future orientation of balancing work and family so important to today's millennial students. The old theme of outdated stereotypes of IT workers and incomplete and inaccurate descriptions of the IT field today may be viewed as the lack of accurate, unbiased, and complete IT career information that is in the hands of their family, teachers, and school counselors. A summary of these themes through the response lens with supporting research is the first goal of this chapter. The second goal is to present strategies, supported by the research literature, that may promote high school girls' interest and choice of an IT career. Suggestions for future research complete the organization of Part II.

Old Themes, New Responses

The themes of time, high school culture, and lack of accurate and up-to-date IT career information appear in the chapters in this section. The authors of the three chapters, using both qualitative and quantitative methodology, agree that negatively gendered stereotypes of the IT worker and time-consuming working conditions in the IT field present formidable barriers to female interest and choice of an IT career path. These barriers are reinforced by the lack of accurate information about IT careers. Throughout their lives, girls learn that being female in our society means that they are expected to be and act in certain ways. Cook (1993) calls this the "gendered context of life" and describes its impact on limiting what careers girls consider as well as their confidence in succeeding. Girls are well aware of the gendered context of life and learn at an early age what careers are appropriate for them to pursue. As early as middle school, girls begin to express preferences for female-dominated careers, especially jobs that are "helping" people or society (Lapan & Jingelski, 1992; Post, Williams, & Brubaker, 1996). This early elimination of careers that fall outside the acceptably gendered options for females precludes their interest and choice of nontraditional careers such as IT even before they know much about those careers. Seeing a career as "too masculine" may have far-reaching consequences if science, math, or IT falls into this category. Even girls with high aptitude for these subjects may opt out of the appropriate courses in high school, thus eliminating IT majors at the college level. This persisting barrier of male stereotype has a new wrinkle as an even larger cultural problem was found in the chapter by Howe, Berenson, and Vouk. Their interviews of high-achieving middle school girls interested in careers in IT revealed that these same girls have abandoned their aspirations when reinterviewed four years later in high school. Rather than citing a male stereotype, the girls had no room in their schedules for IT courses, weren't aware of any IT courses, or the courses were simply not offered at their high school. Raising the awareness of IT careers and working with school administrators may be the response needed so that the interest generated in middle school carries over into high school.

Chapter coauthors Berenson, Williams, Michael, and Vouk examine the theme of time as a factor in understanding girls' IT career decisions. This theme was seen in both time spent on assignments and time required in job responsibilities in an IT career. Earlier research by Berenson, Slaten, Williams, & Ho (2005) also found that time spent completing traditional solo methods of assignments was a factor in considering an IT career. Their work found that agile methods and pair programming methods provided a higher quality product in less time, leading to increased confidence among females in their study. The high school girls interviewed in this chapter echo the themes of this previous work and again identified time as an important variable associated with girls' career decisions. Girls in their study valued their independence in careers not tied to a nine-to-five schedule and sought careers that would provide them with flexible schedules. Howe and Strauss (2000) conclude that time is an important career value of today's millennial students, that is, those born between 1980 and 1999. Time is emerging as an important value for this generation, perhaps as a response to the over-scheduling so prevalent in their lives today. A workplace policy change may be needed to respond to this value.

Meszaros, Lee, and Laughlin add the theme of missing or inaccurate IT career information to the response perspective. When females in their study sought career information from family, teachers, and counselors, their advice led to negative IT interest and choice. This may indicate that girls received stereotyped or inaccurate messages about the appropriateness of this nontraditional career option for them. Silverman and Pritchard (1994) and Adler and Adler (1998) found that negative and inaccurate feedback from significant people in girls' lives was powerful in shaping their beliefs and career choices. Again, the response may be the development of new IT career materials that cover the full range of career opportunities available and continued education of parents, teachers, and school counselors as we seek to change old perceptions.

Summary of the Chapters in this Section

The lead chapter in this section by Howe et al. introduces us to the high school culture and moves our thinking from the lens of girls' characteristics and inadequacies to the response lens of what is going on with access to and the importance of IT courses in many high schools across the United States. The researchers used qualitative methodology to interview high-achieving girls entering seventh or eighth grade who were on a "fast track" in math. Three cohorts of girls participating in a two-week summer program of enrichment activities in mathematics and technology that included meeting regularly with mentors were interviewed at the end of their summer experience. The same girls were reinterviewed four years later when they were in high school. These girls were high achieving, hard working, confident of their math ability, and supported by their families. They enjoyed using computers and looked forward to learning more about computer science. Further, a significant number of them responded that they planned to have careers in computers or engineering. When interviewed later as high school students they had many of the same characteristics exhibited in middle school: e.g., confidence, high achievement, etc. However, they expressed a general lack of interest and information about computer science, computer scientists, and careers in computer science. While not all of the reasons for this decline in interest are known, the influence of the high school curriculum was found to be a major factor for the girls in this study. The American Association of University Women (AAUW) report, How Schools Shortchange Girls, points out that "the formal curriculum is the central message-giving instrument of the school" (AAUW, 1992, p. 105). The message given to the girls in this study was that computer science was either not offered or not considered necessary for acceptance to highly selective colleges.

Cultural aspects of the workplace environment emerged as a concern when Branson and her coauthors attempted to explain why high-achieving girls who are academically advanced in mathematics are not interested in IT careers. Through a series of snapshots taken from a seven-year longitudinal study of more than 300 high-achieving girls from middle school through high school, they followed the strands of careers and time devoted to work from previous studies. Using qualitative methods, they interviewed 39 of the Girls on Track cohort who volunteered to be interviewed in high school. Time emerged as an important variable associated with career decisions. These girls valued their independence and did not want desk jobs that tied them to one place from nine to five. They also wanted flexible schedules and the ability to have part-time jobs that would allow them to pursue other activities, including parenting. Work/family balance is a value of these millennials (Howe & Strauss, 2000), and changing the workplace culture may be a necessary response for the next generation to become part of the IT workforce.

In the last chapter of this section, Meszaros, Lee, and Laughlin use quantitative methodology to examine how female and male high school students make IT career decisions. Using a theoretical model, which also is employed in the description of the model presented in Chapter 1, and survey data from 556 high school students in Virginia, these researchers found two different patterns of information processing among the females and males. The primary difference was found as these young people turned to information sources such as their families, peers, teachers, and counselors for career information. When females sought career information, it often led to negative IT interest and choice, a finding that may indicate either that they received negative messages about the appropriateness of an IT career or that their information sources operated from stereotyped or incomplete views of IT careers. When both young men and women were encouraged to use computers, that experience reinforced their interest in an IT career. Up-to-date, complete, and accurate descriptions of IT career opportunities in various forms may be the response needed, as well as strategies to educate teachers, counselors, and parents in stereotyping and its effect on student interest and career choices.

All of the chapters in this section report studies that have examined the lack of girls in IT courses and careers through the response lens. That is, they all report that girls are capable of entering IT careers and of succeeding in them. However, during their high school years, cultural and social factors impinge negatively on girls' choices. Suggestions are made concerning educating parents, counselors, and teachers so that the advice and information provided to girls will emphasize their ability to enter and to succeed in IT majors in college and careers. One aspect is missing in the reported studies and their recommendations: that is, the importance of peer influence on the choices of girls, particularly for nontraditional courses and careers. As delineated in the next part, each chapter makes specific suggestions for recruiting girls into IT courses and careers.

Research to Practice in Secondary Settings

The chapters in this part clearly identify a persistent problem affecting the recruitment of girls into IT courses and careers, that is, the lack of accurate, unbiased information about the demands of an IT major in college or an IT career. Girls indicate that they want a balanced life and social interaction in the workplace. Unfortunately, the image of an IT career presented in the popular press and media usually presents an isolated work environment that consumes the employee—intellectually and socially. However, each chapter also suggests strategies for encouraging girls in IT as well as suggestions for changing the type of information provided to them. The following suggestions for new strategies offer ideas for recruiting females using a new lens.

Strategies for Recruiting K–12 Females to High Tech Careers

Inspire curiosity about computers by showing them to be fun and exciting. Encourage use and exposure to a variety of computer applications beyond those used for communication. Find ways to show how the computer can be creative and more than a tool. Examine the high school culture and course offerings to be sure students see IT courses offered and their necessity for certain careers. Provide attractive IT career information targeted to females and demonstrate how this career pathway leads to a "helping profession." Provide IT career information that emphasizes flexible work schedules, independent decision-making, and the opportunity to combine career with family. Provide parents, teachers, and school counselors with IT career information for females and strategies for talking with and presenting this information in creative ways. Provide career information that offers profiles of the complete range of IT career options and goes beyond the male stereotype of isolation and boring. Provide professional development workshops, seminars, and other experiences for high school teachers, counselors, and administrators that emphasize changing the high school culture and curriculum to feature the importance of IT courses and career pathways for females. Introduce teachers to practices that promote equity in the classroom. Give girls early and positive exposure to computers. Educate girls about the challenges and rewards of a career in IT. Reinforce workplace policies in business, government, and education that provide flexibility for work/life balance.

Future Research

Clearly there is a need to examine various factors leading to girls' lack of interest in careers in IT. The chapters in this part identify a lack of available, or of valued, courses in high school as well as negative or biased information concerning such careers as two major factors affecting a high school girl's choices. However, research is needed on classroom factors, teacher attitudes, and peer attitudes. Past research in mathematics and science has indicated that teacher attitudes are second only to parent attitudes in affecting a student's course selection in high school and college and career selection after college.

Research specifically focused on classroom factors, an area that proved important in addressing girls' enrollments and success in advanced science and mathematics courses, is needed. Initially, research identified overt teacher and student behaviors that negatively affected girls' interest and attitudes about math and science. Such research examined, for example, who was called on in class (target students), who received adequate time to reply (wait-time), and who received teacher attention (teacher beliefs). Although researchers interested in gender and IT may want to investigate overt factors, it is anticipated that newer, more subtle factors may be of more interest and concern.

Later studies concerning science or mathematics and gender focused on subtle factors. For example, Lee, Marks, & Byrd (1994) assessed the frequency of what they termed gender-related incidents in history, algebra, English, chemistry and one other subject (chosen by the school) in 21 schools. They identified gender-related incidents as very subtle comments or actions that frequently went unnoticed by students or the teacher. They found that the most frequent number of such incidents occurred in chemistry classes and that the number increased as the ratio of boys to girls increased. Given what we know about the ratio of boys to girls in high school computer and other IT classes, research in this area is sorely needed. Likewise, Gaskell (1995) identified a subtle social/cultural factor that he called gender lore that affected girls' participation and confidence in physical science classes. He defined gender lore as "vaguely remembered information from media reports and studies" that is widely accepted and believed by adolescent students of both sexes (Gaskell, p. 22). He concluded that belief and passive acceptance of such lore affects girls' confidence and performance in physical science classes—and eventually their future enrollment in physics. Again, the parallel with IT is obvious, and research is needed to assess any effect of gender lore on girls' choices in the IT area.

Because of the finding that girls receive biased or incorrect information about IT careers, it is important that research identify the most efficient and effective way of providing continuing education to adults, particularly to parents, who do not have the incentives that teachers and counselors may have to take courses. Further, research that investigates both the effectiveness of various types of recruitment materials as well as the efficacy of different modes of delivery is needed.

Conclusion

The chapters in this part successfully identify and explain several factors that affect girls' decisions to take IT courses and to enter IT careers. Further, the research reported examines girls' decisions through the response lens, not the characteristic lens, indicating that the situation may be reversed—if girls' attitudes and beliefs can be modified by appropriate course selection and effective counseling. Yet, the chapters move beyond simply identifying factors affecting girls to provide recommendations of ways to interest and encourage more girls to seek an IT career. Because the field is relatively new, further research is needed to identify other barriers as well as to assess the efficacy of the recommendations. The importance of the high school, or secondary school, in determining a career choice is clear. As the Norwegians found in engineering, the number of women in IT careers will continue to be limited by the number of girls who become literate and interested in IT during their high school days.

References

American Association of University Women. (1992). *How schools shortchange girls.* Washington, DC: Author.

Adler, P., & Adler, P. (1998). *Peer power: Preadolescent culture and identity.* New Brunswick, NJ: Rutgers University Press.

Berenson, S., Slaten, K., Williams, L., & Ho, C. W. (2005). Voices of women in a software engineering course: Reflections on collaboration. *ACM Journal of Educational Resources in Computing* (JERIC), 4(1), Article 3. Retrieved September 29, 2006, from the ACM Digital Library database: http://portal.acm.org/browse_dl.cfm?linked=1&part=journal&idx=J814&coll=ACM&dl=ACM

Boaler, J. (2002). Paying the price for "sugar and spice": Shifting the analytical lens in equity research. *Mathematical Thinking and Learning, 4*(2/3), 127–144.

Cook, E. P. (1993). The gendered context of life: Implications for women's and men's career plans. *Career Development Quarterly, 41*, 227–237.

Eccles, J. (1989). Bringing young women to mathematics and science. In M. Crawford & M. Gentry (Eds.), *Gender and thought: Psychological perspectives* (pp. 36–58). New York: Springer-Verlag.

Gaskell, J. (1995, August). *Gender-equity in science instruction and assessment: A case study of grade 10 electricity in British Columbia,* Canada (A report prepared for the OECD Science/Mathematics/Technology Education project). Unpublished manuscript, Vancouver, Canada: University of British Columbia.

Howe, N., & Strauss, B. (2000). *Millennials rising: The next great generation.* New York: Vintage.

Kahle, J. B., & Lakes, M. K. (1983). The myth of equality in science classrooms. *Journal of Research in Science Teaching, 20*, 131–140.

Kelly, A. (Ed.). (1987). *Science for girls?* Milton Keynes, England: Open University Press.

Lapan, R. T., & Jingelski, J. (1992). Circumscribing vocational aspiration in junior high school. *Journal of Counseling Psychology, 39*, 81–90.

Lee, V. E., Marks, H. M., & Byrd, T. (1994). Sexism in single sex and coeducational secondary school classrooms. *Sociology of Education, 67*, 92–100.

Post, P., Williams, M., & Brubaker, L. (1996). Career and lifestyle expectations of rural eighth-grade students: A second look. *Career Development Quarterly, 44*, 160–172.

Silverman, S., & Pritchard, A. (1994). *Building their future II: High school girls and technology education in Connecticut.* Hartford, CT: Connecticut Women's Education and Legal Fund.

Chapter 2

Changing the High School Culture to Promote Interest in Information Technology Careers among High-Achieving Girls

Ann Howe, Sarah Berenson, and Mladen Vouk

Abstract

Interviews with high-achieving middle school girls enrolled in a math and technology summer program showed that one fourth of the girls were interested in careers in IT. The girls were interviewed four years later when they were in high school. We found that all of them were still interested in math and most of them were taking, or had taken, advanced math courses. However, only several were taking or had taken a computer science course, and only one girl expressed interest in pursuing a career in IT. They showed a general lack of information about computer science, computer scientists and careers in computer science.

Introduction

Girls who have the ability, the persistence, and the interest to be high achievers in math would seem to have unlimited opportunities for careers in IT. Yet few of them are choosing such a career. Although women now make up 20% of graduate students in engineering, recent statistics show that computer engineering, the fastest growing specialty in engineering, still attracts a heavily male enrollment (Laurel, 2003).

The gender gap in interest and participation in IT begins long before graduate school, as shown by a College Board report (quoted in American Association of University Women [AAUW], 2000, p. 42) of high school students who took the Advanced Placement Computer Science tests in 1999. Of those who took the "A" test, 17% were women; of those who took the more difficult "AB" test, only 9% were women. This disparity has led investigators to ask why girls in middle school and high school are not attracted to computer science and what changes can be made to make it more appealing.

A number of ideas and suggestions have been put forward as partial answers to the question of why adolescent girls are not more interested in computer science. A study commissioned by the AAUW (2000) makes a strong case that girls regard computers and computing as a male domain. According to Margolis and Fisher (2002) high school computing belongs to a subset of boys who have been using computers and playing computer games since they were in elementary school. From the age of eight boys spend twice as much time playing computer games as girls do; they form friendships and create communities based on their experience and knowledge so that by the time they get to high school they know more about computers and computing than most of their teachers. They hang out in the computer lab during lunchtime and take over the computers, ignoring anyone else who comes in the room. This computing culture carries over into the classroom, where boys dominate computer science classes and tease the few girls who are brave enough to encroach on their turf (pp. 40-41). Sanders (1995) points out that computer magazines have a preponderance of male authors and use photographs and illustrations aimed exclusively at a male audience. Further observations by Sanders reinforcing the message that computers are for the male domain concern the large libraries of pornography, and what she terms "compusex" (p. 151), readily available on the Web.

Parents and teachers reinforce and sustain the view that boys belong in and to the computer culture while girls do not (AAUW, 2000). Gilbert, Bravo, and Kearney (2004), who conducted a study in two high schools, interpreted the findings of their research to show that boys are expected to be competent and interested in technology but girls are not and, consequently, are not given the same opportunities as boys to learn and excel. "Thus," they write, "rather than lack of interest, key factors in girls' not choosing to be actively involved in technology appear to involve lack of exposure and experience with technology and little opportunity to develop views of themselves as creators of technology" (p. 194).

Several writers have noted that computer games are overwhelmingly made to appeal to boys. Not only the violence and competitiveness of the games appeal to boys, but also appealing is the creation, in the games, of a fantasy world, "an isolated world far removed from domestic space or adult supervision" (Jenkins, 1998, p. 279). Girls, on the other hand, are interested in games with real-life people and real-world settings where friendships can be formed, but Laurel (1998) found that there are few games based on these themes.

Another explanation for girls' not choosing to take computer science courses or plan careers in IT is that girls often underestimate their abilities in math and science and believe that technology is more difficult for them than for boys. For this reason they may avoid taking computer science courses or find, if they do take a course, that the boys are ahead of them; girls then attribute this disparity to their own lack of ability (Margolis & Fisher, 2002, pp. 38-40)

In this chapter we report the results of a study designed to elicit and explore the reasons that a group of high-achieving high school girls gives for their own lack of interest in computer science and in IT careers.

Background

This work is an extension of previous work in which we drew a profile of girls who participated in a program called Girls on Track (GOT) when they were entering seventh or eighth grade. GOT was a program for high-achieving girls who were on the "fast track" in math leading to the study of calculus by their junior or senior years in high school. Participating girls attended a two-week summer program of enrichment activities in mathematics and technology and had opportunities to meet regularly with mentors during the following school year. There were three cohorts who participated during three successive years. Four years later a sample of GOT girls, then in high school, was interviewed again.

Girls Entering Seventh or Eighth Grade

Interviews when girls were entering seventh or eighth grade were conducted with a sample of 15 girls from each GOT cohort (i.e., 1999, 2000, 2001), making a total sample of 45. Purposeful sampling was based on girls' enthusiasm, motivation, interest, and performance during the summer camp experience. Girls were interviewed at or near the end of the two-week summer math camp. Interviews, lasting 15 to 20 minutes, were conducted by interviewers who had not worked with the girls during the summer experience. The prompts in these interviews were: (a) What was math like for you last year? (b) What grade would make you unhappy? (c) Where did you go when you wanted help? (d) What is your favorite subject? and (e) What careers interest you? Follow-up questions were used to prompt interviewees to clarify and/or amplify their responses. The interviews were videotaped; the videotapes were transcribed and analyzed. Content analysis was used to develop categories that were then used to code the transcripts. A questionnaire on attitudes toward computers was also administered to participants, and a survey of participating teachers and counselors was conducted.

Findings

In a preliminary paper (Howe & Berenson, 2003), based on interviews with a sample of 15 girls from the first cohort, we reported that four character-istics were common to all the girls in the sample. In the second and third years we repeated the interviews with 15 girls from each of the second and third cohorts and found that there was remarkable similarity in the responses of girls from each successive cohort. The characteristics common to all GOT girls were these:

Assertiveness. These were not the "good girls" who are passive in class, remaining quietly in the background while the teacher asks the boys the hard questions. Their desire to understand, as well as their desire to get a good grade, prompted them to ask questions in class and to seek help offered by teachers before and after class.

Belief in hard work. What they all did to raise a grade or maintain an A was to work hard or harder. When they got the A that they all worked for and expected, they said that they felt good because "I know I worked for it" or because "I really pushed myself" or because "I worked so hard for that grade." When they didn't get the grade they wanted or expected, they did not blame the teacher but put the onus on themselves. Typical is the girl who said, "If I got a C, I'd just work more and ask the teacher for stuff to review." The interviews confirmed what we have long known: that girls, unlike boys, believe that success comes from hard work rather than innate ability (Wolleat, Pedro, Fennema, & Becker, 1980).

Desire to understand math. These girls all said that they wanted to under-stand what they were doing in math. One said she wanted to know "if I'm really learning and not just memorizing." Another said, "I like a challenge and not just something I can zip through. Something I really have to think about and work hard to get the answer. You have to know how you got the answer. You have to know all kinds of math, not just one type. You have to be good at all the steps, not just knowing the answer."

High expectations. Their high expectations are encouraged and supported by their families and, often, by their teachers. They were confident that they would experience success in mathematics, defined at this point in their lives as achieving high grades. They did not report feeling pressured by their parents but had apparently adopted their parents' expectations as their own.

Table 1. Percent responses indicating middle school girls' interests/attitudes toward computing.

Computer Interest and Attitude Items	% Agree	% Don't Know	% Disagree
Find computer games fun and interesting	95	5	0
Playing computer games makes me want to learn more about computers	60	21	18
Think computer games made to appeal to boys	26	10	63
Look forward to learning more about computers	90	5	5
Know many girls who talk about computers with excitement	42	18	35
Know many boys who talk about computers with excitement	68	18	13
My teachers have interesting and fun ways to do things with computers	55	18	26
My parents encourage me to learn new ways to use computers	76	15	8
In the magazines and TV shows I like, girls use computers	39	42	18
In the magazines and TV shows I like, boys use computers	32	52	15
When I imagine my future career, I see myself using computers in creative and positive ways	76	15	8
When I imagine my future career I see myself learning about computers so I can improve them	32	32	29
If I wanted to make the world a better place, I would find ways to use the computer to help me to do it	68	18	13

Interest in computers. The GOT summer program included learning activities in technology as well as in math. Computers were available throughout the program, and instructors were on hand to help girls learn or increase their skills in using word processing, the Internet, email, Excel, and PowerPoint. At the end of the program a questionnaire was used to gather data on the girls' interest in and attitudes toward computers and computing. The results are shown in Table 1.

The idea that computing belongs to boys was not supported by these results. Nor was the idea that parents believe that computing belongs to boys but not to girls. On the contrary, girls were in strong agreement: they enjoyed computer games, they wanted to learn more about computers, their parents encouraged them to learn more, they saw themselves using computers in creative ways, and they would use computers to "make the world a better place." Overall, at this point in their lives they had a positive attitude and strong interest in computers and computing.

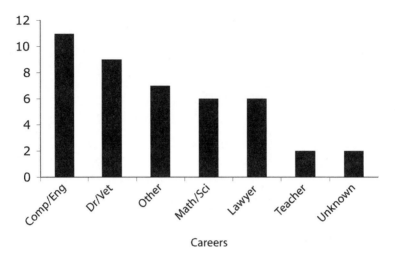

Figure 1. Career choices of middle school girls.

Career interests. Included in the interview protocol was a question on career plans. Some girls had very clear ideas and plans for the future, and others were vague or undecided. Responses to this question are presented in Figure 1. Computers and/or engineering was the most popular career choice, chosen by 11 of the 43 middle schoolgirls who responded to the question concerning careers.

Summary of Middle School Girls

The interviews and questionnaire produced a picture of girls entering eighth, or, in some cases seventh, grade who were high-achieving, hard working, confident, sure of their math ability, and supported by their families. They enjoyed using computers and looked forward to learning more about computer science. A significant number planned to have careers in computers or engineering. Now we turn to the results of interviews of the girls several years later.

Girls in High School

In 2004 we conducted follow-up interviews with a sample of 29 girls who had participated in the GOT program and volunteered to come to campus to be interviewed. When these interviews were conducted, the girls were high school sophomores, juniors, or seniors; the schools represented were one charter school, one private school, and six public schools, all in one large urban school district. The main interview prompts were: (a) What math are you taking this year? (b) How do you feel about computer scientists? (c) Have you taken any computer programming classes? (d) If not, why not? (e) Would you be interested in a computer science career? (e) What career interests you at this point? Interviewers probed for explanations or clarifications after each response. Interviews were audiotaped, transcribed, and analyzed.

Findings

When the girls were interviewed as high school students, they had many of the same characteristics that they exhibited when in middle school. They were still hard working, assertive, confident of their ability in math, and not satisfied with rote learning; they still had strong family support. They had maintained their interest in math, and many were taking, or planned to take, advanced math courses.

A different picture emerges when we examine their interest in computer science and interest in a career in IT. We found a general lack of interest and information about computer science, computer scientists, and careers in computer science.

Interest in computer science. Although 90% of the middle school girls had indicated that they looked forward to learning more about computers, only five of the 29 high school girls are taking or have taken a computer science course beyond the basic eighth-grade requirement. One atypical girl who was taking her second computer science course said she had a great teacher and "loves computers" but had other career plans. The reasons given for not taking a high school course in computer science and the number who gave each reason are shown in Table 2.

The reasons given fall into two categories; the first three are school-based and suggest a culture that puts a low value on technology except as a tool. It suggests that neither counselors nor teachers presented computer science as an attractive option. The three girls who said that their school offered no computer science course attend a public charter school; those in the other schools who "could not fit it in" chose to fit other electives, rather than

Table 2. Reasons high school girls give for avoiding computer science electives.

Reasons Given	Number
No room in schedule	7
Not aware that a course was available	6
No computer science course offered	3
No interest in computer science	4
Presumed difficulty of course	4

computer science, into their schedules. This, too, is an indication of lack of interest. For those who think computer science is too difficult, computing does not seem to be linked with math in their minds, and confidence in their math ability does not transfer to confidence in computer science ability.

Computer science was viewed as difficult not only by those who gave it as the reason for not taking the course but by others as well. In response to the question "What kind of students would you find in a computer science class?" five answered that there would probably be more boys than girls while eight said there would be an even number of boys and girls, but almost all indicated in some way that computer science students would have to be "smart" and that they would need a good teacher. Several said they had heard that the classes were boring, just sitting at the computer following steps in a workbook. Since we know that boys have had more computer experience than girls, the perception of computer science as a very difficult course may well be due to lack of experience and the kind of "fooling around" with computers that boys are more likely to do.

These girls were clearly not part of the computer culture nor aware of it, if it exists, in any of these high schools. Since the girls came from eight high schools, in different parts of the city and surrounding area, it is noteworthy that none of them alluded to boys' "owning" computers or a feeling that they were excluded. They think of computer science, if they think of it at all, as difficult, boring, and unnecessary for their futures. They are aware that boys are more interested in technology than they are but there is no indication that this is a conscious reason that they have opted out. After all, they compete with boys in their other classes every day.

Career interests. The results of asking girls now in high school about their current career interests reflect their lack of interest in taking high school computing. The career interests of the girls are shown in Figure 2.

Although one fourth of the girls planned to pursue a career in computer science or engineering when they were entering eighth grade, only one of the sample of high school girls now wants a career in information technology. Some of the girls told us that they were simply not interested, but a third of the students (nine out of 29) were put off by what they believe the work of computer scientists to be. The prevailing image of a computer scientist is a person whose life is spent in a cubicle in a large office, spending long hours working alone with a computer, in a job that is not creative and not people-oriented. None of the girls mentioned male dominance of IT or gave it as a reason for lack of interest in an IT career.

In addition to lack of information about careers in IT, no one had a clear idea of a career path for computer science. In contrast, some pursuing other

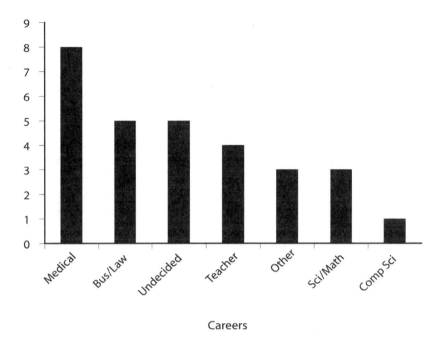

Figure 2. Career choices of high school girls.

careers had set themselves on a clear path and knew the steps they would have to take. This is what one girl told us:

"I actually want to go to medical school. I really want to be a pediatrician. I want to work in a hospital with sick children. I wanted to be a vet a little bit when I was little but ever since I could baby-sit and stuff, I've wanted to be a doctor.... [after college] I'd still be in medical school because you have to take like four or five more years after undergraduate school... [then] either private practice or I'd want to try working in a hospital with cancer patients."

Another girl, who plans to have a career in genetics, has already selected the graduate school she wants to attend for a PhD and has a clear idea of the steps that will lead to her goal. The steps to a career as a doctor, a nurse, or a teacher are also understood, but no student interviewed had any idea of the steps one would take to have a career in information technology.

Summary of High School Girls

We did not find a strong feeling among the girls that they were excluded from computer science or that it was a male domain. They recognized that boys were more interested in and more knowledgeable about computers than they were, but this did not appear to be a factor in their course decisions. They use computers to access the Internet, to write papers, and to make spreadsheets in their classes. They also use them in their everyday lives with no more thought than they give to driving a car or making a phone call, but they seem only mildly interested, if at all, in learning how computers work or how to use computers in creative ways.

These high-achieving girls who are very successful in school appear to know nothing about careers in computer science. Perhaps this is not worthy of note, given the fact that these girls were born into a world where computers were taken for granted. Still, this is somewhat surprising since many of their parents work in technological environments. We found no evidence that parents discourage girls from taking computer courses or planning to have IT careers. However, we found no evidence that parents encouraged girls in these directions. One exception was noted of a girl who was interested in pursuing a career in computer science. She spoke of her father's job in a technology company that is widely recognized for its stellar working conditions, including on-site day care and other employee benefits. Since she envisioned herself working for this company, we believe that her responses indicated a critical event in our longitudinal study, which will be explored further.

Factors in High School Culture

A factor that has not been highlighted in discussions about why girls are not pursuing careers in IT is the high school curriculum. In our study we found that computer courses beyond the basic requirement had to be sought out by students; although students came from eight different schools, no student interviewed had been in any situation where computer science was presented as a course alternative, much less as an attractive career option. It is often noted that the overall design of the academic high school curriculum has changed little in more than a hundred years. The content of courses has changed but few changes have been made in the basic requirements. One of the AAUW reports, How Schools Shortchange Girls, points out that "the formal curriculum is the central message-giving instrument of the school" (AAUW, 1992, p. 105). In the schools attended by the girls in our study the message is that computer science is an add-on, not taught by the best teachers, and not necessary for acceptance to the best colleges. Since it isn't necessary and is thought to be hard, why risk getting a grade below an A to ruin one's grade point average? Although the girls said they couldn't fit computer science in their schedules, they are taking other electives in addition to as many Advanced Placement courses as possible.

A factor that cannot be discounted is the influence of teachers. We heard of no overt negative actions of teachers such as that reported by Schofield (1995), where researchers observed a computer science class in which the teacher did nothing to prevent boys from teasing the few girls who were enrolled in the class. However, we cannot discount the possibility of the more subtle influence of teachers. As part of our study of the Girls on Track program we conducted a survey of the teachers and counselors who participated in that program during three summers. We found that teachers believe that boys and girls have the same aptitude for math, that girls work harder and get better grades, but that boys enjoy math more and have more career opportunities than girls in math-related fields. We cannot generalize this to include career opportunities in IT, but the results are suggestive.

Discussion

Whether a lack of interest, lack of knowledge, or lack of guidance is related to girls' lack of interest in IT careers has yet to be determined. It seems unlikely that many of these high-achieving girls will be drawn to study computer science in college. Also, it appears as if no teacher or parent has intervened to dispel the girls' stereotypes of a computer scientist or a career in IT. Sanders, Koch, and Urso (1997) suggest using a series of activities they designed for preservice teachers to erase some of the negative stereotypes associated with mathematics, science, and technology careers. These activities are easily adaptable to promote thoughtful discussions for teacher enhancement and parent programs.

Although these girls are good math students and interested in math, math is seen as a means to careers rather than the basis of a career. Three decades of effort on the part of mathematics educators and feminists has made ambitious girls aware that they must take math throughout high school if they want to be eligible for college entrance as a step toward careers in science, engineering, and other fields. Girls who have aspirations for these careers must succeed in math throughout their precollege years. There are no such compelling reasons to take computer science. It is not generally required for college admission or as a prerequisite for science or engineering. At this point in their schooling, high school girls do not think of computer science as necessary for the careers they want nor do they think of careers in IT as exciting and creative. Our challenge is to raise their level of awareness and to change the high school culture so that the excitement generated in middle school carries over into high school.

Conclusions

There are several questions that we hope to pursue to help us understand these girls' lack of interest in computer science or information technology (Berenson, Williams, Michael, & Vouk, 2005). Why do they see the value of the computer as a communication tool rather than an object of invention? We have to ask what motivates girls who do choose to major in computer science in college. In a pilot study of North Carolina State students, we noted that many computer science students came from small, rural high schools. Could it be that the experiences of girls in our sample, who are mostly from large, urban high schools, have been in a climate where IT careers are not valued? We also are interested in girls' experiences at home and possible negative influences from parents who work in IT. Could it be that parents spend long hours at work or discuss frustrating incidents in the workplace around the dinner table, and this discourages girls' participation? While we assume that an attribute of computer scientists is their mathematical abilities, we need to test this assumption. Finally, we found little support for the idea that the perception that IT is a boys' world prevents girls from participating in or pursuing IT interests. We do speculate that there are a different set of experiences needed to spark girls' interests in IT careers, and that remains our future challenge.

Acknowledgments

This research was supported in part by National Science Foundation grant 9813902, Girls on Track and National Science Foundation grant 0204222, Women and Information Technology. The views expressed here do not necessarily reflect the views of the National Science Foundation.

References

American Association of University Women. (2000). *Tech-Savvy: Educating girls in the new computer age.* Washington, DC: Author.

American Association of University Women. (1992). *AAUW report: How schools shortchange girls.* New York: Marlowe and Company.

Berenson, S., Williams, L., Michael, J., & Vouk, M. (2005, July/August). *Examining time as a factor in young women's IT career decisions.* Paper presented at the Crossing Cultures, Changing Lives Conference, Mansfield College, Oxford, U.K.

Gilbert, L., Bravo, M., & Kearney, L. (2004). Partnering with teachers to educate girls in the new computer age. *Journal of Women & Minorities in Science & Engineering, 10*(2), 179–202.

Gokhale, A., & Stier, K. (2004). Closing the gender gap in technical disciplines: An investigative study. *Journal of Women & Minorities in Science & Engineering, 10*(2), 149–159.

Howe, A., & Berenson, S. (2003, July). High-achieving girls in mathematics: What's wrong with working hard? In N. Pateman, B. Dougherty, & J. Zilliox (Eds.), *Proceedings of the 2003 Joint Meeting of Psychology of Mathematics Education and PME-NA* (pp. 87–93). Honolulu, HI: University of Hawaii.

Jenkins, H. (1998). Complete freedom of movement: Video games as gendered play spaces. In J. Cassell & H. Jenkins (Eds.), *From Barbie to Mortal Kombat: Gender and computer games* (pp. 262–297). Cambridge, MA: MIT Press.

Laurel, B. (1998). An interview with Brenda Laurel. In J. Cassell & H. Jenkins (Eds.), *From Barbie to Mortal Kombat: Gender and computer games* (pp. 118–135). Cambridge, MA: MIT Press

Laurel, B. (2003, May 16). Down for the count. *Science, 300,* 1072.

Margolis, J., & Fisher, A. (2002). *Unlocking the clubhouse: Women in computing.* Cambridge, MA: MIT Press.

Sanders, J. (1995). Girls and technology. In S. Rosser (Ed.), *Teaching the majority: Breaking the gender barrier in science, mathematics, and engineering* (pp. 147–159). New York: Teachers' College Press.

Sanders, J., Koch, J., & Urso, J. (1997). *Gender equity right from the start.* Mahwah, NJ: Lawrence Erlbaum.

Scholfield, P. (1995). *Quantifying language: A researcher's and teacher's guide to gathering language data and reducing it to figures.* North Somerset, UK: Multilingual Matters Limited.

Spears, J., Dyer, R., Franks, S., & Montelone, B. (2004). Building a network to support girls and women in science, technology, engineering, and mathematics. *Journal of Women & Minorities in Science & Engineering, 10,* 161–177.

Wolleat, P., Pedro, J., Fennema, E., & Becker, A. (1980). Sex differences in high school students' causal attributions of performance in mathematics. *Journal for Research in Mathematics Education, 11*(5), 356–366.

Chapter 3

Examining Time as a Factor in Young Women's Information Technology Career Decisions

Sarah Berenson, Laurie Williams, Joan Michael, and Mladen Vouk

Abstract

The research problem addressed in this chapter is a synthesis of findings from several projects conducted at North Carolina State University. From the synthesis we address possible reasons for young women's disinterest in information technology careers. Interviews with high school girls and college computer science women revealed that time was a major factor in the high school girls' career choices and a possible factor in the retention of some women computer science majors in careers. Our results speak to some of the research findings of those who study the millennium generation, especially around work/life balance issues. While all of these girls and women did not explicitly state the concern, they perceive a need for independence, flexibility, and part-time work that is embedded within issues of work/life balance.

Introduction

As the number of women majoring in computer science, computer engineering, and electrical engineering is falling, there is growing concern that the historical strength of the United States IT workforce may be in danger. Studies of these workforce supply problems have increased attention on young women's attitudes, experiences, and behaviors towards technology in an attempt to stem the tide of women's decreased interest and participation in IT careers (e.g., American Association of University Women [AAUW], 2000; Margolis & Fisher, 2002). The research problem addressed in this chapter is a synthesis of findings from four projects conducted at North Carolina State University. From the synthesis we plan to address possible reasons for young women's disinterest in information technology careers. Two of these projects span seven years of investigations into high-achieving young women's career decisions beginning in middle school, through high school, and into college. The other projects span five years of studying attitudes and achievement of computer science college students towards learning environments that foster collaboration within agile and pair programming methodologies. All four of these projects were funded in large part by the National Science Foundation.

Girls on Track

The first project, started in 1998, was Girls on Track: Increasing Middle Grade Girls' Interest in Math-Related Careers by Engaging them in Computer-Based Mathematical Explorations of Urban Problems in their Communities. Funding for Girls on Track provided a year-round enrichment program for more than 200 high achieving middle school girls who were selected to take Algebra 1 on the fast track. The ages ranged from 11–13 with about 60% Caucasian, 30% African American, and about 10% Asian. The girls attended a two-week summer camp where they investigated community problems using mathematics and information technologies. In addition the program provided tutoring in the fall and math mentoring in the spring. The project also incorporated a professional development component for middle school mathematics teachers, preservice teachers, and guidance counselors. Four years of quantitative and qualitative data were collected during this project, including standardized test results in mathematics and computer literacy, mathematics, science, and computer science course selections, confidence in mathematics and information technologies, proportional reasoning scores, and career interests. The middle school participants reported that they enjoyed working with information technology; many of them had not had extensive prior experience using IT tools. Before coming to summer camp, many girls did not use technology for academic purposes. For example, 82% of the Year 2 girls either had rarely or never used a spreadsheet. Similarly, 65% of these girls had rarely or never used IT tools to solve math or science problems. In the post-camp surveys, 100% of the girls rated their PowerPoint presentations positively, and 96% rated their Web page construction positively. At the end of camp, nearly one quarter of both Year 1 and Year 2 girls reported career interests in computer science or engineering as they prepared to enter seventh and eighth grade (Howe, Berenson, & Vouk, 2005).

Women and Information Technology

The IT Workforce program at the National Science Foundation funded the second study, the Women and Information Technology (WIT) project, that continued to collect data from Girls on Track participants as girls progressed through high school. The goal of the WIT project was to develop and test a model of education persistence of high-achieving young women as they moved through high school towards their undergraduate career choices. Examining school, social, and personal factors, the study prepared to track the development of these girls' career interests as they proceeded through high school. Most Girls on Track participants remained on an advanced mathematics track through their early high school years. After Algebra 2, 75% of these high-achieving girls remained on the advanced mathematics track, taking calculus in their junior or senior years. Much more disappointing was the small number of girls (six out of 39) electing to take computer science courses in high school from the Year 1 cohort. Five of these girls reported negatively on their high school computer science experiences. Those numbers have not changed significantly in our sample of more than 300 girls. In terms of career choices, we interviewed 39 girls from the first three cohorts in Spring 2004 and found that all but one girl were interested in pursuing an IT career path. Following up in Fall 2004 with those in the Year 1 cohort who were going off to their first year of college ($n = 21$), we found eight majors in the arts and humanities, nine majors in engineering/math/science, and three business majors. None of those interested in engineering were pursuing undergraduate majors in computer science.

Agile Development and Pair Programming

This IT Workforce project is led by Dr. Laurie Williams in computer science and is designed to examine the effects of new methods of software development on the retention of women and minorities in computer science majors at the university. Agile software development, a relatively new process model, is rapidly gaining in popularity and use. All the agile methodologies, for example, Extreme Programming, are highly collaborative and social in nature. Specifically, agile methodologies value "individuals and interactions over processes and tools" and value "customer collaboration over contract negotiation." We believe the collaboration and the social component inherent in these methodologies is appealing to people whose learning and training models are socially oriented. There is evidence, for example, that some minority groups, some disabled, and in general a fair fraction of women and men may be helped by this approach in their preparation for and their success/retention in the IT workforce. Changes in the organization of work often have consequences for recruiting and retaining employees. The transition from, for example, solo programming to the more collaborative pair programming may make a career in IT more attractive to people who may have concerns regarding the lack of social interaction in many IT positions.

Focus and Problem

In essence, we have a series of snapshots taken from a seven-year longitudinal study of more than 250 high-achieving girls from middle school through high school. The data reveal that these high-achieving girls lose their initial interests in IT careers upon entering high school. We have reported on a variety of reasons that these girls give for not taking computer science courses in high school (Berenson, Vouk, Michael, Greenspon, & Person, 2004). Generally they state that these courses do not carry advanced standing for grade point averages (A = 5 quality points), schedule conflicts with other electives or AP classes, and are not tied to their career interest. Also, we examined reasons that girls give for their lack of interest in IT careers. A vast majority reported that they knew nothing about these careers. Our problem is to attempt to explain why high achieving girls who are academically advanced in mathematics are not interested in IT careers.

In this analysis, we obtained clues from findings reported by Berenson, Slaten, Williams, and Ho (2005) concerning the voices of women in an upper-level computer science design course at the university. One of the emergent themes reported was that agile methods and pair programming methods saved these women time in comparison to traditional solo methods of assignments. Agile methods require collaboration among pairs of students, where one student assumes the role of "driver" by controlling the keyboard to enter code, and the other the role of "navigator" to observe and question the decisions of the driver. The following are several quotes from computer science women undergraduates published in the Journal on Educational Resources in Computing.

Less time.

A consensus developed among the undergraduate students that paired programming and collaborative development methods took less time than solo work. Since students value time as an important factor in their lives, their opinions concerning structured collaborative experiences were positive. In speaking about her experiences with her partner, Sylvia commented: "We just sat down and programmed and it was just the way we worked. It worked out really well.... We kind of got through this stuff in so much faster time than we would have separately—much, much faster.... If you don't know how to do something and you're going away to search something on the Internet or look it up yourself, it's easier to have someone else explain it to you."

In describing her solo assignment, Beth speaks to feeling somewhat lost without a partner and taking a lot of time just staring at the computer. "Then you go back to the old style of doing solo, it's kind of... a little bit hard. It suddenly feels like the weight is heavier—like you have to do all this stuff on your own and there's nobody to talk to and to ask a question to. So you have to like stare at the computer for hours... thinking all by yourself."

In a similar vein, Stacy infers that working alone can increase the amount of time she may have to spend on an assignment. "I think that it's very common thing to get sort of stumped on something or code something that you just look back at and can't figure out why it's not working. I think that pair programming really helps solve those issues, 'cause you have one other person there looking with you and they can quickly see what you are blind to for whatever reason."

Time management.

The issue of collaborative work taking less time was repeated throughout the transcripts and the retrospectives. Also, students commented that they produced a higher quality product when they work collaboratively in pairs or teams (pp. 8-9).

These data led to the conjecture that the methodology produced a higher quality product in less time, therefore leading to increased confidence among these women undergraduates. Based on these results, we decided to return to the 39 interviews of our high school high achievers to examine the interview data for comments related to the strands of careers and time.

Data Collection and Analysis

Girls on Track girls who were rising seventh and eighth graders in summers 1999, 2000, and 2001 and who were in high school during spring of 2004 volunteered to be interviewed about their career choices. Thirty-nine semi-structured interviews were tape-recorded and transcribed from these sophomores, juniors, and seniors. Most of the data about their career visions and aspirations were gleaned from a prompt asking about their interest in future careers and then probes to uncover the girls' perceptions of these careers in relation to their values and interests. We employ grounded theory methods of inquiry in order to develop propositions related to women's low participation in IT careers. Grounded theory methodology requires that researchers make multiple collections of data "in the field" and conduct interviews to identify theoretical propositions or hypotheses. Then these propositions are tested. The method involves continuously collecting data until a category is saturated and no new information is added. We used an iterative and dynamic process with propositions developed and then tested over time as younger girls move through middle grades and high school. The problem that this chapter addresses is to identify possible reasons for the drop in interest in IT careers. The proposition we are testing in this chapter began with findings from the agile development and pair programming project and the importance of time (Berenson, Vouk, Michael, Greenspon, & Person, 2004). We analyzed the data using categorical aggregation where time was mentioned in conjunction with career choices in the interviews. Then constant comparison methods were used to identify themes within the strands of career and time.

The Evidence

Of the 39 girls interviewed, 16 mentioned "time" as an important variable associated with their career decisions. The first theme to emerge within time was the value these girls placed on their independence. Further analysis revealed that some of these girls wanted careers that would provide them with flexible schedules. Another theme associated with time and career options was that of part-time work. We consider the evidence under each of these themes to draw some conjectures about the strands of time and career.

Independence. Ten of the girls wanted jobs where they would be independent from careers that they envision to be the in nine-to-five, desk job workplace. Rather than pursue traditional careers within established organizations, girls mentioned careers where they would direct the job-related activities themselves or have opportunities to make decisions in dynamic environments.

Student 1: [five years after college graduation] "I would say living still in North Carolina near family. Working hard to have my own house or place. Something like that. And still working probably, I would want to pull up on my own ... having my own office and working myself, trying to get that started. And having other people working with me ... or working under somebody."

Student 2: "You know, I just want to sit behind some screen and sell stuff over the Internet. That's another thing I've sort of wanted to be. To like run my own store or something. But you know it's just sort of a free schedule...."

Student 3: "Well I would probably not want to work with a company. I'd probably want to start my own business because then I can work on my own time. And I guess have a nice little business where I have everything that I would need and my computer...."

Student 4: "I like business. I took a small business class and I really like everything that has to do with like the whole business."

Student 5: "And if you go into business you can do almost anything so I was thinking about that."

Student 6: "A lawyer, I might want to be one just because it's something you're working at instead of having some boss tell you this is how you're going to do it and you come in every day and sit down and do the same thing."

Student 7: "I'd probably want to interact with people a lot. And I want like a real hands-on job where I can, I guess move around a lot. Like I don't actually want to sit around at a desk all day and do those things. I want to interact with people a lot and travel would be a lot of fun too."

Student 8: [Speaking about her career as a pediatrician] "Either a private practice … I'd want to try. Or working in a hospital with like cancer patients."

Student 9: "What I really want to do now is [the kind of project] that you go and oversee rebuilding houses, substandard housing and stuff and make sure it's safe and they kind of are a go-between for churches and other organizations."

Student 9: "Interact with people a lot. Like I kind of want a job where there's not a typical day. That you kind of have to go with the flow and change and interact and not a desk job."

Student 10: "I would like to work in something hands-on. I wouldn't like to be in an office too often and I would like to have a job where change was involved … like I didn't do the same thing every day."

Independence means several different things to these girls in terms of their careers. Some are considering careers where they can be their own boss [Student 1, Student 2, Student 3, Student 4, Student 5, and Student 8]. Others want the independence of determining their own work tasks rather than being controlled by a "boss" [Student 6 and Student 7]. Student 8 and Student 9 want to be their own bosses within organizations. Independence for these girls is further defined as jobs with tasks that change rapidly as opposed to careers that involve repetition. [Student 9 and Student 10].

Flexibility. A second strand to emerge within the time factors associated with careers is that of flexibility. Several girls mentioned this as a factor to consider when making their career decisions.

Student 11: "Before I wanted to be a neurologist, but I thought that was too hard."

Interviewer: "What kind of … I mean where are the difficulties in the work?"

Student 11: "I guess maybe because you have to put a lot of time into doing it and I guess with psychology you can pick your own times like if you have your own clinic or something. You can set your own schedule."

Student 11: "I wouldn't want it to be hectic or anything. Because I have another friend … so that maybe we can one day open a clinic or something and she wanted to do child psychology so we could split it up sort of and then like have our own schedules and not be too stressed out."

Student 12: "I've dreamed I would be on the radio or something. Because that seems really fun to me. I'd also like to have a job that doesn't require me to sit in an office for eight hours a day and you know, I don't want a boring job."

Student 2: [in speaking about her own business] "But you know it's just sort of a free schedule and you know … I don't like anything nine to five, but that's not really what I mean. Not like a cubicle job or anything like that."

Student 13: "Well I also … I really like acting. So I'm hoping I can do Community Theater aside from teaching. Because I know some … I've had a substitute teacher once that I saw at a play and I thought that was really interesting. You know if I could like do that in my spare time, that would keep me excited."

Student 12: "I guess I would look for a job that didn't involve too much work. Obviously every job involves work but not a job that required me to be there 12 hours a day six or seven days a week. I really think that even if you love a job, it shouldn't be more than eight to nine hours a day and you should have weekends and free time and you know a life separate from work. So something that can accommodate that and a good salary."

Student 14: [Speaking about her image of a career in computer science] "… but I think it'd be an interesting job. I think the difference being it's not as structured I'd say from what I've heard. It's not as structured … but I think it's almost a little more free than most careers."

In the second time theme, girls voice their preferences for careers that are flexible in several ways. Several girls expressed their distaste for nine-to-five working hours [Student 12 and Student 2]. For some, flexibility is expressed as a desire to set their own schedule, overlapping somewhat with the independence strand, but also as a counter to the nine-to-five work environment [Student 11]. Another thought expressed was the flexibility to balance time at work with time for other things in their lives [Student 12 and Student 13]. It is interesting to note that even though she does not select computer science as a possible career option, Student 14 perceives computer science to require less structure in terms of time at work.

Part-time. In the third time strand several girls expressed the desire for a job that was only part-time, allowing them to pursue activities they enjoyed more fully. Their passions seemed to lie within these other activities rather than in having a career.

Student 15: [In speaking of a career in dental hygiene] "So I just think it would be kind of a good job and they only work, oh I think the place … they don't work Fridays and they only have half days on Wednesdays. So it would be very good hours if I ever wanted to have a family. And the computer people, they usually have to work after-hours, like after business closes, you have to go in and just make sure everything's ok after everyone's out which is like kind of clean up if any errors happened during the day. So I just think that would be very time consuming."

Student 16: "And I'll probably getting some random job and then doing arts on the side. My mom is actually a substitute teacher right now."

These two girls' values do not seem to reflect that having a career is of great importance. Student 15 is looking to a future where she has a family and work will need to fit into whatever time she needs to devote to her family. Student 16 on the other hand seems to think that she cannot earn a living in the arts, so a part-time job will enable her to pursue her art activities.

Discussion

For 16 out of 39 high-achieving high school girls, time is a critical factor in career decisions. Among these 16, it appeared that independence and flexibility were important values. Making their own schedules, avoiding the nine-to-five workplace, and being their own bosses were attractive features of future jobs. Tied into these girls' time and career expressions was the idea of work/life balance. They wanted time for other things in their lives, and, therefore, careers that required large amounts of time at work were stricken from their lists of future careers. The part-time job notions expressed by two girls were to free up time for families or art, and are somewhat expected. What is surprising is that only two out of 39 girls expressed this preference for a "job" rather than a career. In our initial study of time in relation to pair programming methods (Berenson, Slaten, Williams, & Ho, 2005), undergraduates in this case study indicated a preference for methods that saved time. We question why time is such an important variable for high school girls when considering their futures.

We turn to the sociology literature to first study the values of this millennial generation to which these high-achieving girls belong. Next we examine disciplines, such as physics and computer science, that are viewed as time "greedy." Finally, we attempt to reconcile the future of the millennial generation with respect to IT careers.

The millennial generation, those born between 1980 and 1999, are studied by a number of sociologists who otherwise refer to this generation as "echo boomers," "generation y," and "nexters." The girls in this study are part of this generation that has just begun to enter the workplace. A number of descriptors have been given to the millennial generation including "realistic" and "entitled" (Lancaster & Stillman, 2002), "practical" and "religious" (Howe & Strauss, 2000), and "self-confident" and "good communicators" (Raines, 1997). Unlike the previous generation, millennials respect authority, especially their parents; and accept principles of diversity, have a strong sense of community, and exhibit behaviors of social responsibility (Tapscott, 1998). Referencing time, Howe and Strauss (2000) concluded that millennials are over scheduled in terms of homework and outside activities, yet have a strong sense of following the rules of changing school cultures. Laughlin and Barling (2001) speak to the changing nature of the workplace for this next generation of workers where they report that in North America and Europe, 30% of the workforce is employed in part-time or contractual employment, Zemke, Raines, and Filipczak (2000) conjecture that young workers may be more interested in work/life balance than rising in the leadership ranks. Our results speak to some of these dimensions especially the work/life balance issues. While the concern is not explicitly stated by all of these girls, the need for independence, flexibility, and part-time work are embedded within issues of work/life balance. We previously reported that these girls do respect the opinions of their parents, and take their cues about careers and education from their parents (Berenson, Vouk, Michael, Greenspon, & Person, 2004).

Next we examine disciplines and careers that require more time or that are perceived to require more time than other disciplines or careers. Reporting on the contrast between undergraduate physics majors and business majors, Nespor (1994) concluded that physics was a highly individualized endeavor requiring inordinate amounts of students' time for studying or lab work. Margolis and Fisher (2002) cite instances where undergraduate women's confidence in their abilities to succeed in computer science declines after spending hours and hours on assignments that fellow students appeared to finish in comparatively little time. In their comments on persistence in computer science, Margolis and Fisher advise that women who work hard in computer science should negate the belief in a computer gene. The implications are that time, lots of time, is needed to work hard in computer science.

Finally, we report on the work of Walker and O'Neill (2002) who question whether the future IT workforce will come from the millennium generation. They state that both males and females in this generation appear disinterested in the IT industry. Also, Costa (2000) reported that family and flexibility are highly prized by the millennium generation, "shunning traditional work schedules" (Walker & O'Neill, p. 697). With the perception among both males and females that IT is "boring," Walker and O'Neill (2002) imply that changing the culture in the IT workplace is necessary if the millennium generation is to be attracted to IT careers.

Acknowledgments

This research was funded in part by National Science Foundation grants 9813902, 0204222, and 00305917. The views expressed here do not necessarily reflect the views of the funding agency.

References

American Association of University Women. (2000). *Tech-Savvy: Educating girls in the new computer age*. Washington, DC: Author.

Berenson, S., Vouk, M., Michael, J., Greenspon, P., & Person, A. (2004, April). *Women and Information Technology: A seven-year longitudinal study of young women from middle grades into college*. Paper presented at the annual meeting of American Educational Research Association, San Diego, CA.

Berenson, S., Slaten, K., Williams, L., and Ho, C. (2005). Voices of women in a software engineering course: Reflections on collaboration. *ACM Journal on Educational Resources in Computing (JERIC)*, 4(1), Article 3. Retrieved September 25, 2006, from the ACM Digital Library database: http://portal.acm.org/browse_dl.cfm?linked=1&part=journal&idx=J814&coll=ACM&dl=ACM

Costa, G. (2000, May 8). Generation Y, the gentle age. *The Age*, p. 1.

Howe, A., Berenson, S., & Vouk, M. (2005, July). *Changing the high school culture to promote interest in IT careers among high achieving girls*. Paper presented at the Crossing Cultures Changing Lives Conference, Oxford, U.K.

Howe, N., & Strauss, B. (2000). *Millennials rising: The next great generation*. New York: Vintage.

Lancaster, L., & Stillman, D. (2002). *When generations collide: Who they are. Why they clash. How to solve the generational puzzle at work*. New York: Harper-Collins.

Laughlin, C., & Barling, J. (2001). Young workers' work values, attitudes, and behaviors. *Journal of Occupational and Organizational Psychology, 74*, 543–558.

Margolis, J., & Fisher, A. (2002). *Unlocking the clubhouse: Women in computing*. Cambridge, MA: MIT Press.

Nespor, J. (1994). Knowledge in motion: Space, time, and curriculum in undergraduate physics and management. Washington, DC: Falmer.

Raines, C. (1997). Beyond generation X. Menlo Park, CA: Crisp.

Tapscott, D. (1998). Growing up digital: The rise of the net generation. New York: McGraw Hill.

Vouk, M., Berenson, S., & Michael, J. (2004). *Women in information technology* (Second Year Report to the National Science Foundation). Raleigh, NC: North Carolina State University.

Walker, E., & O'Neill, L. (2002). IT courses and the IT industry: Does the future rely on gender or generation? In A. Goody, J. Herrington & M. Northcote (Eds.), *Proceedings of the Annual International Conference of the Higher Education Research and Development Society of Australsia (HERDSA): Vol. 25. Quality Conversations* (pp. 695–703). Milperra, Austria: HERDSA Inc.

Zemke, R., Raines, C., & Filipczak, R. (2000). Generations at work: Managing the clash of veterans, boomers, xers, and nexters in your workplace. New York: American Management.

Chapter 4

Information Processing and Information Technology Career Interest and Choice among High School Students

Peggy S. Meszaros, Soyoung Lee, and Anne Laughlin

Abstract

The purpose of this study was to examine how female and male high school students make IT career decisions. Using a theoretically driven and empirically supported model and survey data from 556 high school students in Virginia, this chapter explains patterns found in information processing (decision orientation, receptivity to advice, information creditability, and information sources) and computer-related characteristics (attitudes towards IT workers and computer use) among female and male high school students. Information processing is at the center of the model showing the process students use to make educational and career decisions. Findings have direct implications for support to females for information processing and the connection between interests in computing and career choice.

Introduction

The United States is facing a serious technology workforce problem. We simply do not have enough workers in the technology pipeline. We are losing ground in IT world leadership as Europe, Japan, and other Asian countries are challenging our edge in science and technology. Much of the cause of this low workforce dilemma is due to underutilizing a valuable human resource for the IT field—females. Fewer and fewer women are making up the IT workforce, which has declined by 18.5% in eight years (Information Technology Association of America, 2005).

Although the problem of attracting females to nontraditional careers such as IT is not a new one, most published studies relate to college women and women already in the IT workforce, while career-oriented decisions are made much earlier, possibly at ages 11–17 (Tang & Cook, 2001). The small number of adolescent females choosing an IT career path and preparing to enter the field further compounds this attrition of women in IT. By adolescence many of the girls have already decided against the science, technology, engineering, and math (STEM) fields, and their high school course choices preclude science and technology careers. A study of the influences on career decisions in early teens, as well as possible gender differences in career decision-making, may add to what we know about solving the underrepresentation problem. Chapter 1 in this book explains a theoretically driven and empirically supported combined model of high school and college women's interest and choice in a career in IT. This chapter deals only with a subsample of high school female and male students discussed in Chapter 1 in an attempt to understand adolescent career information processing. The purpose of this study is to examine how male and female high school students process information, view IT computer workers, and use computers as they think about their interest and choice of IT careers. The career decision-making path analysis model developed and tested in the larger study used the theoretical framework of self-authorship developed by Marcia Baxter Magolda (2001). In this study we used this same theoretical framework and examined only information processing with the four variables: decision orientation, receptivity to career information, information credibility, and information source, from the high school females and males in the larger study. We also investigated the attitudes towards IT workers and computer use of our study participants. The dependent variable was IT career interest and choice. There were significant differences between our female and male high school students (n = 556) in their career decision-making processes. Male students followed a direct pathway from computer interest and ability to IT career interest and choice, whereas females followed a more complicated pathway with significant differences in information processing.

The research questions address finding answers for this difference:

How do career decision-making processes differ for female and male adolescent high school students?

What roles do the information processing variables (decision orientation, receptivity to career information, information credibility, and information source) and computer-related variables (computer use, and positive attitudes towards IT career workers) play in understanding adolescent female IT career interest and choice?

Related Literature

Self-authorship and adolescent decision-making. The developmental theory of self-authorship offers a lens to understand the processes that young people use to make a wide range of decisions, including about careers (Baxter Magolda, 2002). In this study, the theory was used as a conceptual guide for quantitative questions related to the decision-making process. Baxter Magolda defines self-authorship as "the ability to collect, interpret, and analyze information and reflect on one's own beliefs in order to form judgments" (1998, p. 143). Self-authorship addresses the criteria individuals use to weigh evidence (cognitive dimension); the role that an internally defined sense of self plays in making personal decisions (intrapersonal dimension); and the role of others in the decision-making process (interpersonal dimension). Self-authorship is linked to decision-making because it influences how individuals make meaning of the advice they receive from others and the extent to which the reasoning they employ reflects an internally grounded sense of self (Baxter Magolda, 1998, 1999, 2001). A self-authored decision process is one that is based on an internally generated sense of self and involves genuinely considering the input of others without being unduly influenced by them.

The journey toward self-authorship starts with a reliance on external formulas, progresses through a developmental crossroads, and leads to cognitive, intrapersonal, and interpersonal maturity. Individuals at different phases of the journey employ different strategies to make decisions. Past research using self-authorship as a framework has not focused on high school students; however, many studies have explored development in college students and found the majority of traditionally aged college freshmen to be in the earliest phases of development, characterized by an unquestioning reliance on external formulas (e.g., Baxter Magolda, 1992, 1998). Based on these studies, it follows that most high school students are just beginning their developmental journey. At this place, individuals lack reflective awareness of their values and identity. Their identity is largely externally defined and, consequently, they are readily influenced by the opinions of others. Viewing knowledge as certain and lacking an internal grounding for evaluating knowledge, these individuals rely on similar others to provide the "right answers." Decisions are often motivated by a need for approval.

The influence of IT career information in information processing. Adolescent females from all ethnic backgrounds need extensive support for developing and implementing career plans, especially nontraditional career plans (De Leon, 1996). Through gender role stereotyping, girls and boys learn early which careers are suitable for them, with the result often limiting career choice and planning. In addition, girls suffer from limited career awareness because they lack information on nontraditional career choices, including those related to IT (Julien, 1999; Newmarch, Taylor-Steele, & Cumpston,

2000). Parents, teachers, school counselors, and peers can play an important role in providing IT career development support for females if the information they give is accurate, up-to-date, and free from stereotypes.

The influence of teachers and school counselors starts early for females and continues through the middle school and high school years. Silverman and Pritchard (1994) studied girls and technology education in Connecticut and found that middle school girls were discouraged from taking more technology education in high school because of two major factors which tend to reinforce each other. First, technology has been a field dominated by men. They found evidence that traditional stereotypes about male-female occupations were still operating and were strong enough to outweigh girls' positive feeling about their experiences in technology classes. They also found that the girls were uninformed about economic realities and the world of work. They lacked basic information about careers, including expected salaries and education needed to pursue IT careers.

In focus group interviews the girls in this study revealed their confidence in being as good as the boys in all areas, including science, math, and technology. However, researchers found that if by eighth grade the girls were not informed about the requirements of careers, they did not make the connection between what they were doing in the classroom and the world of work. If they are unaware of the kind of classes they can take in high school to further their interest in IT, they may close off options that could lead to high-wage IT careers.

This same study found students reported getting little advice or information about technology education from their school counselors. This lack of information was particularly difficult for girls to overcome since they were less likely to have experience with technology outside of school and must be willing to fight stereotypes about appropriate subjects for girls. Stereotypes were also found operating in a 1990 ERIC educational digest research review that revealed school counselors often worked with teachers to channel students into certain educational paths, which sometimes meant that girls were discouraged from taking advanced math or science (Durham, 1990).

Peers are a powerful influence on females' beliefs and choices. This influence starts early and is amplified as they enter teenage years. The career stereotypes held by peers exert themselves as various personas such as geeks and nerds and are applied to IT career fields (Adler & Adler, 1998). As adolescent females make choices about who they want to be when they grow up, a negative stereotype that is applied to IT by their friends may influence the courses they take as they try to fit into the norm for their gender. This lack of preparation may preclude the IT career field from consideration regardless of their interest in computers.

Families, specifically parents and siblings, shape the belief systems and provide role models of adult behavior for adolescents. Females learn about appropriate roles for boys and girls in these early strong relationships that persist over time. Gendered messages about careers that are appropriate for either sex are communicated by family members in explicit and implicit ways. The images in popular culture may reinforce the male model in IT careers through traditional gender-role depictions, and the lack of career information that presents a different, more open and accurate view of non-traditional careers may continue to influence family communication (Gupta & Houtz, 2000).

Gender differences in information technology. Many studies have examined gender issues related to computers such as computer anxiety, skills, attitudes toward computers, and types and amount of computer use (for example studies, see Teo & Lim, 2000). In recent years, a growing body of studies that focus on gender differences in the fields of IT has also emerged. These studies examine gender differences in IT career success (Baroudi & Igbaria, 1994/1995; Isaacs, 1995), IT work stress and barriers (Allen, Reid, & Riemenschneider, 2004; Lim & Teo, 1996), preferred IT job characteristics (Creamer, Burger, & Meszaros, 2004; Smits, McLean, & Tanner, 1993), IT acceptance and use (Sánchez-Franco, 2006), and women's exclusion from IT related fields (Henwood, 1993).

Studies about gender and technology, in general, reported that males were more likely to use computers and technology, have a positive attitude toward computers and technology, and be more confident and interested in learning computers and technology than females (Elder, Gardner, & Ruth, 1987; Harrison & Rainer, 1992; Krendl, Broihier, & Fleetwood, 1989; Qureshi & Hoppel, 1995; Teo & Lim, 1996; Volman & van Eck, 2001). Also, these studies showed that gender differences existed in the types of technology use. For example, males were more likely to use the Internet in order to obtain information, whereas females were more likely to use the Internet for messaging activities (Teo & Lim, 2000). When using the Internet for searching specific information, males performed significantly better than females (Roy & Chi, 2003/2004). Females were less likely to know about software packages and less confident in IT skills (Kent & Facer, 2004). A weaker link also existed between perceived usefulness and the intention to use the Internet among females than males (Sánchez-Franco, 2006).

However, some studies showed contradictory findings from the previous studies. For example, Kaplan (1994) reported that females thought that computers were more fun than males did. Chen (1986) found that male high school students had more positive attitudes and confidence in using computers than females, but when controlling the degree to which they experienced computers, both males and females had similar levels of interest in using the computer.

Methods

Three phases of data collection. The overall data collection and analysis procedures of the Women and Information Technology (WIT) project consisted of three phases. During the spring of 2002, the first phase of the quantitative data collection was conducted. Survey questionnaires about participants' computer-related attitudes, career influencers, and career decisions were distributed to ten high schools, two community colleges, and four colleges in rural and urban areas in Virginia. A total of 467 participants returned usable questionnaires for a 62% response rate (467 of 750). The first-year survey participants consisted of 346 females (74.1%) and 121 males (25.9%); 177 high school students (37.9%), 118 community college students (25.3%), and 172 college students (36.8%); and 322 whites (69.0%), 139 minorities (29.7%), and six unidentified races (1.3%). During the fall of 2002, one-on-one 30-minute telephone interviews with a total of 119 female students (46 high school, 40 college, and 33 community college women) and 25 parents of the high school interview participants were completed.

In 2003, the second phase of data collection was conducted. The main purpose of the second data collection was to refine the data collection instruments. The Career Interest and Choice Questionnaire was revised based on the analysis of the first year survey and interview data. More comprehensive items about related to decision orientation, self-authorship, parental support, information credibility, and IT career interest and choice were developed. The survey questionnaire was also reformatted to be more user-friendly. Questions about the role of parents and the decision-making processes related to IT career interest and choice were added to the interview protocol. During spring 2003, the revised survey questionnaire was distributed to those who participated in the first-year survey data collections. Among 467 first-year survey participants, 423 students who had provided their mailing addresses while completing the first year survey were selected as our potential survey participants. A total of 124 completed survey questionnaires were returned from 63 high school (50.8%), 31 community college (25.0%), and 30 college students (24.2%). Our final survey response rate for the second phase was 33.3% (124 of 372). Second-year survey participants consisted of 103 females (83.1%) and 21 males (16.9%). Also, 92 whites (74.2%) and 30 minorities (24.2%) participated in this second-year study, and two students' racial information was unidentified

(1.3%). The follow-up telephone interviews were also conducted with 13 female high school students and 12 parents, and each interview took from 30 minutes to one hour.

The third phase of the larger research project was intended to test reliability and validity of the revised survey questionnaire and to confirm our theoretical model of women's IT career interest and choice. Ten high schools in Virginia participated in the first phase of the WIT project, and four of them agreed to participate in the third phase of the study. A total of 845 survey questionnaires were mailed and 556 completed surveys were returned from these four high schools (66% response rate). Findings in this chapter are based on these 556 high school respondents. Table 1 provides the demographic characteristics of our respondents. Participants in this study were 293 female (52.7%) and 263 male (47.3%) high school students in Virginia. Caucasians (n = 196) and African Americans (n = 196) were the largest groups in our survey, making up 72.8%. About 12% of the participants were Asian Americans (n = 66), and 4.8% (n = 26) were Hispanic American. There were three native Hawaiians or Pacific islanders (0.6%) and 51 participants listing ethnicity as "other" or "multiracial" (9.5%). A total of 18 participants did not report their race or ethnic information. A majority of our participants (n = 510, 92.6%) were between the ages of 15 and 20, and juniors (23.8%) or seniors (55.3%) in high school. Over 80% of our participants' parents had high school or college degrees.

Measurements. Seven four-point Likert scales were designed to measure (a) information processing variables (decision orientation, receptivity, information sources, and information credibility), (b) computer-related variables (positive attitudes towards IT workers and the amount of computer use), and (c) our dependent variable (IT career interest and choice among high school students). Item options were disagree, slightly disagree, slightly agree, agree. All measures were coded such that the higher the value, the more positive the interpretation. Also, items asking about general demographic information, such as gender, race, birth years, parents' educational levels, and school years, were included in this questionnaire.

To address content and construct validities of each scale, all the survey scales were constructed based on the relevant literature and our team members' expertise. We also conducted face validity tests. In particular, to address the information processing variables' (decision orientation, receptivity, information sources, and information credibility) content and construct validities, the original items were developed in collaboration with Dr. Marcia Baxter Magolda, who is a recognized expert on the theory of self-authorship (1998, 1999, 2001). The developmental theory of self-authorship

Table 1. Demographic information ($n = 556$).

Race	Females ($n = 293$)	Males (n = 263)	Total (%)
Caucasian American	92	104	196 (36.4)
African American	122	74	196 (36.4)
Asian American	37	29	66 (12.3)
Hispanic American	11	15	26 (4.8)
Native Hawaiian/Pacific Islander	2	1	3 (0.6)
Others	25	26	51 (9.5)
Total (%)	289 (53.7)	249 (46.3)	538 (100.0)
Missing	4	14	18

Age	Females ($n = 293$)	Males (n = 263)	Total (%)
Younger than 14 years old	22	15	37 (6.7)
15-20	271	239	510 (92.6)
Older than 20 years old	0	4	4 (0.7)
Total (%)	293 (53.2)	258 (46.8)	551 (100.0)
Missing	0	5	5

School Years	Females ($n = 293$)	Males ($n = 263$)	Total (%)
1st year student	32	25	57 (10.3)
2nd year student	20	39	59 (10.6)
3rd year student	70	62	132 (23.8)
4th year student	170	137	307 (55.3)
Total (%)	292 (52.6)	263 (47.4)	555 (100.0)
Missing	1	0	1

Mother's Level of Education	Females ($n = 293$)	Males ($n = 263$)	Total (%)
Less than high school or high school	114	94	208 (40.7)
Community college or college	125	110	235 (46.0)
More than master's degree	26	42	68 (13.3)
Total (%)	265 (51.9)	246 (48.1)	511 (100.0)
Missing	28	17	45

Father's Level of Education	Females ($n = 293$)	Males ($n = 263$)	Total (%)
Less than high school or high school	132	94	226 (44.3)
Community college or college	81	98	179 (35.1)
More than master's degree	49	56	105 (20.6)
Total (%)	262 (51.4)	248 (48.6)	510 (100.0)
Missing	31	15	46

was a conceptual guide as we constructed the questions related to information processing, although these items are not a complete measure of self-authorship. Each of our scales' internal consistencies is reasonable. Cronbach's alpha of each measurement with our high school sample was .644 for decision orientation, .738 for receptivity, .850 for information credibility, .804 for information source, .710 for positive attitudes toward IT workers, .582 for computer use, and .708 for IT career interest and choice, establishing high reliabilities of the survey measurements. Example items are presented in Table 2. Information about all variables in the full model, measurements, and research procedures are presented in Chapter 1 of this volume.

Data analysis. Using the independent *t*-test, we examined gender differences in seven key variables in our research: information processing variables (decision orientation, receptivity, information sources, and information credibility), computer-related variables (positive attitudes towards IT workers and computer use), and IT career interest and choice. To test our theoretical model we conducted path analysis. Path analysis is a unidirectional causal flow model (Maruyama, 1998), which explains relationships between observed variables by arrows (Raykov & Marcoulides, 2000). Path analysis is very useful for researchers to articulate theoretical models underlying their logic. It is also beneficial to show direct and indirect causal effects of each independent variable on dependent variables (Maruyama; Raykov & Marcoulides). Due to our theoretical rationale and significant gender differences in variables, we tested our model of IT career interest and choice separately for males and females.

Results. The group differences by gender suggested that males and females were significantly different in each of the five variables. Females were less likely to rely on external formulas in decision orientation, were more receptive to others' advice, communicated with more people, were more likely to consider others' opinions, and had more positive attitudes than males. However, male students used computers more often and were more interested in IT careers than female students. Table 3 shows a summary of the independent t-test analysis results.

  Figures 1 and 2 and Tables 4 and 5 present the results of path analyses for female and male high school student models. In order to clarify direct and indirect effects of variables, only the statistically significant path coefficients are presented in the figures. All the results of path analyses are summarized in the tables. First, Figures 1 and 2 present separate pictures of IT career decision-making procedures among female and male high school students. For female students, information source, as well as posi-

Table 2. Items in five key variables.

Items	Cronbach's alpha
IT Career Interest and Choice	
1. I have a good idea about what people in computer-related fields do in their jobs. 2. I feel a sense of satisfaction when I am able to use a computer to solve a problem. 3. If I chose to, I probably have the ability to be successful in a job in a computer-related field. 4. I have family, friends, and/or acquaintances who work in information technology or a computer-related job. 5. I would be comfortable working in a male-dominated occupation. 6. Working in a computer-related field is one of the career options I am considering. 7. My parents would probably consider a career in a computer-related field a good choice for me.	.708
Information Processing Variables	
A. Decision Orientation	
A1. I have given a good deal of thought to choosing a career that is compatible with my values, interests, and abilities. A2. I have a plan for what I would like to do as a career. A3. When it comes to choice of a career, my parents know what is best for me so I am inclined to go with what they suggest. (Recoded) A4. I am confident about my ability to set my own priorities about schoolwork. A5. I am confident about my ability to set my own priorities about my personal life. A6. I am confident about my ability to choose a career. A7. I am unsure about my ability to make my own decisions about a future job. (Recoded) A8. I am unsure about my ability to make my own decisions about my personal life. (Recoded) A9. If my parents disagree with a decision I have made, I am likely to change my decision. (Recoded) A10. If my close friends disagree with a decision I have made, I am likely to change my decision. (Recoded) A11. I am most likely to trust the advice of people who know me best. (Recoded) A12. There are times when even authorities are uncertain about the truth.	.644

Table 2. Items in five key variables (continued).

Items		Cronbach's alpha
B. Receptivity		
B1. I like to have my parents' input before I make a big decision. B2. Even when the advice is contradictory, I try to synthesize the information people give me before I make a big decision. B3. I find it helpful to listen to the input of others before I make an important decision. B4. When I make an important decision, I often seek the input of members of my family. B5. When I make an important decision, I often seek the input of my friends.		.738
C. Information Credibility How often have you discussed your career options or plans with others?	1. Mother/female guardian 2. Father/male guardian 3. Teacher or professor 4. Counselor or advisor	.850
D. Information Source How likely are you to consider career advice when these people offer it?	5. Other family members 6. Male friends 7. Female friends 8. Significant other 9. Employer or boss 10. Family friends	.804
Computer-Related Variables		
A. Positive Attitudes towards IT Workers		
I think people who chose careers in computers are: 1. Geeks (Recoded) 2. Likely to be male (Recoded) 3. Loners/antisocial (Recoded) 4. Interesting 5. Hard-working 6. Smart 7. Creative		.710
B. The Amount of Computer Use		
How often do you use a computer for the following activities? 1. Communication (such as email, instant messages, or chat rooms) 2. Games (any computer-based game) 3. General entertainment (such as internet surfing or music downloads) 4. News and current events (news sites, online magazines) 5. General tasks (such as word processing or creation of databases or spread sheets) 6. Development or design (such as creating web pages or graphics, programming) 7. Educational purposes (such as to conduct research or complete a homework assignment)		.582

Table 3. Gender differences in key variables (n = 556).

Variables	M		SD		t
	Females (n = 293)	Males (n = 263)	Females (n = 293)	Males (n = 263)	
Decision orientation	38.29	37.06	4.51	5.06	3.022**
Receptivity	15.74	14.82	3.07	3.01	3.542***
Information credibility	28.56	27.53	5.68	5.68	2.129*
Information source	16.37	14.71	5.84	5.88	3.316**
Positive attitudes	23.30	22.39	3.20	3.35	3.271**
Computer use	13.72	14.58	4.06	4.24	-2.458*
IT career interest & choice	20.01	21.46	4.39	4.21	-3.961***

* p < 0.05, ** p < 0.01, *** p < 0.001

Note. Code: females = 1 & males = 2 so that negative t values mean that male students have higher mean scores than female students.

tive attitudes and computer use, directly impacted IT career interest and choice (see Figure 1). Computer use was the strongest predictor of female students' IT career interest and choice. In addition, decision orientation, receptivity, and information credibility indirectly influenced IT career interest and choice through information source, positive attitudes, and computer use. Decision orientation did not have a direct effect on receptivity, but it had direct effects on information source, positive attitudes, and computer use. These four information processing variables, positive attitudes, and computer use explained 26.6% of female high school students' IT career interest and choice.

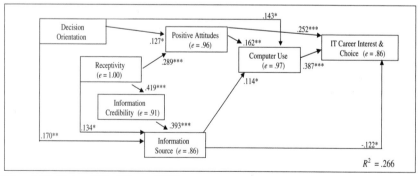

* p < 0.05, ** p < 0.01, *** p < 0.001

Figure 1. Statistically significant standardized coefficients and error variances for model of female students' IT career interest and choice (n = 293).

Table 4. Summary of path analysis for model of female students' IT career interest and choice ($n = 293$).

Variable	B	SE B	β
Step 1			
Decision orientation	-.028	.052	-.029
Receptivity	.046	.083	.032
Information credibility	.071	.048	.091
Information source	-.092	.044	-.122*
Positive attitudes	.347	.074	.252***
Computer use	.419	.057	.381***
R^2		.266	
Step 2			
Decision orientation	.128	.053	.143*
Receptivity	.003	.086	.002
Information credibility	.067	.050	.094
Information source	.015	.046	.021
Positive attitudes	.205	.076	.162**
R^2		.065	
Step 3			
Decision orientation	.090	.041	.127*
Receptivity	.301	.065	.289***
Information credibility	-.021	.039	-.038
Information source	-.014	.036	-.026
R^2		.081	
Step 4			
Decision orientation	.230	.066	.178**
Receptivity	.092	.106	.048
Information credibility	.471	.057	.458***
R^2		.260	
Step 5			
Decision orientation	.063	.068	.050
Receptivity	.759	.100	.411***
R^2		.166	
Step 6			
Decision orientation	-.083	.040	-.122*
R^2		.015	

* $p < 0.05$, ** $p < 0.01$, *** $p < 0.001$

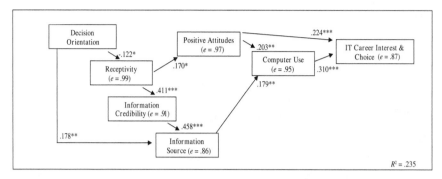

* $p < 0.05$, ** $p < 0.01$, *** $p < 0.001$

Figure 2. Statistically significant standardized coefficients and error variances for model of male students' IT career interest and choice ($n = 263$).

In Figure 2, male students' positive attitudes and computer use had direct impacts on IT career interest and choice (see Figure 2). The male student model did not show direct influences from the four information processing variables on IT career interest and choice. These four variables influenced IT career interest and choice only through positive attitudes toward IT workers and computer use. About 24% of male students' IT career interest and choice was explained by the information processing variables, positive attitudes, and computer use.

Discussion

The purpose of this research was to understand how career decision-making processes differ for female and male adolescent high school students and what roles information processing variables and computer-related variables play in understanding female IT career interest and choice. Many of the factors found to characterize high school female and male similarities and differences in career decision-making processes were consistent with those previously cited in the literature. Specifically, our findings indicate a major similarity between females and males in that both appear to be making decisions based on external formulas, much like the early college students in Baxter Magolda's work (1992, 1998). Individuals processing information at this early stage in their journey toward self-authorship rely heavily on the opinions of others and are motivated by a need for approval.

A primary difference in male and female information processing was found as they turned in our model to information sources such as their families, peers, teachers, counselors for career information (see Figures 1 and 2). When females in our study sought career information, it led to

Table 5. Summary of path analysis for model of male students' IT career interest and choice ($n = 263$).

Variable	B	$SE\ B$	β
Step 1			
Decision orientation	-.007	.046	-.009
Receptivity	.033	.087	.024
Information credibility	.039	.048	.053
Information source	.067	.046	.093
Positive attitudes	.282	.072	.224***
Computer use	.308	.057	.310***
R^2		.235	
Step 2			
Decision orientation	.021	.050	.025
Receptivity	.031	.094	.022
Information credibility	.029	.053	.039
Information source	.147	.049	.203**
Positive attitudes	.226	.077	.179**
R^2		.105	
Step 3			
Decision orientation	-.003	.040	-.004
Receptivity	.189	.075	.170*
Information credibility	.044	.042	.075
Information source	.050	.040	.087
R^2		.068	
Step 4			
Decision orientation	.156	.062	.134*
Receptivity	.332	.115	.170**
Information credibility	.406	.061	.393***
R^2		.254	
Step 5			
Decision orientation	-.040	.063	-.036
Receptivity	.790	.106	.419***
R^2		.176	
Step 6			
Decision orientation	.005	.037	.008
R^2		.000	

*$p < 0.05$, ** $p < 0.01$, *** $p < 0.001$

negative IT interest and choice, which may indicate that they got negative messages about the appropriateness of this nontraditional career option for them or that the sources they talked with were operating from stereotyped or incomplete views of IT careers. This finding is consistent with findings in the Silverman and Pritchard (1994) study of girls and technology and the 1998 study by Adler and Adler. This negative feedback from significant people in their lives is powerful in shaping the beliefs and choices of females and may account for the negative relationship in our model.

On the other hand, males and females seeking career information from significant others may have been reinforced in the appropriateness of the IT career field for them, as the direct link between information source to computer use in Figures 1 and 2 also directly influences their IT career interest and choice. This finding may again reveal the powerful messages about IT related careers that are appropriate for either gender, given by family members, peers, teachers, and the media, based on their interest and ability. In addition, using computers leads both female and male students to be more likely to be interested in IT careers. This finding reveals that encouraging students to use computers helps them to develop their interest in IT and consider IT as a future career option. Therefore, significant others who are generally engaged in career discussions with adolescents can encourage them to use computers and consider IT career choices not based on their gender but on their interest.

Consistent with previous studies (Teo & Lim, 1996, 2000; Volman & van Eck, 2001) males in our sample used computers more and had more interest in an IT career. However, females had more positive attitudes toward IT workers. For both males and females, using the computer often and for a variety of purposes resulted in greater IT career interest and choice.

As we look at the role of information processing variables, we see that female students had higher scores for all of the four variables than males and were more active in interacting with others in their information seeking. This finding of a negative link between information source and IT career interest and choice poses some interesting implications from this study:

1. Females need extensive support for developing and implementing nontraditional career plans (De Leon, 1996). Gender-neutral IT career materials are needed as well as materials with complete information about the range of IT career options that go beyond the male stereotype in isolation.

2. The influence of parents, peers, teachers, and counselors is powerful in advising and shaping girls' career choices. We need more information about the power of these partners and help for them in developing self-authorship in young girls as they move beyond external formulas to develop their internal belief systems and confidence in their decision-making. The DVD and Facilitator's Guide (Meszaros & Laughlin, 2006) developed by the WIT research team may be a useful resource.

3. Computer use and exposure to a variety of applications is important to sustain female IT career interest and choice. While female and

male use is at the same rate today, females should be encouraged to experiment with a variety of applications beyond those used only for communication.

Although this study of high school adolescents does make important contributions to the literature, further research is needed to clarify the influences on IT career interest and choice at an early age, perhaps beginning at the elementary grades. If we are ever to see an increase in females entering the IT field, we cannot afford to wait until they reach college age to attack this problem. Career decisions are being made at very early ages, and our culture continues to send mixed messages about appropriate and inappropriate gendered career choices.

Acknowledgments

This research was supported by funds from the National Science Foundation under grant HRD-0120458.

References

Adler, P., & Adler, P. (1998). *Peer power: Preadolescent culture and identity.* New Brunswick, NJ: Rutgers University Press.

Allen, M. W., Reid, M., & Riemenschneider, C. (2004). The role of laughter when discussing workplace barriers: Women in information technology job. *Sex Roles, 50*(3/4), 177–189.

Baroudi, J. J., & Igbaria, M. (1994/1995). An examination of gender effects on career success of information systems employees. *Journal of Management Information Systems, 11,* 181–201.

Baxter Magolda, M. B. (1992). Knowing and reasoning in college: Gender-related patterns in students' intellectual development. San Francisco: Jossey-Bass.

Baxter Magolda, M. B. (1998). Developing self-authorship in young adult life. *Journal of College Student Development, 39*(2), 143–156.

Baxter Magolda, M. B. (1999). *Creating contexts for learning and self-authorship.* Nashville, TN: Vanderbilt University Press.

Baxter Magolda, M. B. (2001). Making their own way: Naratives for transforming higher education to promote self-development. Sterling, VA: Stylus.

Baxter Magolda, M. B. (2002, April). *The central role of self in learning: Transforming higher education.* Paper presented at the annual meeting of the American Educational Research Association, New Orleans, LA.

Chen, M. (1986). Gender and computers: The beneficial effects of experience on attitudes. *Journal of Educational Computing Research, 2,* 265–282.

Creamer, E. G., Burger, C. J., & Meszaros, P. S. (2004). Characteristics of high school and college women interested in information technology. *Journal of Women and Minorities in Science and Engineering, 10,* 67–78.

De Leon, B. (1996). Career development of hispanic adolescent girls. In B. Leadbeater & N. Way (Eds.), *Urban girls: Resisting stereotypes, creating identities* (pp. 380–398). New York: New York University Press.

Durham, P. H. (1990). *Procedures to increase the entry of women in mathematics-related careers.* Columbus, OH: ERIC Clearinghouse for Science, Mathematics, and Environmental Education.

Elder, V. B., Gardner, E. P., & Ruth, S. R. (1987). Gender and age in techno stress: Effects on white-collar productivity. *Government Finance Review, 3*, 17–21.

Gupta, U., & Houtz, L. (2000). High school students' perception of information technology skills and careers. *Journal of Industrial Technology, 16*, 2–8.

Harrison, A. W., & Rainer, R. J. Jr. (1992). The influence of individual differences on skill in end-user computing. *Journal of Management Information Systems, 9*, 93–111.

Henwood, F. (1993). Establishing gender perspectives on information technology: Problems, issues, and opportunities. In E. Green, J. Owen, & D. Pain (Eds.), *Gendered by design* (pp. 67–96). London: Taylor & Francis.

Information Technology Association of America. (2005). *Untapped talent: Diversity, competition and America's high tech future.* Retrieved September 6, 2006, from http://www.itaa.org/eweb/upload/execsummdr05.pdf

Isaacs, E. (1995). Gender discrimination in the workplace: A literature review. *Communications of the ACM, 38*, 58–59.

Julien, H. (1999). Barriers to adolescents' information seeking for career decision-making. *Journal of the American Society for Information Science, 50*, 38–48.

Kaplan, R. (1994). The gender gap at the PC keyboard. *American Demographics, 16*, 18.

Kent, N., & Facer, K. (2004). Different world? A comparison of young people's home and school ICT use. *Journal of Computer Assisted Learning, 20*, 440–455.

Krendl, K., Broihier, M., & Fleetwood, C. (1989). Children and computers: Do sex-related differences persist? *Journal of Communications, 39*, 85–93.

Lim, V. K. G., & Teo, T. S. H. (1996). Gender differences in occupational stress and coping strategies among IT personnel. *Women in Management Review, 11*, 20–28.

Maruyama, G. M. (1998). *Basics of structural equation modeling.* Thousand Oaks, CA: Sage.

Meszaros, P. (Executive Producer) & Laughlin, A. (Associate Producer). (2006). *The power of partners: Helping females find their way to high tech careers.* [DVD]. Washington, DC: National Science Foundation. (Available from http://www.witvideo.org.vt.edu).

Newmarch, E., Taylor-Steele, S., & Cumpston, A. (2000, March). *Women in IT: What are the barriers?* Paper presented at the Network of Women in Further Education Conference, Sydney, Australia.

Qureshi, S., & Hoppel, C. (1995). Profiling computer predispositions. *Journal of Professional Services Marketing, 12*, 73–83.

Raykov, T., & Marcoulides, G. A. (2000). *A first course in structural equation modeling.* Mahwah, NJ: Lawrence Erlbaum Associates, Inc.

Roy, M., & Chi, M. T. H. (2003/2004), Gender differences in patterns of searching the Web. *Journal of Educational Computing Research, 29,* 335–348.

Sánchez-Franco, M. J. (2006). Exploring the influence of gender on the web usage via partial least squares. *Behaviour & Information Technology, 25*(1), 19–36.

Silverman, S., & Pritchard, A. (1994). Building their future II: High school girls and technology education in Connecticut. Hartford, CT: Connecticut Women's Education and Legal Fund.

Smits, S. J., McLean, E. R., & Tanner, J. R. (1993). Managing high-achieving information systems professionals. *Journal of Management Information Systems, 9,* 103–120.

Tang, M. & Cook, E.P. (2001). Understanding the relationship and career concerns of middle school girls. In P. O'Reilly & E. M. Penn (Eds.), *Educating young adolescent girls* (pp. 213–229). Mahwah, NJ: Erlbaum.

Teo, T. S. H., & Lim, V. K. G. (1996). Factors influencing personal computer usage: The gender gap. *Women in Management Review, 11,* 18–26.

Teo, T. S. H., & Lim, V. K. G. (2000). Gender differences in Internet usage and task preferences. *Behaviour & Information Technology, 19*(4), 283–295.

Volman, M., & van Eck, E. (2001). Gender equity in information technology in education: The second decade. *Review of Educational Research, 71*(4), 613–634.

Part III

The Post-Secondary Level

Considering Individual, Social, and Cultural Factors in the Construction of Women's Interest and Persistence In Information Technology at the Post-Secondary Level

Elizabeth G. Creamer and Lesley H. Parker

A complex set of factors that reflect individual, social, and cultural elements is required to understand women's participation in IT in a global context. Failures to adopt this perspective often result in accounts that implicitly or explicitly blame women for their underrepresentation in many STEM fields, excluding rather than considering teaching and learning experiences that fail to motivate young girls. This is a point made by one of the discussants, Jane Butler Kahle, at the 2005 international IT conference.

Key individual qualities related to IT include attitudes about computers and computing fields, and qualities of parents, particularly their familiarity with IT and their views about the appropriateness of IT as a career choice. Social qualities relate to structural dimensions of the environment, such as encouragement from educators, family and friends, role models, and peer culture. They also include elements of family, community, and educational environment that influence opportunity to experience creative applications of computing. The stereotyping of IT as an inherently unfeminine field is a key cultural dimension that impacts women's perceptions of the opportunity for success and advancement in the field.

Social construction theory has been used to understand how individuals respond to culture and social expectations (Trauth, 2002). From this individualistic framework, how individuals experience and respond to the social shaping of both gender and IT is key to understanding women's interest and persistence in computing fields. A similar framework shapes the model presented in Chapter 1 and is a characteristic captured empirically in the variable, "decision orientation," that derives from Marcia Baxter Magolda's work about the developmental construct of self-authorship (1999, 2001). Self-authorship shapes the strategies students deploy to process or disregard diverse viewpoints and to make judgments. This is an instrumental dimension of how both men and women respond to gender stereotyping of occupational fields.

This chapter has several goals. The first is to identify key themes that link the four chapters presented in this section and to ground them with key findings from the research literature about women's interest and persistence in computing majors at the post-secondary level. The second goal is to identify strategies supported by the research literature that promote the recruitment and retention of women in computing fields at the post-secondary level. This section also addresses some implications for instructional pedagogy and policy. The third goal and section of the chapter identifies critical areas for future research.

Section Themes

The authors of three of the four chapters in this section emphasize the impact of social, cultural, and environmental support for women's interest in IT. One clear indication of the impact of the socialization process embedded in this wider environment is that in the US views about the nature of work in IT and the attributes of workers in the field grow more stereotypical as students get older (Sanders, 2005). One explanation for this socialization process lies not so much with qualities of the student and their immediate environment but in the exposure they get to computing as primary and secondary students. A lack of exposure to informal activities and anything but the most mundane aspects of computing in coursework is one reason why women are particularly likely to view computing as "boring" (Cohoon & Aspray, 2006).

The themes in this chapter link back to an issue raised very early in the 2005 international IT conference in the UK. That issue questions the usefulness of continuing to focus on gender differences. Trauth (2002) maintains that a natural consequence of literature that focuses on male/female differences and an "essentialist" theoretical perspective is the assumption that women and men should be treated differently. Similarly, Thorne argues that a focus on separate but different cultures, and on dualisms associated with these, leads to a sense of loss of the whole. She points to the self-perpetuating nature of the paradigm when she observes: "[I]f we begin by assuming different [male and female] cultures, separate spheres, or contrastive differences, we will also end up with a sharp sense of dichotomy rather than attending to multiple differences and sources of commonality" (2001, p. 108).

Chapter coauthors Lenore Blum, Carol Frieze, Orit Hazzan, and M. Bernardine Dias join the spirit of Trauth's conclusion by their stout conviction that neither the women nor the field needs changing. They argue that "women do not need hand-holding or a 'female friendly' curriculum in order for them to enter and be successful in CS or related fields, nor is there need to change the fields to suit women. To the contrary, curricular changes based on presumed differences can be misguided, particularly if they do not provide the skills and depth needed to succeed and lead in the field. Such changes will only serve to reinforce, even perpetuate stereotypes and promote further marginalization."

An important subtlety of Blum et al.'s argument is that it does not dismiss the salience of considerations of gender or gender differences, but reframes them with an environmental rather than individual perspective. This perspective approaches gender by locating gender differences in the environment or culture. Defining culture as a "complex and broad set of relationships, values, attitudes, and behaviors (along with the micro-culture and counter-cultures that also may exist) that bind a specific community consciously and unconsciously," Blum et al. point to microclimates/communities that counter the social construction of IT as a masculine field.

Summary of the Chapters in this Section

The lead chapter in this section by Blum et al. makes a persuasive case for a cultural framework. The authors use literature and case studies of microclimates in several different settings to demonstrate that the underrepresentation of women in IT is far from a universal problem. Case studies—including of the computer science program at Carnegie Mellon, the culture inspired by agile software development, of Jewish and Arab high school students in Israel, and an extension of Carnegie Mellon in Qatar—document how perception of IT as a male activity is successfully offset in some microcultures. As with the findings reported by Creamer, Lee, and Meszaros in the second chapter in this volume, culture appears often to be mediated through parents. Parental encouragement is a key element of college student's interest in IT in a variety of settings, both in the US and internationally.

Cecille Marsh, from a university in South Africa, also considers the influence of both social and cultural factors in her chapter, Sociopolitical Factors and Female Students' Choice of Information Technology Careers: A South African Perspective. During the course of research comparing students from two dramatically different secondary locations, Marsh found a number of things that contrast with what is generally reported from studies with Western women. Strikingly absent was the gender gap in confidence in ability to learn to use computers effectively. Also in contrast to what is found in the West, women expressed significantly more interest in IT than men. Both of these findings support Blum et al.'s contention that what is often attributed to gender differences is, in fact, a byproduct of culture or localized microcultures.

Marsh interprets her findings to reflect both social and cultural elements of the environment in South Africa today. This includes a post-apartheid political environment that demonstrates a commitment to empowering women with the goal of economic development. Marsh maintains that an important byproduct of this policy position has been to elevate the status of women in the home. This links interest in IT to elements of the environment, including social and political support. Marsh underscores the influence of strong women role models in the home who carry primary responsibility for the financial well-being of the family and interest in IT.

Joining with authors of several other chapters in this section, Marsh's work challenges the assumption that prior exposure to computing is a necessary precondition for post-secondary enrollment in a computing field. In this research, students from more impoverished school settings where there was less exposure to computers, either at home or in school, expressed significantly more positive attitudes toward their ability to learn to use computers than respondents from a more affluent secondary school. Unlike their peers attending more affluent schools in South Africa, these women may well have had fewer encounters with the idea that an IT career was an inappropriate choice.

Cohoon and Lord's work has direct implications for practices designed to recruit women to computing fields. In a study of 46 computer science and computer engineering graduate programs in the U.S., Cohoon and Lord determined that many practices commonly expected to have a positive impact on increasing the enrollment of women actually work against the goal of achieving gender balance. While even a relatively small amount of effort was associated with greater than average enrollments of women, only one strategy was consistently related to improved outcomes. That was flexibility in program requirements. Cohoon and Lord speculate that one explanation for the failure of many recommended practices to have the desired effect is that successful interventions are likely to require a multi-faceted approach that involves the commitment of the whole unit, rather than a designated few.

Cohoon and Lord's work yields some additional findings that are consistent with the puzzling conclusion reported in other chapters in this volume, that the more interaction women in the US have with information about computing fields as a career, the less their interest. Their findings challenge the idea that meeting with prospective female students is always an effective strategy in redressing the gender imbalance. Women applicants rated impressions of departmental climate as being significantly more influential to program choice than did men applicants. There was a moderately negative relationship between women's representation in a program and recruiting by male faculty and students. In circumstances where there is not uniform commitment to the importance of diversifying the student body, encounters between faculty, graduate students, and prospective graduate students may reinforce the image of the field and program as one that is not conducive to the success of women. Cohoon and Lord speculate that the actions of an individual or subgroup designated to recruit and retain women may be insufficient to counteract routine practices and broader cultural norms in the department.

The last chapter in this part, by Bettina Bair and Miranda Marcus, narrows the focus from the broader social-cultural framework to individual attitudes and interest in IT jobs in the US. The findings from their research reinforce that most undergraduates in the US show a low level of familiarity with IT jobs, except for those associated with the most routine activities like Web design, data entry, or word processing. Bair and Marcus's data demonstrate that most male and female undergraduates in the US are looking for jobs that are fun and enjoyable, and women in particular cannot imagine IT as a field they are likely to enjoy. This chapter weaves back in the themes of earlier chapters in this part in its conclusion that lack of prior exposure to creative applications of computing in the primary and secondary grades is one explanation for negative views about IT. This argument returns the focus from individual characteristics to opportunities in the environment.

The cross-cultural framework provided in this text offers a critical vantage point for considering the implications of Bair's and Marcus' finding about the importance of the "fun factor" in career interests in the US. Their findings are consistent with Sanders' (2005) conclusion that the wider body of literature about IT supports that enjoyment in using computers is a key factor that attracts both male and female undergraduates to computing fields. Marsh's and Blum et al.'s chapters convincingly demonstrate, however, that women in other countries not only live within cultural contexts that communicate different messages about the suitability of IT for women, but also that other factors, most notably economic security, are more salient in women's career interest in many other settings. Middle-class undergraduate females in the US attending predominantly white colleges may have the privilege of pursuing careers for "fun," rather than potential for income, and this may not be an option in the priorities of women from many other countries.

Converting Research to Practice in the Post-Secondary Settings

A range of suggestions to improve recruiting and retention practices in post-secondary settings emerges from these chapters. A key question about recruiting is: What strategies are effective in building on an interest in and enjoyment of computers to an interest in a job or career in a computing field? For retention, a critical question is how to manufacture microclimates that communicate the message that there is an "IT-women fit."

As Lesley Parker pointed out in her introductory comments at the international conference in Oxford, there has been a transition, both in definitional and practical terms, from a narrow focus on computers in learning to a broader perspective that considers the many different facets of the whole educational prism, including the ways in which students engage in learning, both formally and informally. While access to informal and formal opportunities to experiment with computers remains an important issue, the processes of learning and the outcomes of that learning are also matters important to our consideration. Processes cover all aspects of the content, pedagogy, and assessment of computer-related learning.

The following sections of the chapter list suggestions to improve recruiting and retention practices in post-secondary settings.

Implications for recruiting. Units determined to recruit women to undergraduate majors in computing fields are not likely to be successful without widespread commitment from all members of the unit and careful consideration of elements of the climate and personal interactions that might inadvertently communicate that IT is a not a field where women are likely to be successful.

Opportunities for women to engage in creative computer applications in informal settings are critical to promoting interest.

Because women are more likely to "fall into" an IT career than to plan for it, recruiting efforts have to be broad-based and targeted at populations in a variety of settings, not just high school seniors as they are making their decisions about college choice.

Exposure is linked to interest, but authors of two chapters in this part document how the expectation for prior experience in programming is negatively related to the enrollment of women in computing majors, both at the graduate and undergraduate level.

Emphasizing the creative, interactive, and social significance, as well as the potential for flexibility in work schedule, speaks to dimensions of IT jobs that are likely to be most attractive to women in the US.

Faculty and graduate student interactions with prospective students may deter, rather than attract, women to IT. Colleges and universities seeking to enroll more women in computing fields will find it fruitful to look to identify strategies that institutions funded by the National Science Foundations ADVANCE Grant program have found to be effective in promoting the development of more gender inclusive environments.

Implications for retention, including pedagogy. Although math-based comput-ing, unlike math, is generally taught in a lab setting (Cohoon & Aspray, 2006), centers designed to enhance undergraduate teaching effectiveness could play an important role by coaching instructors in STEM field about strategies that promote positive peer interaction in these settings.

Same-sex pairing in coed classes with a significant lab or group project component has the potential to reduce the impact of gender stereotyping of IT as a masculine field.

Implications for policy. Schools and communities have a responsibility to off-set differences in the socioeconomic status of their citizens by providing ready access to computers and up-to-date software.

Opportunities to gain skills using a computer in ways that extend beyond keyboarding should be a core requirement in both the high school and col-lege curricula.

Implications for future research. Research presented in this part documents that differences in fundamental aspects of IT interest and choice can vary dramatically by setting and that IT is by no means a male-dominated field in all settings. It is critical that such research simultaneously considers gen-der with race, class, and other major status variables and that it is framed by a theoretical perspective. Future research can build on the emerging body of knowledge about women and IT by maintaining the international perspective offered by this volume. The impact of specific microclimates cannot be determined conclusively, however, until more systematic data is collected that matches women with similar individual qualities from across a variety of national and international locations.

In the US, much of what students learn about computers occurs in infor-mal settings. This includes the lab setting or out-of-class experiences with group projects and cooperative educational activities, such as LEGO® con-tests. In IT, as in engineering, peer interactions in these informal settings play a particularly instrumental role in attracting or deterring women from the field. This is one type of interaction where stereotypes about the field are likely to be perpetuated. Continued research that involves systematic observation of same-sex and cross-sex peer interactions in these informal settings will provide important insight into the shaping of microclimates that support women.

Conclusions

The international perspective offered by this volume adds important new insight to issues related to women's interest in IT. The studies in this part challenge the idea that a love of computing and the type of logic it teaches is a major determinant of undergraduate women's choice of an academic major at the post-secondary level. While Cohoon and Lord demonstrate in a chapter in this section that a love of computing is clearly a major attractor for both men and women to graduate programs in computing, other researchers in this section suggest that other motivators may be more salient to women at the undergraduate level. This suggestion is supported by the findings reported elsewhere that women's career choices are less directly motivated than are men's by interest and enjoyment of a field (O'Brien & Fassinger, 1993). In two separate chapters reporting on research in an international context, Marsh and Blum et al. provide convincing documentation that, with encouragement, women chose to pursue the field for reasons such as to provide support for a family or to promote the economic and social development of the country. These studies provide strong support for the argument that the lack of interest and confidence in computing is a byproduct of culture and socialization. They also provide strong support for the idea that career choice cannot be understood solely as an individual decision, but one that is made within a social and cultural context.

Interactions about careers in computing with faculty, advisors, and others within and outside the classroom seem to have a surprisingly negative impact on women's interest in IT in the US. This conclusion is supported by the negative relationship between interactions and career interest in IT reported in the Chapter 4 by Meszaros, Lee, and Laughlin, and by the findings of Cohoon and Lord, in which interactions with male faculty and students were negatively related to achieving gender balance in enrollment in graduate computing programs. It is difficult to avoid interpreting this puzzling finding as an indication that it is not uncommon for women to walk away from such interactions questioning their ability to succeed in the field in that setting. Offsetting unintentionally negative messages about computing as a masculine field requires concerted effort, attention to departmental climate, and an array of activities that involve everyone in a program. It also involves an interest in creating a research program that shifts from the question of access and gender differences at the individual level, to a broader more comprehensive framework that considers cultural and environmental supports and deterrents, and learning processes along with individual qualities.

References

Baxter Magolda, M. B. (1999). Creating contexts for learning and self-authorship: Constructive-developmental pedagogy. Nashville: Vanderbilt University Press.

Baxter Magolda, M. B. (2001). Making their own way: Narratives for transforming higher education to promote self-development. Sterling, VA: Stylus.

Cohoon, J. M., & Aspray, W. (Eds.). (2006). *Women and information technology: Research on under-representation.* Cambridge, MA. MIT Press.

O'Brien, K. M., & Fassinger, R. E. (1993). A causal model of the career orientation and career choice of adolescent women. *Journal of Counseling Psychology, 40,* 456-469.

Sanders, J. (2005, July). *Gender and technology in education: A research review.* Paper presented at the Crossing Cultures, Changing Lives International Conference, Oxford, England.

Thorne, B. (2001). Gender and interaction: Widening the conceptual scope. In B. Baron & H. Kotthoff (Eds.), *Gender in Interaction: Perspectives on femininity and masculinity in ethnography and discourse* (pp. 3–18). Amsterdam/Philadelphia: John Benjamins Publishing Company.

Trauth, E. M. (2002). Odd girl out: An individual differences perspective on women in the IT profession. *Information Technology & People, 15*(2), 99–118.

Chapter 5

A Cultural Perspective on Gender Diversity in Computing

Lenore Blum, Carol Frieze, Orit Hazzan, and
M. Bernardine Dias

Abstract

This chapter presents a cultural perspective for thinking about, and acting on, issues concerning gender and computer science and related fields. We posit and demonstrate that the notion of a gender divide in how men and women relate to computing, traditionally attributed to gender differences, is largely a result of cultural and environmental conditions. Indeed, the reasons for women entering—or not entering—the field of computer science have little to do with gender and a lot to do with environment and culture as well as the perception of the field. Appropriate outreach, education, and interventions in the microculture can have broad impact, increasing participation in computing and creating environments where both men and women can flourish. Thus, we refute the popular notion that focusing on gender differences will enhance greater participation in computing, and we propose an alternative, more constructive approach that focuses on culture. We illustrate the cultural perspective using specific case studies based in different geographical and cultural regions.

Introduction

For some time now there has been rising concern in the US and in many of the developed nations over the declining numbers of women entering and succeeding in computing related fields. More recently, young men have also been turning away from these fields. Indeed, we are somehow failing to attract, educate, and encourage the next generations of computer scientists, men and women,[1] particularly at a time when computing technology is becoming even more integral to our scientific, economic and social infrastructure. Increased attention to declining numbers has brought a much needed reexamination of these fields and how they are perceived in the public consciousness. At the same time it has highlighted common grounds of concern (Morris & Lee, 2004). The situation presents an ideal opportunity for broadening the scope of how we account for determinants of participation—or lack of participation—in computing related fields.

This chapter presents a cultural perspective toward thinking about, and acting on, issues concerning women and computer science (CS) and related fields. We posit and demonstrate that the notion of a gender divide in how men and women relate to computing, traditionally attributed to gender differences, is largely a result of cultural and environmental conditions. We illustrate that under specific cultural and environmental situations, women fit very well into CS. Indeed, where cultural conditions allow for diversity, and where women are perceived as capable of doing computer science (or any science), the "women-CS fit" is visible and active (Adams, Bauer, & Baichoo, 2003; Schinzel 2002; Vashti, 2002; Eidelman, 2005). The implications are that women do not need handholding or a "female friendly" curriculum in order for them to enter and be successful in CS or related fields, nor is there need to change the fields to suit women. To the contrary, curricular changes, for example, based on presumed gender differences can be misguided, particularly if they do not provide the skills and depth needed to succeed and lead in the field. Such changes will only serve to reinforce, even perpetuate, stereotypes and promote further marginalization.[2]

Here we share findings from specific case studies that illustrate culture and environment as determinants in participation in CS and ask: (a) How can such knowledge best be used? and (b) Can such discussions lead us away from the gender differences debates (which seem to be going round in circles) and open the way for more productive directions?

We argue that our understanding and experience with successful interventions that promote microcultural change have broad implications for increasing participation in computing and for creating environments where both men and women can flourish.

At the same time, it is also important to recognize the crucial role played by the public's perception and misconception of CS in attracting (or not) students to the field. For the most part, CS has been equated with programming, particularly in the US. This is largely due to the dearth of pre- or entry level college/university curricula that present the depth and breadth of computer science and computational thinking. While curricula and perception are not the focus of this chapter, we have also been working to develop curricular materials, teacher training programs, and outreach efforts to broaden and correct the image of what computer science is and who computer scientists are (Blum & Frieze, 2005b; Frieze & Treat, 2006).

In discussions about participation in CS and related fields, there is often ambiguity about what fields we are actually talking about. This is not surprising, because of the newness and interdisciplinary nature of the fields and the changing and expanding boundaries.[3] But it can lead to confusion, particularly when data and findings about (and programs to increase) participation in "computer science" are sometimes used interchangeably with like data about "information technology." While many of the issues are similar, not all are, and the fields they refer to are not the same. The National Center for Women and IT (NCWIT) defines[4] IT broadly as: "1) all forms of technology used to create, store, exchange and use information in its various forms; and 2) the design and use of computers and communications to improve the way we live, learn, work and play." Computer scientists might or might not agree that this includes "computer science."[5] For example, computer scientists who work in the more theoretical and foundational aspects of computer science—such as complexity theory or the theory of computation—might not agree that their work is included in the definition of IT. Other computer scientists might think that areas often considered as IT, such as managing information in large corporations, are far removed from core CS. We do not attempt to resolve this debate, but instead, we clarify that the case studies presented here would mostly be considered within the realm of what might be called traditional computer science.

Our first case study looks at undergraduates majoring in computer science at Carnegie Mellon University in the US. We show as the environment has become more balanced, the culture of computing has changed in such a way that both men and women can thrive. Thus, under specific changes in the microculture, the gender divide is shown to dissolve with students presenting a spectrum of relationships to computing (Blum & Frieze, 2005a, 2005b). Our second case study shows how the agile approach for software development (Cockburn, 2001), which is becoming more and more predominant in the software industry, allows for a situation in which both men and women are equally communicative and more effective (Hazzan & Dubinsky, 2006). Finally, we illustrate how certain Eastern microcultures highlight the women-CS fit. We hope these illustrations suggest both new perspectives and avenues for further exploration.

Culture and Gender: The Dynamics and Distinctions

With respect to all our case studies, we explore cultural factors, acknowledging that culture is a very complex concept and that the term is open to various interpretations. Here we are using the term culture to refer to the complex and broad set of relationships, values, attitudes and behaviors (along with the microcultures and countercultures that also may exist) that bind a specific community consciously and unconsciously. Our definition posits that culture is bound by context and history and that we are born into specific cultures with prevailing values and structures of opportunity.

But culture, like history, allows for change. Culture is dynamic, shaping and being shaped by those who occupy it, in a synergistic diffusive process. Indeed, while a dominant culture may embrace and influence a community, counter- or microcultures may exhibit unexpected features. As individuals, and/or as groups, we contribute to culture(s) in different ways to different degrees and are impacted by culture(s) in different ways to different degrees. In this sense we view culture, and cultural occupants, as agents of change, and environments as appropriate sites for interventions and opportunities.

In this chapter, therefore, we propose moving away from discussing gender issues toward talking about cultural issues. This raises an obvious but interesting point: Isn't gender a cultural issue? Here we try to explain the distinction and why our suggestion to focus on culture is a pragmatic and positive move.

First, we should explain that we are using the term gender to refer, in addition to biology, to the roles, behaviors, attitudes, etc., attributed to men and women as they are born into specific cultures and moments in history. Thus, our working definition of gender embraces the complex dynamics of both natural and cultural factors and influences. At the same time we suggest that the gender differences arguments, such as the nature/nurture debates, serve to perpetuate a model of oppositional thinking, a model which begins and ends with dividing men and women, rather than looking at the dynamics of diversity and the common ground they may reveal. Even more, programs designed to "accommodate" presumed gender differences can promote further marginalization.

We suggest a need to escape self-limiting categories and convey the message that gender issues are really cultural issues that concern us all. The discourse of culture tends to be more inclusive, for examining not only gender issues but also issues of race and class. In terms of gender issues, "thinking culturally" means thinking that embraces gender similarities and intragender differences. We suggest that thinking culturally broadens the scope for examining inequities in the light of other models of possibilities while also serving to focus our attention on the factors at work in specific environments. In this way, gender issues are not reduced to a simplistic oppositional model that pits men against women and vice versa. Examining gender within the larger, or even localized, parameters of culture can help reinvigorate our research as we learn from other cultures, and share approaches and models of effective practices.

A particularly significant way in which gender issues have become self-limiting lies in the popularity and dominance of theories of gender "differences" that are used indiscriminately to account for our behaviors and attitudes. We have observed that research on gender and CS tends to be driven by the search for gender differences. Indeed, a crucial component of NSF funding criteria for gender studies has been to find such differences.[6] Barrie Thorne long ago pointed out the potential for flawed findings inherent in this model when "the strategy of contrast is often built into the research" (Thorne, 1993). She explains how many studies begin by separating boys and girls into single-sex groups and proceed by working with each group separately to find differences, differences that then are attributed to gender. This is just one of the many ways in which gender issues, driven by the search for gender differences, can become self-limiting, self-sustaining, and self-fulfilling.

We need to pay close attention and be wary of attributing differences to gender when they are the outcome of cultural and environmental factors. The significance of this problem is illustrated in the section of this chapter on CS undergraduates where we note that most studies on gender and CS have been conducted in situations where, by default, there are very few girls and women. Findings from such studies have often revealed strong gender differences. In contrast, we show that such differences tend to dissolve and gender similarities emerge when the environment becomes more balanced. Our findings illustrate Rosabeth Kanter's argument that "[w]hen men and women are in similar situations, operating under similar expectations, they tend to behave in similar ways" (Kanter, 1977, p. 312). Echoing this perspective, Cynthia Fuchs Epstein advocates the "structural approach [which] looks at the ways in which factors external to the individual explain even those attributes ordinarily regarded as wholly internal, such as motivation and aspiration" (Epstein, 1990, p. 100). As she points out, the structural approach is critical to counter a trend in social science research "to find support and justification for gender distinctions and inequality rather than locate the sources of these distinctions and understand the dynamics. In this sense, scientists have also been active agents in perpetuating distinctions based on mainstream viewpoints" (Epstein, p. 4).

A related concern for keeping culture in the foreground of our discussions, and our thinking, is to raise awareness of how easily we buy into myths about gender differences. In the book, *Same Difference: How Gender Myths Are Hurting Our Relationships, Our Children, and Our Jobs* (Barnett & Rivers, 2004), the title of the first chapter, "The Seduction of Difference," caught our attention. Gender differences are indeed seductive in that they form so much of the exciting, fun, and attractive dynamics of relationships, as well as fueling our fires as we argue for fairness and against inequity. Yet, as authors Barnett and Rivers point out, so many of these differences turn out to be myths. Boys and girls (and men and women) may well act differently because of the cultural messages they have received and taken on board. The danger of the seduction of difference lies in closing our eyes to gender similarities, to cross-gender dynamics, and to recognizing "that people's behavior today is determined more by situation than by gender" (Barnett & Rivers). Gender myths based on differences are also easy to buy into since they feed on stereotypes; in addition, based on limited experiences, they seem to ring true on many levels.

Like Barnett and Rivers, other researchers have questioned the dominance of theories of gender differences by "going back to the data" and noting that much of it is misinterpreted, amplifying differences and ignoring gender similarities. Diane Halpern's review of math and cognitive tests led her to conclude that any differences in boys' and girls' cognitive skills are so small as to be insignificant (Halpern, 2000). Janet Shibley Hyde's extensive meta-analysis of psychological gender differences led her to write "The Gender Similarities Hypothesis," in which she affirms that "men and women, as well as boys and girls, are more alike than they are different" (Hyde, 2005, p. 581). Hyde also reminds us of the important effects of timing and context. Test results can "fluctuate with age" and vary, "creating or erasing gender differences in math performance" when test takers have preconceived views on the outcome of their performance (Hyde, p. 588-9).

Clearly, as our approach suggests, we need to look beyond gender to account for differences in the experiences and perspectives of men and women. "It is time to consider the costs of over-inflated claims of gender differences. Arguably, they cause harm in numerous realms, including women's opportunities in the workplace.... Most important, these claims are not consistent with the scientific data" (Hyde, 2005, p. 590).

We illustrate gender myths further in our section on software engineering and the practice of collaboration. It has been suggested that collaboration fits "women's style" because women are more communicative. However, the agile approach for software engineering, which promotes communication and gives rise to collaboration, was designed to improve software development in general, not to suit women's style. The agile approach provides us with an example of work practices that allow for both men and women to be successful. The example also serves to show that the style attributed to women is actually a style developed within the culture of the software development industry, which is currently male dominated.

With regards to the larger cultural picture illustrated in our section on Eastern cultures, there is ample evidence to show that "gender distribution (in CS) is culturally diversified" (Schinzel, 2002). The work of Adams et al. showed that on the tiny island of Mauritius, women were entering and graduating in computing related fields at rates comparable to their proportion in the general population (Adams et al., 2003). The same appears to be the case in Malaysia (Othman & Latih, 2006). Britta Schinzel has looked at female enrollment in CS around the world and notes a multiplicity of reasons that account for higher and lower rates of female participation. She describes how in countries with good gender distribution in computing, such as India, Brazil, and Argentina, "there seems to be no conviction like in the Northwest stereotyping women as less capable of pursuing education in science and technology." In the North African and Arabic countries where there is an "extremely high participation of women in CS," she highlights the fact that there is "no coeducation at any level of education in these countries" (Schinzel, 2002, p. 10).

In the US, a study by Antonio Lopez and Lisa Schulte looked at African American students of CS in historically black colleges and universities (HBCUs) and in non-HBCUs during the period 1989–1997. They found that at HBCUs, consistently more African American females were awarded bachelor's degrees in CS than their male counterparts, while the opposite was true for African Americans (as well as for non-African Americans) at non-HBCUs. They concluded: "For African American females, this might suggest that being awarded a bachelor's degree in computer science has less to do with gender differences and more to do with cultural factors" (Lopez & Schulte, 2002).

There seems to be no single theory that covers all cases, nor should we expect to find one when the variables are so numerous, but what these studies reveal is a multitude of complex cultural factors—some specific and some more general—playing a significant role. "While the problem is widespread, the under-representation of women in computer science is not a universal problem. It is a problem confined to specific countries and cultures" (Adams et al., 2003, p. 59).

Thus we argue that yes, gender is a cultural issue, and as such, gender should be approached through culture. The arguments we make cannot be contained within the umbrella of gender or the framework of gender differences. Barrie Thorne points out the need "to develop concepts that will help us grasp the diversity, overlap, contradictions, and ambiguities in the larger cultural fields in which gender relations, and the dynamics of power, are constructed" (Thorne, 1993, p. 108). We propose that thinking about culture, whether of geographical magnitude or a localized microculture, can embrace such concepts and remind us of the wealth of evidence relating to culture as determinant of how we perceive and experience the world around us. Ultimately we suggest that the reasons for women entering—or not entering—the field of computer science have little to do with gender and a lot to do with culture.

Case Studies: Western Cultures

In this section we examine how a microculture within an academic CS department in the US has evolved. We also look at the agile subculture within the software development industry. In each case we discuss the cultural factors that allow for the women-CS fit to present itself. In the next section we discuss two cases within Eastern cultures.

Case Study 1: Undergraduate CS at Carnegie Mellon University

This case study is based on the work of Blum and Frieze (2005a, 2005b) at Carnegie Mellon University in Pittsburgh and illustrates how women's (and men's) relationship to computing is shaped by the ambient microculture. Specifically, this case study illustrates the evolvement of a computing culture—and its synergistic impact—as the environment shifted from an unbalanced to a more balanced environment in three critical domains: 1) gender, 2) the range of student personalities and interests, and 3) professional support afforded to all students.

Prior to 1999, the undergraduate CS environment at Carnegie Mellon was unbalanced in these domains. Indeed, in the mid-1990s less than 10% of the undergraduate CS students were women. The admissions policies, as well as the culture of computing at that time, supported a specific type of (male) student, in particular those who had exhibited great programming proclivity. And women students, being in the minority, did not have access to the various informal professional support systems available to the majority male students.

Early research, conducted by Margolis and Fisher during 1995–1999, which examined the perspectives of this specific student body, found a gender divide in the way men and women related to computer science (Margolis & Fisher, 2002). The core of the divide, in particular their findings that women wanted to do useful things with computing while men liked to focus on programming and the machine itself, was summarized by Margolis and Fisher as "computing with a purpose" and "dreaming in code," respectively.[7] They also found that women's confidence was extremely low (even "extinguished"). Not surprisingly, women in their cohort felt they did not fit into the computing culture. Not surprisingly, given that most undergraduate computing environments were similar to that of Carnegie Mellon's in the 1990s, these findings rang true with many in the CS community.

By the fall of 1999 new admissions criteria were in place at Carnegie Mellon that deemphasized prior programming experience[8] while at the same time placing more emphasis on breadth and leadership promise[9] (without reducing the high academic criteria). This change allowed for diversity in the student body, in particular an increase in the numbers of women[10] and an increase in the numbers of students with broad interests, both men and women. It is important to note that the Carnegie Mellon CS academic curriculum was not adapted to become "female-friendly" and in fact continues to be one of the most rigorous CS programs in the US.

Subsequently, the student body became more balanced in terms of gender and in terms of students with a broader range of interests. In 1999, the organization Women@SCS[11] was established to formalize a program of professional, networking, and mentoring opportunities for women. In this way female students were formally provided with those opportunities that had been available naturally for the majority (male) students (Frieze & Blum, 2002). Thus, the environment became more balanced in the three critical domains.

A primary reason for establishing Women@SCS was to provide a structure that would help ensure the retention and success of our new undergraduate student body. At the same time, impetus came from our women graduate students' perceived need for community; already they had initiated pot-luck dinners and get-togethers with women faculty.

It is important to emphasize that Women@SCS has evolved not as a "handholding" support group, but rather as an action-oriented organization in which women have taken leadership roles that have enhanced the entire CS community. We emphasize further:

> Women@SCS explicitly provides crucial educational and professional experiences generally taken for granted by the majority in the community, but typically not available for the minority participants. Many of these experiences are casual and often happen in social settings. For example, in an undergraduate CS program, male students often have the opportunity to discuss homework with roommates and friends late at night or over meals. Course and job information and recommendations are passed down from upperclassmen, from fraternity files and from friends. Women students, being in the minority, do not have access to, in fact are often excluded from, these implicit and important advantages. As one proceeds into the professional world, similar phenomena occur (Blum & Frieze, 2005a, 2005b).

These changes in the "local environment" in a few short years have provided us an opportunity to examine how men and women relate to CS in a more balanced situation and to compare with earlier studies.

Here we illustrate this shift with our most recent data collected from interviews with computer science seniors from the class of 2004, a class which consisted of 156 students, 104 men and 52 women. Fifty-five of these seniors were interviewed, 23 men and 32 women (including all 12 active members of Women@SCS). All interviews were transcribed. From the 55 total, we selected a sample of 20 men and 20 women (which included 5 of the active 12 Women@SCS members) to arrive at a representative cohort for which transcripts were analyzed. The analysis involved reading each transcript in its entirety and reading sets of responses to each question. This allowed us to identify and compare prominent themes, common issues, and patterns of perspectives. Figures 1, 2, and 3 present data derived from this analysis. These figures point to some post-1999 specififc changes with regard to *confidence levels* and *perspectives on programming*. Figure 4 uses data from a general student survey to illustrate the post-1999 change in students' *sense of fitting in*.

Confidence levels. In our 2004 studies we found that while men were still reporting higher confidence levels than women, most women in our cohort reported an increase in their confidence levels. The confidence gap had narrowed significantly (see Figure 1). Students, men and women, stated that although their confidence increased overall, levels varied greatly over the years, depending on the classes they were taking. Several students, three men and three women, said their confidence had fluctuated or remained stable, or as this woman says, it could do both: "It's probably remained about the same actually. I was pretty confident coming in and I'm pretty confident now; in between it has gone up and down." We categorized this group under *stabilized*. One woman in the class of 2004 acknowledges "bumps along the road, but overall I think I'm pretty happy with the way

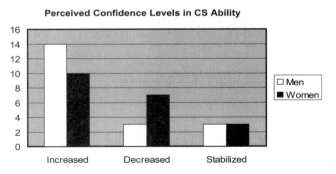

Figure 1. Perceived confidence levels in CS ability.

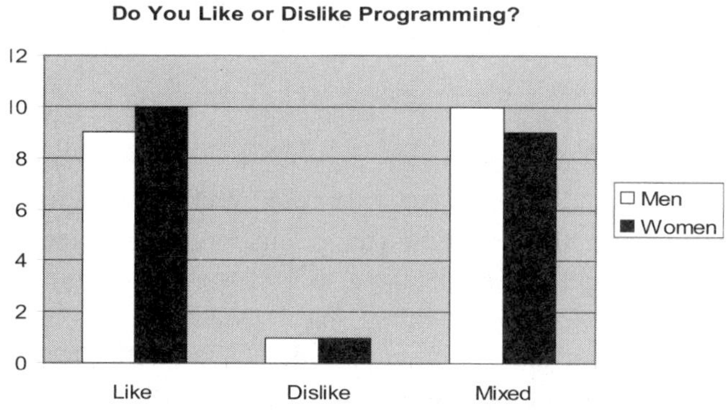

Do You Like or Dislike Programming?

Figure 2. Liking or disliking programming.

it went." Another woman in that class gives a roadmap for her increased confidence: "Once you start working on different projects or having more projects under your belt you just feel a little better.... Public speaking and having a more professional front is all part of it. And joining a group like Women@SCS really helps because there are plenty of chances to speak, talk and I think just growing more as an individual" (Blum & Frieze, 2005a, 2005b).

Attitudes toward programming. Perhaps one of the strongest illustrations of emerging similarities and the women-CS fit is found in the data relating to programming. Our representative cohort of 20 men and 20 women were specifically asked about their attitudes towards programming. In answer to the question, "Do you like or dislike programming?" the responses from students revealed some striking similarities with ten women and nine men saying they liked programming, while just one man and one woman said they disliked programming (see Figure 2).

One woman explains her attachment to coding: "I like programming. I guess it's also this kind of instant gratification feeling again where if you can code something and then just clicking that one button and seeing it actually happen right there it just kind of okay, wow, I got that to [work] ... the feedback that you get that quickly is what I like about it. And then there's all this problem solving skill that you have to go through, and if you can do that yourself and by coding it you prove to yourself that you could do it, that you could solve the problem. I think that's what I like about it." This man shows a similar attachment: "I love programming, very much.... In programming you are limited by the time you spend, not the computer. And, so I like that sort of fast feedback and being able to see things immediately."

Initially, we sorted the responses into two main categories, *like* and *dislike*, but it soon became clear that this was an oversimplification; indeed it was quite obvious that a third category had emerged, a category in which the responses were mixed.

The *mixed* category is particularly interesting in that it shows the limitations of a simple oppositional yes/no answer. Gender similarities emerged again with nine women and ten men providing thoughtful, mixed responses as they tried to explain the complexity of their views. This woman answered, "a little bit of both," while this man said, "I have to say I'm kind of in the middle." Another woman pointed out, "I like higher level programming ... [but] I dislike systems level programming, so it's a mixed bag"; this man also qualified his response: "I think it more depends on actually what I'm programming. It depends on the language and the field that it's being applied in ... so, yes, I like programming in some cases, but not for everything."

Answers to the question of liking or disliking programming revealed a spectrum of attitudes that cut across gender, and many students qualified their attitudes. Thus, liking and/or disliking programming was determined by a variety of factors, primarily what kind of programming was involved, what the purpose of the programming was, and the number of hours spent actually programming. While most students in this cohort say they like programming, or have mixed responses, most do not see themselves in future careers focused solely on programming. As one woman in the class of 2004 put it, "I enjoy programming.... I really like it. I guess I don't really enjoy it on a daily basis, for example if I had to do it 50 hours a week I don't think I would enjoy myself."

The findings illustrated in Figures 1 and 2 led us to look at the correlation between confidence and programming skills.

Confidence and programming skills. When asked if they had the skills for good programming, this same cohort of women and men reported a set of very similar skill factors: you have to be well-organized and able to think ahead; you need good problem-solving skills; you need to be able to think logically and analytically and have lots of patience. Women reported slightly ahead of men, 11 and ten respectively, in rating they had good programming skills (see Figure 3). This woman suggests that good programming skills develop with increased experience: "as you get more exposure to programming it's impossible not to develop these skills." Once more, an interesting category emerged as we tried to understand the complexity of students' answers. This category, which we called Yes, But/Doubts, covered a range of attitudes in which students either qualified their sense of having good skills with com-

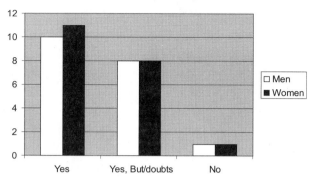

Figure 3. Rating of programming skills.

ments such as "yes, to an extent" or expressed some doubts saying such things as "I did at some point." Again a strong gender similarity emerged, with eight men and eight women falling into this middle ground category. Clearly, this cohort of women shows a high level of confidence when it comes to programming skills; and strong gender similarities emerged in all categories.

At the same time, almost all students, men and women, reported programming as one part of their CS interests and the computer as a "tool" for their primary focus, which often was applications. The images of "dreaming in code" as the dominant characteristic of male CS students and "computing with a purpose" as a primary focus for women were clearly being challenged. As one woman in the class of 2004 put it, "It's always fun to sit down in front of a computer and kind of producing code until something is done and it's such a good feeling. A lot of time once I sit down and do programming I find myself living in the cluster for a day without eating or sleeping." A male student showed his interest in the applications of programming: "I like programming. I think it's a good tool to reach an end. But I mean, on that note, I don't like programming just for the sake of programming … if I'm not interested in what the ultimate goal is, then I don't like programming." When students were asked to define CS, one of the predominant responses overall was "problem solving" and "a way of thinking." As one women in the class of 2004 put it, "I look at computer science as a sort of logic-based way to solve problems" (Blum & Frieze, 2005a, 2005b).

These findings suggest that any gender divide in how students relate to CS, particularly with respect to programming versus applications, is not a product of gender but rather a product of microcultural and environmental conditions.

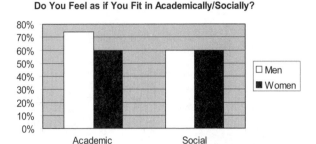

Figure 4. Sense of fitting in after freshman year.

Sense of fitting in. The data for assessing students' sense of fitting in was collected during the academic year 2004–2005 as part of a CREU[12] project (Frieze, Chang & Fan, 2005). Figure 4 represents survey responses from 88 sophomores through seniors (60 men and 28 women). The surveys showed that in this cohort, both men and women claimed to feel that they fit in well both academically and socially.

These findings indicate a marked change from the earlier studies at Carnegie Mellon (Margolis & Fisher, 2002). Indeed, the early studies showed that in the pre-1999 atmosphere, women did not feel comfortable, academically or socially, while male students were found to have great camaraderie and, by virtue of their programming strengths, could perform well academically.

Furthermore, in contrast to the early Carnegie Mellon studies, and others that have been conducted in situations where there have been very few girls and women, our findings show a similar spectrum of attitudes and attachments amongst women and men rather than a gender divide. We argue: the experiences and perspectives of the women in these other studies were in part shaped by their minority, and sometimes token, status rather than by gender. To borrow Kanter's analysis of men and women (from the Indsco corporation), we might say, "It was rarity and scarcity, rather than femaleness *per se*, that shaped the environment for women in the [departments] mostly populated by men" (Kanter, 1977, p. 207). Likewise, our findings serve to confirm the importance of microculture and environment as significant contributors to student perspectives on computing.

Our conclusion here is that the observed gender differences from the 1995–1999 study tell more about the biases in the former admissions criteria into the CS program at Carnegie Mellon, and a narrow conception of the undergraduate program, than about significant or intrinsic gender differences in potential computer scientists. During the latter half of the 1990s, the undergraduate CS program fed primarily into the booming high tech industry; thus the high school computer "geek" had a definite admissions advantage. Women and men with potential to become computer science leaders, but without long-standing programming experience or commitment, had little chance. The very few women who managed to get in had exceptional academic records. It is worth noting that the identification of programming with computer science is mostly a late twentieth-century phase in the field, one that unfortunately persists in the public's mind. Very few of the pioneers and current professors of computer science were "hackers." Many were motivated by their interest in logic and in understanding intelligence and problem solving. Today, in the twenty-first century, with the increasing ubiquity of computing, women and men with this broader and deeper perspective are critical for the field and will drive its future (Blum & Frieze, 2005a, 2005b).

Case Study 2: Agile Software Development

This case study illustrates how the culture inspired by agile software development (Cockburn, 2001) enables women to gain new and better positions in the high-tech industry in general, and in software development teams in particular.

During the 1990s, the agile approach toward software development started to emerge in response to problems in the software industry. Specifically, the agile software development approach, composed of several methods, formalizes software development methods that aim at overcoming characteristic problems of software projects (Highsmith, 2002). The "Manifesto for Agile Software Development" (http://agilemanifesto.org/) appears in Table 1.

The agile approach reflects the notion that development environments should support communication and information sharing, in addition to heavy testing, short releases, customer satisfaction, and sustainable workpace for all individuals involved. Recent managerial research studies attri-

Table 1. Manifesto for agile software development.

We are uncovering better ways of developing software by doing it and helping others do it. Through this work we have come to value:
- **Individuals and interactions** over processes and tools
- **Working software** over comprehensive documentation
- **Customer collaboration** over contract negotiation
- **Responding to change** over following a plan

That is, while there is value in the items on the right, we value the items on the left more.

bute similar characteristics to "women's management style." Here are two examples from the literature.[12]

1. "Women's style of management is based on sharing power, on inclusion, consultation, consensus, and collaboration. Women work interactively and swap information more freely than men do. Women managers encourage their employees by listening to, supporting, and encouraging them" (Fisher, 1999, p. 32).

2. "Recent research indicates women's management style, which is centered on communication and building positive relationships, is well suited to the leadership paradigm of the 90's" (Peters, 2003).

As the following data shows, agile software development environments can enable women's equal participation in agile teams. This data was gathered by observing a project-based operating-systems course in the Computer Science Department of Technion—Israel Institute of Technology (Dubinsky & Hazzan, 2005). The agile method has been used in this course since the summer semester 2002 by four teams of ten to 12 students each semester. Each team is guided by an academic coach.

An examination of the communicative behavior of 294 students, who worked according to the agile method during eight semesters in 27 different groups, reveals that females are equally communicative in this setting. For example, when the communicative behavior was measured by monitoring the electronic forum used by students in the course, it was observed that the percentage of messages sent by females (22.8% or 1391 out of 6093) was essentially the same as the percentage of females in the cohort (22.4% or 66 out of 294) (see Figure 5).

Based on this analysis, as well as on additional findings (Hazzan & Dubinsky, 2006), it is suggested that the agile method reflects a women-CS

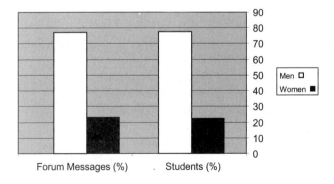

Figure 5. Men's and women's communicative behavior in agile teams.

fit. For example, in addition to being a software developer in the team, each student plays an auxiliary role on his or her team, such as coach, tracker, or customer. Roles are distributed uniformly among males and females, which in turn reinforces the female students' voice in these teams.

In summary, this case study briefly illustrates how the agile approach towards software development, formulated to address problems in the software industry and not in order to meet women's needs, creates an environment in which women and men behave similarly to the benefit of all.

Case Studies: Eastern Cultures

The two case studies presented in the previous section illustrate how subcultures can counter prevailing trends in their broader (Western) culture and demonstrate the women-CS fit. In this section we briefly consider two cases that show similar phenomenon within Eastern cultures.

Case Study 3: Israeli High School Advanced Placement CS Classes

Our main case study within an Eastern culture focuses on Jewish and Arab Israeli high school Advanced Placement (AP) CS classes. Most Jewish and Arab students in Israel attend separate educational systems with similar curricula in most subjects. Specifically, the AP CS classes are all coed, the syllabus is identical in both systems, and the only differences are in the teaching language and the language of the matriculation exam.

Eidelman and Hazzan (2005) studied a population of 146 twelfth-grade AP CS students from nine typical high schools from both sectors (5 schools from the Jewish sector, 4 schools from the Arab sector).[14] In the Jewish sector, 25 of the 90 AP CS students (i.e., 28%) were female; in the Arab sector, 34 of the 56 students (i.e., 61%) were female. That is, while female high school students in the Jewish sector are underrepresented in AP CS classes, they are highly represented in the Arab sector.

We focus here on the cultural factor *support and encouragement*, which is one explanation for the difference in the participation of female students in the two sectors (Eidelman & Hazzan, 2005). One of the questions students were asked was: "Who encouraged you to choose computer science studies?" Figure 6 presents the distribution of the answers to this question.

Figure 6 reflects an unequivocal conclusion: Arab female high school students receive much more encouragement to choose CS than do their Jewish counterparts. Specifically, Arab female high school students are encouraged more by their mothers (56% vs. 40%), fathers (44% vs. 40%), siblings (44% vs. 16%), friends (44% vs. 20%), acquaintances who had studied CS (50% vs. 20%), and—with the greatest difference—by their teachers (56% vs. 8%).

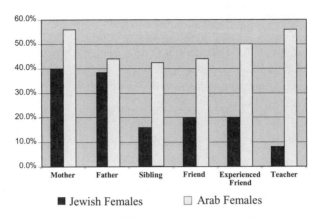

Figure 6. Percentage of females' encouragement by others.

The broad-based network of encouragement that the Arab female students receive is supported by additional data (see Eidelman & Hazzan, 2005).

The noticeable differences in the extent of encouragement Arab female students receive from various agents can be explained by looking at findings from other studies that have explored cultural and familial differences between Arab and Jewish adolescents (Peleg-Popko, Klingman, & Abu-Hanna Nahhas, 2003). According to these studies, since Arab students are part of an Eastern collective culture, as well as a minority group in Israel, it is likely that they are strongly encouraged by their parents to higher scholastic achievement in order to improve their social status. In addition, Arab students perceive their family environment as more authoritarian than do their Jewish counterparts. The hierarchical structure of the Arab family is based on age and traditionally requires the young to obey the old and adhere to their expectations (Peleg-Popko et al.).

As can be seen, different social and cultural characteristics stimulate the extensive encouragement the Arab female students receive. This might lead us to the intermediate conclusion that in a culture that supports positive attitudes towards CS, we can probably attract more female students to study advanced levels of CS.

Case Study 4: Undergraduate CS at Carnegie Mellon–Qatar

Another Eastern case is taken from Qatar. In the fall of 2004, Carnegie Mellon opened a campus in Qatar (CMU-Q), offering an undergraduate major in CS with the same curriculum as its campus in Pittsburgh. We have yet to determine how cohorts of students on each campus can be compared, because of newness of the Qatar program and since there are so many variables to consider. Certainly, as the program progresses and evolves, this will be interesting to study. But in the cultural context of this chapter, we can already present some interesting observations, particularly since women outnumber men in the Qatar CS program. While the reasons for larger percentages of women students are not entirely known, this is most likely due in part to families traditionally allowing more sons to travel overseas for their higher education while encouraging daughters to study in Qatar. Although this tradition appears to be changing, it most likely accounts for the higher percentage of women undergraduate students in Qatar. As for CS attracting more women, anecdotal evidence suggests that women in Qatar see CS as a means of interacting with, impacting, and experiencing the world without defying their cultural traditions.

Preliminary observations at Carnegie Mellon Qatar indicate that Qatar Arab students' perceptions of CS and of women's ability in math and science studies align with many of the observations from our case studies of the Israeli-Arab AP CS classes and of the new microculture in the School of Computer Science at Carnegie Mellon Pittsburgh. While some students are more excited by programming and debugging, others are more excited by applications such as robotics. Also, the CS women are certainly multidimensional, and many are active in several other endeavors, including student government (the student-elected president is a CS woman), and take leadership roles in many ways. Moreover, responses to initial questionnaires given to the Qatar CS students are quite interesting. Women students completed the sentence "I chose to learn computer science because" with "it has to do with logic," "I loved computers since I was a kid," and "computer science is important in every domain of life." Family and teachers were the most important influencers for all students, men and women, in their decision to study CS. Another strong influencing factor is that all of the Qatari students are fully sponsored by industry to obtain their degrees at CMU-Q, and it is apparent that these industry partners are willing to sponsor women to obtain CS degrees.

Surveyed women students overwhelmingly disagreed with the statement: "In my country, an equal number of men and women choose to study computer science." The reasons were surprising, elaborated as follows: "I believe in my country females feel that computer science is more important; men go to engineering and business field[s]" and "Women are [represented] more than men because they are 'more genius' than men." When asked why more women seemed to be interested in CS, one woman student responded, "I think that the women here probably have more patience.... So yes, while the guys are drawn to engineering ... the women are discovering a new path through computer science."

Surprising to some, prior programming experience was not a factor that influenced these women (or men) to pursue a degree in CS—many of them had no prior programming experience, and more women than men had some exposure to programming in high school. Future careers also did not influence most women to pursue a CS degree—in fact, most of them are unsure what career, if any, they will pursue following their graduation. While the men generally have more options and direction for what they wish to do post-graduation, many of the women wish to make a significant impact on their country or in the Gulf region or globally and are seeking ways in which they can do so within their cultural boundaries. Most of them seem to have selected and continue in CS (despite very heavy workloads compared to their peers in some other undergraduate programs) because they wish to succeed in the challenge they undertook and because they enjoy the intellectual challenge of CS.

Longer-term discussions with students revealed that most of the CS students feel torn between their families and their educational demands. While their families are supportive of their higher education, CS is not a well-understood discipline in Qatar, and cultural requirements in terms of time spent with family, relatives, friends, and in community service are very high. Thus, the highly demanding CS program causes friction between the students and their families because the families do not fully understand why their children need to spend so much time on academic work. Despite the tremendous pressures that arise from feeling like they are not understood by anyone, the students rely on each other for support and encouragement and persevere in their quest for a degree in CS with courage and determination against many odds.

Some endeavors by the faculty are also helping to ease this friction between students and their parents by giving parents opportunities to witness the accomplishments of their children and to understand more about the challenges in computer science and related fields. One example was a poster session that allowed students to present their final projects from a robotics course to parents and colleagues. Students described the poster session as an empowering experience, and parents enthusiastically hailed it as a learning experience that demonstrated the knowledge and accomplishments of the students. One father thanked the professors and said, "I am so proud of my daughter ... [and the fact that] she is learning to think in creative ways.... I now understand why she spends so much time in the lab."

We will be investigating further such similarities, and differences, and the roles they play in the success—or lack of success—of women and men in CS in the Qatar campus.

Conclusion

Whether referring to attitudes within larger cultures, such as the Israeli and Qatari-Arab subcultures, or a microculture, such as the computing culture of a specific undergraduate department, we hope to have illustrated the impact of culture and environment as determinants of women's (and men's) choices and participation in computing. We have offered evidence for an alternative model of thinking about gender issues rooted in the dynamics of culture rather than the self-limiting, and often misleading, oppositional model of gender differences. Our work leads to various questions for consideration. Two questions with clear implications for constructive and effective action are:

1. How might thinking about culture (as opposed to gender) help us understand and impact women's and girls' (and men's and boys') choices of CS and computing-related careers?
2. What can different cultures learn from each other with regards to CS education?

Based on the perspective presented in this chapter, we suggest that we should look to the environmental and cultural conditions that enable the women-CS fit. This chapter presents several specific examples of such conditions and of interventions that help create them. Clearly there is more to investigate with the goal of enabling women and other underrepresented groups to enter CS studies and contribute to computing-related fields. These findings will also have broader implications both for opening up CS to a wider population and for the health and future of the field itself.

Acknowledgments

We thank Carnegie Mellon University and the Sloan Foundation for their support of the recent research at Carnegie Mellon. We also thank the Samuel Neaman Institute for Advanced Studies in Science and Technology, the Technion MANLAM Fund and the Technion Fund for the Promotion of Research at the Technion for their generous support of the research about the high school AP CS studies in Israel and about agile software development. Finally, we wish to thank the Qatar Foundation for Education, Science and Community Development for partially sponsoring this research, and the Carnegie Mellon University Qatar campus for their support.

A brief and preliminary version of this chapter was presented at SIGCSE 2006.

References

Adams, J. C., Bauer, V., & Baichoo, S. (2003). An expanding pipeline: Gender in Mauritius. *Proceedings of the SIGCSE Technical Symposium on Computer Science Education, USA, 34*, 59–63.

Barnett, R., & Rivers, C. (2004). *Same difference: How gender myths are hurting our relationships, our children, and our jobs.* New York: Basic Books.

Blum, L. (2004). Women in computer science: The Carnegie Mellon experience. In D. P. Resnick & D. Scott (Eds.), *The innovative university* (pp.). Pittsburgh, PA: Carnegie Mellon University Press, 111–129.

Blum, L., & Frieze, C. (2005a). The evolving culture of computing: Similarity is the difference. *Frontiers, 26*(1), 110–125.

Blum, L., & Frieze, C. (2005b). In a more balanced computer science environment, similarity is the difference and computer science is the winner. *Computing Research News, 17*(3). Retrieved September 20, 2006, from http://www.cra.org/CRN/articles/may05/blum.frieze.html

Camp, T. (1997). The incredible shrinking pipeline. *Communications of the ACM, 40*(10), 103–110. Retrieved September 20, 2006, from http://www.mines.edu/fs_home/tcamp/cacm/paper.html

Cockburn, A. (2001). *Agile software development.* Reading, MA: Addison-Wesley.

Dubinsky, Y., & Hazzan, O. (2005). The construction process of a framework for teaching software development methods. *Computer Science Education, 15*(4), 275–296.

Eidelman, L. (2005). *Gender- and sector-based analysis of Israeli high school computer science studies.* Unpublished master's thesis, Technion—Israel Institute of Technology, Israel.

Eidelman, L., & Hazzan, O. (2005). Factors influencing the shrinking pipeline in high schools: A sector-based analysis of the Israeli high school system. *Proceedings of the SIGCSE Technical Symposium on Computer Science Education, USA, 36*, 406–410.

Epstein, C. F. (1990). *Deceptive distinctions: Sex, gender and the social order.* New Haven, CT: Yale University Press.

Fisher, H. (1999). *The first sex: The natural talents of women and how they are changing the world.* New York: Ballantine Books.

Frieze, C., & Blum, L. (2002). Building an effective computer science student organization: The Carnegie Mellon Women@SCS action plan. *Inroads SIGCSE Bulletin Women in Computing, 34*(2), 74–78.

Frieze, C., Chang, B., & Fan, C. (2005). *Motivation, persistence and success in computer science: What can computer science seniors tell us?* Final report to CREU 2004–2005. Retrieved September 21, 2006, from the Computer Research Association's Committee on the Status of Women in Computing Research (CRA-W) Web site: http://www.cra.org/Activities/craw/creu/crewReports/2005.php

Frieze, C., & Treat, E. (2006). Diversifying the images of computer science: Carnegie Mellon students take on the challenge! *Proceedings of the 2006 WEPAN National Conference.* Retrieved September 20, 2006, from http://www.x-cd.com/wepan06/pdfs/10.pdf

Halpern, D. (2000). *Sex differences in cognitive abilities* (3rd ed.). Mahwah, NJ: Lawrence Erlbaum Associates.

Hazzan, O., & Dubinsky, Y. (2006). Empower gender diversity with agile software development. In E. M. Trauth (Ed.), *The encyclopedia of gender and information technology* (pp. 249–256). Hershey, PA: Idea Group Inc.

Highsmith, J. (2002). *Agile software developments ecosystems.* Reading, MA: Addison-Wesley.

Hyde, J. S. (2005). The gender similarities hypothesis. *American Psychologist, 60*(6), 581–592. Retrieved September 20, 2006, from http://www.apa.org/journals/amp/

Kanter, R. M. (1977). *Men and women of the corporation.* New York: Harper Torchbooks.

Lopez, A. M., & Schulte, L. J. (2002). African American women in the computing sciences: A group to be studied. *Inroads SIGCSE Bulletin Women in Computing, 34*(1), 87–90.

Margolis, J., & Fisher, A. (2002). *Unlocking the clubhouse: Women in computing.* Cambridge, MA: MIT Press.

Morris, J. H., & Lee, P. (2004). The incredibly shrinking pipeline is not just for women anymore. *Computing Research News, 16*(3), 20. Retrieved September 20, 2006, from http://www.cra.org/CRN/articles/may04/morris.lee.html

Othman, M., & Latih, R. (2006). Women in computer science: No shortage here! *Communications of the ACM, 49*(3), 111–114.

Peleg-Popko, O., Klingman, A., & Abu-Hanna Nahhas, I. (2003). Cross-cultural and familial differences between Arab and Jewish adolescents in test anxiety. *International Journal of Intercultural Relations, 27*, 525–541.

Peters, H. (2003). Risk, rescue and righteousness: How women prevent themselves from breaking through the glass ceiling, Hagberg Consulting Group.

Schinzel, B. (2002). Cultural differences of female enrollment in tertiary education in computer science. In K. Brunnstein & J. Berleur (Eds.), *Proceedings of the IFIP: Vol. 225. Human Choice and Computers: Issues of Choice and Quality of Life in the Information Society* (pp. 283–292). Deventer, the Netherlands: Kluwer.

Thorne, B. (1993). *Gender play: Girls and boys in school.* New Brunswick. NJ: Rutgers University Press.

Vashti, G. (2002). Women in computing around the world. *SIGCSE Bulletin, 34*(2), 94–100.

Vegso, J. (2005). Interest in CS as a major drops among incoming freshmen. *Computing Research News, 17*(3). Retrieved September 20, 2006, from http://www.cra.org/CRN/articles/may05/vegso.

Wing, J. (2006). Computational thinking [Viewpoint]. *Communications of the ACM, 49*(3), 33–35.

Zweben, S. (2006). Ph.D. production at an all-time high with more new graduates going abroad; Undergraduate enrollments again drop significantly [2004-2005 Taulbee survey]. *Computing Research News, 18*(3). Retrieved September 20, 2006, from http://www.cra.org/CRN/articles/may06/taulbee.html.

Notes

1. The 2004–2005 CRA Taulbee Survey reports that the number of new undergraduate CS majors in the US dropped by more than 30% since 2001-2002 (Zweben, 2006). Even more alarming, according to the UCLA/HERI (Higher Education Research Institute) survey, the percentage of incoming undergraduates among all degree-granting institutions who indicated they would major in CS declined by 70% between fall 2000 and 2005 (Vegso, 2005).

2. We note that recent conferences on gender and IT have also brought culture to the foreground, indicating a timely momentum for our perspective. Examples of such conferences include "Women and ICT: Creating Global Transformation," Baltimore, USA, June 2005, and "Crossing Cultures, Changing Lives: Integrating Research on Girls' Choices in IT Careers," Oxford, England, July/August 2005.

3. For example, the Carnegie Mellon School of Computer Science (SCS) is comprised of seven interrelated departments. In addition to "core" CS, these departments include robotics, software engineering, human computer interaction, language technologies, machine learning, and entertainment technology.

4. See: http://www.ncwit.org/Prospectus.pdf.

5. Herbert Simon defined computer science as "the theory and design of computers, as well as the phenomena arising from them." The Wikipedia is a source of various views of the fields (http://en.wikipedia.org/wiki/Computer_science): "Computer science rarely refers to the study of computers themselves. The renowned computer scientist Edsger Dijkstra is often quoted as saying, 'Computer science is no more about computers than astronomy is about telescopes.' The study of computer hardware is usually called computer engineering, and the study of commercial computer systems and their deployment is often called information technology or information systems."

6. The synopsis of the NSF program, "EHR (Education and Human Resources): Research on Gender in Science and Engineering" illustrates this point: "Typical projects will contribute to the knowledge base addressing gender-related differences in learning and in the educational experiences" (http://www.nsf.gov/funding/pgm_summ.jsp?pims_id=5475). The goals of the program include: "To discover and describe gender-based differences and preferences in learning science and mathematics" (http://www.nsf.gov/pubs/2005/nsf05614/nsf05614.htm).

7. These findings led Margolis and Fisher to recommend a female-friendly and contextual approach to revamping the CS curriculum (Margolis & Fisher, 2002). Our findings lead us to question such a recommendation. Whether or not it is a good idea to incorporate applications into a particular course should depend on whether it makes sense for the subject matter, for the intellectual and technical skills to be developed, or for pedagogical purposes, not as a presumed means to promote gender equity (Blum & Frieze, 2005a, 2005b).

8. This was an important pragmatic consequence of the Margolis and Fisher finding that the amount of prior programming experience did not affect graduation rates.

9. Raj Reddy, then Dean of the School of Computer Science, asked the undergraduate Admissions Office to develop criteria that would select for future leaders and visionaries in the field. One subsequent criterion gave value to "evidence of giving back to the community."

10. See Blum (2004), Margolis and Fisher (2002), and Blum and Frieze (2005a, 2005b) for fuller details on the key factors that resulted in the change in the undergraduate CS population at Carnegie Mellon. A particularly key factor was a series of workshops held on the university campus for high school teachers of Advanced Placement CS, funded by the National Science Foundation. These workshops ran for three summers during the late 1990s and integrated discussions about women and CS along with technical CS training. Indeed, without such focused outreach, it would be hard to buck downward national trends of dramatic declines in computer science enrollments (Camp, 1997; Vegso, 2005; Zweben, 2006). Support (including funds) for teachers to participate in such programs is crucial. Unfortunately, for a number of years, government support for these important hands-on workshops has not been as forthcoming.

    Based on our belief that the reasons for underrepresentation of women in CS are very much the same as the reasons for the huge decline in interest in the field generally, in the summer of 2006, with support from Google, Carnegie Mellon sponsored a pilot workshop for high school CS teachers (CS4HS) that focused on computational thinking (Wing, 2006) and changing the image of what computer science is, and who computer scientists are (Frieze & Treat, 2006). Currently, we are working to expand this program nationally and internationally. (See: http://www.cs.cmu.edu/cs4hs.)

11. Women@SCS is an organization of undergraduate and graduate students, and faculty, in Carnegie Mellon's School of Computer Science (SCS), working on-campus and off-campus to create, encourage, and support women's academic, social, and professional opportunities in the computer sciences and to promote the breadth of the field and its diverse community. The Women@SCS program of activities is designed and implemented by an informal advisory council made up of core Women@SCS members. Women@SCS also runs an informative Web site: http://women.cs.cmus.edu/.

12. The Collaborative Research Experience for Undergraduates in Computer Science and Engineering (CREU) Program is sponsored by the Computing Research Association's Committee on the Status of Women (CRA-W). See: http://www.cra.org/Activities/craw/creu/.

13. We note that these quotes about women's management style further highlight the tendency to investigate gender differences—in this case with respect to management style. Moreover we note that these observations were found in a culture in which women are in a minority of management positions. But we also note that many attributions of "women's style," such as the ones highlighted in the quotes, are ones that men employ to advantage as well. The agile software development environment discussed here provides one such example.

14. The gender mix in both Jewish and Arab high schools is about 50%-50%. See, e.g., data from the Israeli Central Bureau of Statistics: http://www1.cbs.gov.il/shnaton56/st08_19x.pdf.

Chapter 6

Sociopolitical Factors and Female Students' Choice of Information Technology Careers

A South African Perspective

Cecille Marsh

Abstract

This chapter investigates the reasons behind the large number of black South African females from technologically disadvantaged backgrounds enrolling for IT-related courses at universities. Samples consisting of female students from distinctly different backgrounds and enrolled at two institutions with very different legacies are the units of analysis of the study. A postulate put forth is that sociopolitical factors play a significant role in the females' decision to study IT courses.

Introduction

Previously, I undertook research into the effectiveness of teaching the strategic use of computer applications in general computer literacy courses to students from technologically disadvantaged backgrounds in a South African Technikon (an institution of higher education). During the course of this study I investigated the computer self-efficacy levels of the students in the sample groups. The reason for this investigation was that studies have shown that there is a distinct relationship between a student's belief structure (self-efficacy) and his or her performance (Bandura, 1977) and that self-efficacy is influenced by a person's expectations about his or her capacity to accomplish certain tasks (Betz & Hackett, 1981). During this investigation I discovered that the female students did not have significantly different scores when compared with the males on either pre- or post-computer self-efficacy tests (Marsh, 2003). This was contradictory to several studies in the developed world that have shown strong gender differences in levels of computing self-efficacy expectations (Miura, 1987; Harrison & Rainer, 1992; Vasil, Hesketh, & Podd, 1987). For example, a freshman survey conducted by the University of California found that 46% of male freshmen rated themselves as having above average computer ability as compared to 23% of female freshmen students (UCLA Higher Education Research Institute, 2001).

Together with the above finding was a parallel finding that within this institution, and in two similarly historically disadvantaged sister institutions, there were more female students (between 56% and 61%) than male students registered for the first year of IT related courses. Were there lessons to be learned from female black South African students that could inform those who are currently looking for ways to boost the numbers of females entering post-secondary IT courses elsewhere in the world?

Socioeconomic Context of Black African Women

Migrant labor started in South Africa with the discovery of gold and diamonds. The institutionalization of apartheid in South Africa ensured that the black African majority was kept from the centers of economic power. Through the creation of the so-called homelands, apartheid barricaded Africans inside the four walls of the impoverished and overcrowded rural areas and townships and exploited the men as a reliable source of cheap migratory labor. There was one notable result of these years of male migration: the power of rural women has been markedly increased as they have become de-facto heads of households. In 1993 South Africa's population was 40.3 million people; 53% were women. Of all the households in the rural areas, 59% were headed by females. In 1999, 65% of South African rural households were managed and maintained by women (Statistics South Africa, n.d.).

The repudiation of apartheid did not end South Africa's economic and social problems. Racially discriminatory policies enforced by successive governments throughout the twentieth century left the African majority of the population in possession of only about 13 percent of the nation's land, and most of that of poor quality. Black Africans, male and female, unable to achieve sustainable agricultural development, continue to flock to cities where many live in sprawling squatter camps. In these squatter camps, the nuclear family is not the norm, and it is common for women as single parents, or the widowed, divorced, and deserted, to head families.

Political Empowerment of Black African Women

When Former President Nelson Mandela opened the first sitting of parliament after South Africa's first democratic elections in April 1994, he said, "It is vitally important that all structures of government, including the president himself, should understand this fully: that freedom cannot be achieved unless women have been emancipated from all forms of oppression."

The South African government continues to be committed to gender equity and gender equality. Of the total of 28 ministers in government, ten are females. Among 21 deputy-ministers, ten are females. In 2004, in choosing the provincial premiers who are regarded as engines of delivery, especially in building and protecting the economies of major cities with the collaboration of local municipalities, President Thabo Mbeki appointed four women out of nine premiers. In the legislature, one third of the members of the National Assembly are now female, and slightly more women, 35%, are sitting in the National Council of Provinces. The most recent female political appointment by the president was that of a female deputy-president.

In South Africa a number of measures have been taken to establish national machinery that would effectively implement gender equality and nonsexism at various levels of government. An Office on the Status of Women has been established in the presidency to oversee and coordinate policy on women at the national level. This office has also been established in premiers' offices to coordinate policy in seven of the nine provinces. The task of the office is to take forward the National Empowerment Policy document, determining baseline information and launching gender mainstreaming activities at the national and provincial levels.

In addition, parliament has passed legislation to create a National Commission on Gender Equality. The commission commenced its work in 1997. The task of this commission is to promote gender equality in society and to ensure that government and other nonstatutory bodies implement their commitment to gender equality. The Human Rights Commission and the Office of the Public Protector, established by parliament, also play a major role in protecting women's human rights, as outlined in the constitution.

Methods

I hypothesized that within a political environment of high-level awareness and support for gender equity, socioeconomic influences on black South African women play a significant role in the choice of females studying IT courses at historically disadvantaged universities.

A questionnaire was administered to female students in IT programs at two different post-secondary institutions. Institution A was typical of what is termed a "historically disadvantaged institution," and Institution B is a "historically advantaged institution". The reason for doing a comparative study was that Institution B was fairly typical of a university campus in the developed world and that any differences in the findings could be significant for that group. The percentage of first-year female students enrolling for IT in Institution A was 59% and in Institution B it was 29%. The sample size from Institution A was 39 students, and from Institution B it was 22 students.

The questionnaire was designed to capture data about the female students' socioeconomic background, influences on choice of study course, computer self-efficacy, role-models, and attitude towards gender roles in computing. Audiotaped interviews were held with a smaller, random sample of seven females from Institution A in order to obtain broader and deeper information on the same areas as the questionnaire.

Characteristics of the Respondents

Students attending Institution A typically come from underresourced schools in rural areas in the Eastern Cape Province, the most impoverished area of South Africa, which is still suffering from the ravages of the homeland policy of the apartheid regime. Most of these students are only partially financially supported by family and community and cannot pay their fees without government loans. In an earlier survey I had found that these students came from a poor technological environment with little exposure to digital devices in general and to computers in particular. They did not have a developed awareness of the importance of the computer in the society in which they were to study and later find employment (Marsh, 2000).

Students attending Institution B typically come from "Former Model-C" schools in a city. These schools have high levels of tuition and are well-resourced having previously been those that served the white population under the apartheid regime. Most of these students come from homes equipped with a variety of digital devices and computers.

Findings

Socioeconomic Factors

Figure 1 depicts the percentage of the sample who (a) have access to a computer in the home, (b) had access to a school computer when a pupil, (c) are in a household with a female head, (d) felt confident of their computer studies in their ability to use a computer effectively, and (e) were influenced by a female to choose an IT course. The rationale for using access to a computer in the home and at school as indicators of a student's economic status arose from the fact that many of the students registered at Institution A come from the impoverished rural areas of the Eastern Cape. In these areas many homes still do not have electricity and running water. A prelimi-

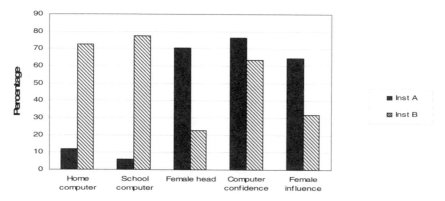

Figure 1. Socioeconomic factors.

nary analysis of the Eastern Cape student background questionnaires from the Third International Mathematics and Science Study (TIMSS) found that only 54% of the children surveyed had electricity in their homes (Howie, 1998). Their schools were similarly without essential services and were very poorly equipped.

The third item of analysis, the students' computer confidence, was included for comparative purposes since, according to Bernstein (1994), individuals who have used computers during their youth, whether as an educational or a recreational tool, will be more experienced in computer use and should thus display a resulting comfort with, and affinity for, computing and also because positive past experience with computers will increase computer self-efficacy beliefs (Ertmer, Evenbeck, Cennamo, & Lehman, 1994).

The presence of a female head of household and female influence over the choice of an IT course of study were chosen for investigation because they would indicate the strength of the female role model in the students' formative years and either support or negate my hypothesis that an emerging matriarchal society, underpinned by a robust affirmation of gender equity, was a significant factor in the high number of female black South African students enrolling for IT courses at universities.

Figure 1 confirms the economic disparity between the females at the two institutions in that very few, only 12%, of those at Institution A had a computer at home, as compared to 72% of females at Institution B. The disparity between their access to computers while at school is even greater, with only 6% of females at Institution A having had this advantage as opposed to 78% of females at Institution B. The interviews that were conducted confirmed the poverty and financial distress in which many of the students at Institution A found themselves. The verbatim excerpts below are typical.

It must be noted that these students are not native English speakers but largely speak Xhosa, and therefore their grammar is often awkward. Where necessary I have inserted words in brackets to add to the meaning:

Student 5: "My grandmother is the head of the house, I do have a grandfather but he is just there as a grandfather but the main person who is doing everything is my grandmother. Okay they do get a pension, both of them, but my grandmother always tries to do something else, like she also has this small loan [business], then she lends money and she looks after us very much but most of us are her grandchildren and I am here because of her."

Student 7: "No she's not working, she's unemployed, she got the pension now, but she got the money for the children who have got no father so she managed to raise us with that money—but the money stops when you are eighteen years [old]. So she managed with that money at that time."

This disadvantage surprisingly did not have a negative effect on the attitude towards computers of the females at Institution A. In fact, their initial confidence in their ability to use computers effectively was greater than that of the females at Institution B: 77% of them had responded positively to this section of the questionnaire as opposed to 63% of those at Institution B. This finding contradicts findings by researchers such as Bernstein (1994) and Ertmer et al. (1994) referred to above.

The chart also indicates very strongly that the females at Institution A were very likely to have a strong female role model in their homes in that 70% of them had a female head of household, compared with 23% of females at Institution B. When asked as to the gender of the person(s) who had influenced them most to undertake studies in IT, 64% of the females at Institution A answered "female," as compared with only 32% of the females at Institution B. The following verbatim excerpt from the interviews is typical:

Student 5: "I heard about IT from most of them [who] were males, then she came and because of [her] referring to computers so I thought maybe this was a man thing, she told me, no man [SA slang expression], even females can do this. Then I will do it. I will go for it."

The interviews that were conducted with the random sample of females from Institution A also strongly supported the premise that they were inspired to succeed by a female role model(s) who often were mothers but in some cases were grandmothers, aunts, or older sisters. Some verbatim excerpts from each of the seven interviews are below:

Student 1: "I have always looked upon my mother as an achiever because even at home there are eight, from my mother's family there are eight, three other brothers and five sisters. My mother [has] always been the one taking care at home, taking care of my grandmother and stuff like that."

Student 2: "My father left us I think when I was 14 and I was doing standard seven. So I'm left with my mother, my sisters and my brothers. So she is the head of the family, she is the one who brings something to the home, she is the one who supports me."

Student 3: "The role she [mother] plays is mother and father because I don't have a father, I have a father but I have never seen my father. I have seen him in the streets. I grew up without a father."

Student 4: "She's [aunt] a very harsh person but she's got her days when she's nice and everything. She's a good parent because I grew up with my grandmother and then at high school she took over."

Student 5: "She [grandmother] is a very strong [person] and I rely on her and one day I hope I can be as strong as she is. She always told me that there's nothing specifically for males, if a male could do it then a female could do it."

Student 6: "...they are taking the responsibility of being the women and also being the man. Because they have to take [care of] us—they have to do the work that a man has to do, go to work and work hard for their children. In Xhosa culture it was always the man who has to go to work and work for their children. But our mothers have to go to take care of us. They are doing a great job."

Student 7: "I have five brothers....Three brothers, elder brother, then my sister, then me, the fifth, then I have two brothers after me. They are doing grade 10 this year.... My mother [looks after us]."

Attitudes toward Gender Roles in Computing

I was interested to find out whether the females at the two institutions shared similar attitudes with their Western peers when asked questions relating to whether males were better at IT studies than females. Figure 2 depicts the percentages of the samples who (a) thought that males knew more about computers than they when they embarked upon their computer course, (b) thought that males were better programmers than they, and (c) thought that females and males were better at different IT areas

From Figure 2 it can be seen that overall the respondents from the two institutions concurred in their responses to these particular questions. Only close to 50% of each of the samples thought when they started their IT studies that the male students knew more about computers than they did. A similar percentage (52% of females at Institution A and 47% of those at Institution B) stated that males were better at programming than females. When asked if they thought males or females were better at different areas of computing, there was a more conclusively positive response from the females at both institutions (71% from Institution A and 68% from Institu-

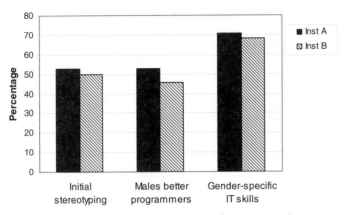

Figure 2. Attitudes to and gender roles in computing.

tion B). In examining the positive answers to a question on the question-naire that was administered to both samples, "Do you think that males and females are better at different IT areas? If so, explain which," it was found that the majority of females indicated that males were better in the technical areas and that females were better at applications design and software engineering. However, there was no hint of inferiority feelings in their responses. The following answer from a student at Institution B is rep-resentative of the majority of the questionnaire responses: "I do think that women are better listeners—therefore better at requirements solicitation. Other than that they are evenly matched. Some might say that women are better at multitasking and project management too."

The interviews bore out this finding. as the following verbatim excerpt shows:

Student 1: "We have had projects for DS (Development Software III) and there was a male in our group who was very good at programming ... but I was not feeling cold or shy to stand out because he could do well [in] pro-gramming but there some other things he can't do well. So we as women in our group we stood out and did our best in what we could."

I took the opportunity afforded by the interviews of probing the female students' attitudes towards gender-related general ability and found that most of the interviewees were adamant that they were as able as their male counterparts:

Student 1: "I think, yes, there is nothing that will [be] stopping me from doing anything I want to do. I could perform as well as guys could."

Student 5: "It's being different, like in South Africa. Because ... in the past, most of the women [were] like depressed. Men were dominating on both sides. Women were there to be like wives, cook and bear children, but now things have changed now we have this power that you can do whatever you can do. I'm so glad that I'm a woman doing IT so that I can prove it that women have this ability to do whatever men do."

Discussion

The importance of self-efficacy, together with a student's attitude toward and prior experience with computers, has often been maintained as an important influence on that learner's decision about whether to undertake a computer-related course of post-secondary study. What is noteworthy from the findings is that, although less than 12% of the respondents from Institution A had had prior experience with a computer, 77% of them had a positive attitude toward their ability to learn to use a computer effectively and succeed in an IT course. This was 14% higher than the respondents from Institution B, the vast majority (78%) of whom had had prior computer experience. I postulate that one reason for this anomaly is that these black African females' overall self-confidence in their ability to perform has been encouraged by strong female role models in their formative years, that this self-efficacy has been affirmed by determined efforts of the South African government to promote women, particularly previously disadvantaged women, throughout its own apparatus at national, provincial, and local levels, and that this is serving as an example to South African society as a whole. Further investigation on a larger sample drawn from a wider spectrum of institutions of higher learning both within South Africa and in other African countries would confirm or dispute this claim.

I acknowledge, however, that there might be another reason for the high computer confidence of the black African female students in that, since they had had little or no contact with computers during their primary and secondary schooling, their confidence could have been based on a lack of information and prior experience. Further investigation into this possibility needs to be carried out.

Another interesting finding is that only half the respondents from both institutions started their IT courses with the belief that males knew more about computers than themselves. This is not typical of females in Western cultures, as Margolis and Fisher (2002, p. 109) maintain. They state that by the time those females enter high school, "their natural curiosity about how and why things work may have been destroyed. By then, gender stereotypes may be too deeply engrained for females to feel comfortable moving into a male-dominated culture." The females in both the samples who indicated that they thought males and females were better at different IT areas intimated by their responses that they were comfortable with these differences, and there was no indication that they thought that males had a higher status in the IT field. In addition to this, the interviews revealed that in general black African women students were confident that they could do anything that their male counterparts could do.

This self-confidence and corresponding feelings of affirmation of many black South African women can be summed up by an extract from The Sowetan, a major South African newspaper. This paper published the story of Noluthando Luzipo, a female contractor from Port Elizabeth who had just been awarded a building contract worth 1.3 million South African rands in the Coega Development Initiative (a major designated industrial development zone in South Africa). When asked how she had managed to achieve that, Luzipo said: "Women can compete in the field of construction [because] they have the ability to do whatever they put their minds to."

Conclusion

Self-confidence is critical for success not only in IT courses at universities, but also in an IT career. In the developed world there seems to be a confidence gap between male and female IT students. However, this gap does not appear to be evident among the black South African IT students surveyed in this study. I postulate that major reasons for female black South African IT students' firm belief in their ability are the strong female role-models in their homes and communities and a political environment that aggressively promotes and empowers women. Providing positive role models for girls considering studying post-secondary IT courses is not a new intervention. I suggest, however, that there needs to be a more holistic approach that goes beyond the confines of a particular discipline or career—an approach that targets a girl's overall self-image and understanding of her capacities. Otherwise, she is conditioned from birth to uphold male superiority in fields such as science, engineering and, particularly, IT. Perhaps what I am seeing in the black South African sociopolitical environment is a change within the household, albeit, ironically, forced by the socioeconomic engineering policies of the apartheid regime, which has radically changed women's status within the family, and a present-day government that is vigorously creating enabling conditions that legitimize that change.

References

Bandura, A. (1977). Self-efficacy: Toward a unifying theory of behavioral change. *Psychological Review, 84*, 42–64.

Bernstein, D. (1994). The effects of previous computer exposure, computer owner-ship and gender on computing skills and comfort: Two countries' experiences. *New Zealand Journal of Computing, 5,* 77–84.

Betz, N. E., & Hackett, G. (1981). The relationship of career-related self-efficacy expectations to perceived career options in college women and men. *Journal of Counseling Psychology, 28,* 399–410.

Ertmer, P. A., Evenbeck, E., Cennamo, K. S., & Lehman, J. D. (1994). Enhancing self-efficacy for computer technologies through the use of positive classroom experiences. *Educational Technology, Research & Development, 42*(3), 45–62.

Harrison, A. W., & Rainer, R. K., Jr. (1992). The influence of individual differences on skill in end-user computing. *Journal of Management Information Systems, 9,* 93–111.

Howie, S. J. (Ed.). (1998). Mathematics and science performance in the middle school years in the Eastern Cape Province of South Africa. The performance of students in the Eastern Cape Province in the Third International Mathematics and Science Study (TIMSS). Pretoria, South Africa: Human Sciences Research Council.

Margolis, J., & Fisher, A. (2002). *Unlocking the clubhouse: Women in computing.* Cambridge, MA: MIT Press.

Marsh, C. J. A. (2000, September). *End user computing at a South African Tech-nikon: Enabling disadvantaged students to meet employers' requirements.* Paper presented at the 2000 Annual Conference of the European Educational Research Association (EERA), Edinburgh, U.K. Abstract retrieved September 23, 2006, from the EERA Web site: http://www.eera.ac.uk/

Marsh, C. (2003, July). *Boosting computer self-efficacy by teaching strategic use of computer applications: A preliminary investigation.* Paper presented at the Elev-enth International Conference of Gender and Science and Technology (GASAT) Association, Brighton, U.K.

Miura, I. T. (1987). The relationship of self-efficacy expectations to computer interest and course enrolment at college. *Sex Roles, 16,* 303–311.

Statistics South Africa. (n.d.). Retrieved September 23, 2006, from http://www.statssa.gov.za

UCLA Higher Education Research Institute. (2001). *The American freshman: National norms for fall 2000.* Retrieved September 23, 2006, from http://www.gseis.ucla.edu/heri/norms_pr_00.html

Vasil, L., Hesketh, B., & Podd, J. (1987). Sex differences in computing behaviour among secondary school pupils. *New Zealand Journal of Educational Studies, 22,* 201–214.

Chapter 7

Women's Entry to Graduate Study in Computer Science and Computer Engineering in the United States

J. McGrath Cohoon and Holly Lord

Abstract

What factors are related to the gender composition of graduate computer science and computer engineering programs? Data from a nationwide survey of graduate computer science (CS) departments in the US address this question. Our exploratory analyses indicate that program flexibility, active recruitment, and effort to recruit women are all associated with the gender composition of these departments, but not necessarily in the predicted manner. Women's representation appears to be highest in flexible programs that put effort into recruiting women. But when men in the department meet with prospective students, recruitment of male students is likely to far outpace recruitment of women.

Research Objective and Theoretical Perspective

Our objective is to identify factors related to women's representation in graduate programs in computer science and computer engineering (CSE) in the United States. Minimal previous research exists on this topic. As a consequence, we look to research from other science, technology, engineering, and mathematics (STEM) disciplines, the workforce, and undergraduate computing to guide our work and suggest hypotheses. From graduate programs in STEM, we know that women's representation varies with the type of student-faculty interactions prevalent in a department (Fox, 2001). From the workforce, we know that women's representation in a firm is affected by formal and informal hiring practices (Reskin, 2003), social networks (Reskin and McBrier 2000; McPherson, Smith-Lovin, & Cook, 2001), and employer and employee preferences and stereotypes (Reskin, McBrier, & Kmec, 1999; Gorman 2005). From undergraduate computing, we know that institutional gender composition is related to department gender composition, and that college men and women are drawn to computing under very similar circumstances (Tillberg & Cohoon, 2005; Cohoon, 2006). It is unclear, however, which, if any, findings transfer from these arenas to graduate CSE.

This chapter describes some findings from the first large-scale empirical study of women's representation in graduate CSE programs. For our analysis, we consider how student preferences and departmental recruitment practices influence the gender composition of graduate enrollment. Consideration of other factors is deferred to future analyses. If the effects of preferences and recruitment practices follow patterns observed in other settings, we should see that there are few differences in the program features that men and women find attractive, that faculty attitudes and behaviors regarding diversity affect women's representation, and that formalized recruitment practices increase women's representation.

Research Methods

We recruited departments for the survey from a stratified random sample of all the US post-secondary institutions with active doctoral programs in computer science or computer engineering. Forty-nine departments participated in the data collection, but the doctoral program in one institution was inactive, so this program was dropped from the analysis. Two outlier departments were also dropped from the current analysis because of apparent problems with the data for their dependent variable. The resulting data set is thus from 46 CSE departments, with 18 considered top-tier and the rest divided equally into middle and bottom tiers in academic quality. Tiers are based on 1993 National Research Council rankings, with departments divided into thirds to comprise tiers.

In the spring of 2003, we collected survey data using three instruments: chairpersons, faculty, and graduate students. All full-time graduate faculty, and in most cases all students, in a department were invited to participate. In especially large departments, we randomly sampled up to 85 students, oversampling women up to 50%. The surveys were implemented through the Web. We sent out multiple email reminders, and nonrespondents received a paper questionnaire follow-up. The subsequent response rates from the original sample were 94% for chairpersons (46 chairs, 43 in the data used for analysis), 63% for faculty (789 faculty, 749 in the data used for analysis), and 55% for students (2012 students, 1949 students in the data used for analysis). Response rates for particular questions varied.

Survey questions used a five-point scale to measure the attitudes and practices of students and faculty. Students were asked to rate the importance of various factors in their decision to pursue a graduate degree in computer science or computer engineering (CSE) and in the selection of their current program. Another set of student questions measured their level of agreement with various statements about their intended career. The student survey also asked if students had ever helped recruit new graduate students. The faculty questionnaire asked how often they engaged in different recruitment activities and how much importance they placed on various criteria when evaluating applicants. To measure the outcomes of faculty recruiting practices, we asked chairpersons how many part- and full-time male and female students were enrolled in their program.

Initial analyses for male/female differences were done on the individual level. For all analyses relating recruitment practices to the female proportion of enrollment, data were aggregated to the department level. Program tier was investigated as a relevant factor in women's representation but was dropped from the analysis when no significant findings were obtained.

Findings

We considered two issues—how men and women are similar and different in what they seek in a graduate CS education and a particular program, and what recruitment and admission practices are employed by graduate CS programs. For both preferences and recruitment and admission practices, we measure correlation with women's representation.

Program Choice

Program choice for men and women is based on similar, but differently weighted, features. Descriptive statistics from individual responses identified the leading factors that graduate students thought affected their choice of program and the features that particularly appealed to female students. In this section, we report the most influential factors, along with some factors that students considered less important but that show some potentially interesting gender differences. The full set of program choice factors considered by survey respondents is given in Appendix C.

On average, the men and women who pursue graduate study in CSE do so for very similar reasons. The factors that respondents rate as most important in their decision to pursue the degree and in their selection of a program are the same for both sexes. Men and women both put "interest in or enjoyment of computing" as their number one reason for graduate study of this discipline. But, although sex was not a factor in the ranking of factors that influenced student decisions to pursue a graduate degree in CSE, there were sex differences in ratings. Men rated interest and enjoyment as 4.2 on a scale where 1 is not at all important and 5 is extremely important, and women rated it 4.1. Analysis of variance indicated that this gender difference was statistically significant at the .01 level, and it persists when degree program is taken into consideration.

As with decision to study CSE at the graduate level, men and women also chose their particular program for similar reasons. Table 1 shows that their most important consideration was reputation—of the institution and of the program or professor(s). For women, the next most important factor in selecting a graduate program was the availability of financial aid, followed by research opportunities and area of specialization. For men, the next most important factor after reputation was research opportunities, followed by the availability of financial aid. Among these most influential factors, only the gender differences in the importance of financial aid and area of specialization were statistically significant.

Table 1 also shows other potentially consequential gender differences that exist for program choice factors that were rated only moderately important. For example, environment in the department was more important to women's decisions than to those of men. Impressions of faculty and department culture were both moderately important to women but slightly less important to men. Women also placed more importance than men on flexibility in program content and geographic preferences or constraints. All of the gender differences in these factors were statistically significant.

Finally, women cared more than men did about the presence of women among faculty and students, but neither group thought this factor was

Table 1. Factors that influenced choice of program.

Importance of Selected Factors Influencing Choice of Program, by Sex	Male Mean Rating	Female Mean Rating
Institution reputation	3.9	3.9
Program or professor reputation	3.8	3.9
Financial aid available*	3.7	3.9
Research opportunities	3.8	3.7
Particular computing specialization*	3.6	3.7
Geographic preferences or constraints**	3.0	3.3
Impression of faculty from campus visit**	2.9	3.1
Department culture**	2.9	3.1
Flexibility in program content**	2.8	3.0

Ratings are on a scale where 1 = not at all important and 5 = extremely important.

*Statistically significant at the .05 level.

**Statistically significant at the .01 level.

very important. Women rated the importance of women's presence among students as between slightly and moderately important (2.4), and rated women's presence on the faculty at about the same level of importance (2.3). Men thought these factors were less important still (1.9 and 1.6, respectively).

Flexibility is the only program feature with evidence of a positive relation to women's representation. Correlations between the items in Table 1 and women's representation (measured as the percent of enrolled female graduate students according to chairperson reports) show only one significant relationship: a moderately strong positive correlation between "flexibility in program content" and women's representation in a program ($r = .35, p < .01$). This correlation indicates that CSE departments with flexible programs are particularly attractive to women.

Recruitment and Admission Practices

Recruitment and admission practices that lead to gender balance are difficult to identify. In addition to asking students what attracted them to departments, we asked faculty members about their recruitment practices. We aggregated their responses by department to assess how common each practice was in each department. The recruitment practices are listed in Table 2 with measures of their mean reported frequency on a scale where 1 represents *never* and 5 represents *always*. Table 2 also lists correlations between recruitment practices and a department's effort devoted to enrolling women graduate students (aggregated mean responses to "In your opinion, how much effort does your department devote to enrolling women graduate students?" with response options on a five-point scale from "no effort" to "very extensive effort.") These correlations indicate some positive associations with effort, but none with women's representation (not shown). Women's representation is positively correlated with department effort to enroll women, although the specific practices that lead to gender balance are difficult to identify.

Effort departments put into enrolling women graduate students appears to pay off—departments that put more than "a little effort" into women's recruitment tended to enroll higher percentages of women.

Faculty responses to the question about effort showed that the average department put slightly less than a "moderate" amount of effort toward enrolling women. Departments ranged from "a little" effort to effort rated between "moderate" and "extensive." No departments were rated by their faculty as exerting "extensive" or "very extensive" effort.

Among departments putting more than "a little" effort into enrolling women, greater effort was associated with greater women's representation

Table 2. Recruitment and admission actions.

	Mean frequency of action on 1–5 scale	Correlation with dept. mean effort to enroll women
Actions Related to Amount of Effort Expended for Enrolling Women		
Actively recruit from liberal arts colleges	1.89	.52**
Actively recruit from women's colleges	1.67	.43**
Admission criteria emphasized academic letters of recommendation	4.24	.41**
Meet prospective students	3.62	.33*
Involve undergraduates in my own research	3.52	.33*
Admission criteria emphasized maturity	3.42	.33*
Admission criteria emphasized undergrad degree from this institution	1.99	-.32*
Recruit through personal contacts in undergraduate depts.	2.61	.30*
Faculty actively recruit graduate students	3.08	.28*
Admission criteria emphasized research experience	3.82	.27*
Actively recruit at conferences	2.60	.26*
Admission criteria emphasized prior graduate degree	2.39	-.25*
*Significant at the .05 level. **Significant at the .01 level.*		
Actions Unrelated to Amount of Effort Expended for Enrolling Women		
Teach summer research courses	1.41	.17
Sent personal letters/email to prospectives	3.21	.19
Presentations to cs/ce undergrads	2.72	.04
Personally call prospectives	2.63	.14
Encourage undergrads to go to grad school	4.17	.07
Encourage masters to go on to PhD	4.12	-.07
Assist students with grad applications	3.06	.20
Admission criteria emphasized students who desired to use tech skills for social good	2.36	.10
Admission criteria emphasized US citizenship	1.97	.01
Admission criteria emphasized undergrad computing degree	3.46	.12
Admission criteria emphasized reputation of undergrad program	3.95	-.07
Admission criteria emphasized quality of academic record	4.43	-.14
Admission criteria emphasized noncomp. work/volunteer experience	1.81	.14
Admission criteria emphasized motivation	4.25	-.01
Admission criteria emphasized member of underrepresented group	2.64	.22

Table 2. Recruitment and admission actions (continued).

	Mean frequency of action on 1–5 scale	Correlation with dept. mean effort to enroll women
Admission criteria emphasized math background	3.81	-.07
Admission criteria emphasized leadership experience	2.54	.15
Admission criteria emphasized GRE score	3.55	.00
Admission criteria emphasized GRE CS subject exam score	2.72	-.10
Admission criteria emphasized grades in noncomputing courses	3.09	.22
Admission criteria emphasized grades in computing courses	4.21	.22
Admission criteria emphasized gave special consideration to applicants away from formal education for a time	2.05	-.18
Admission criteria emphasized EE background	2.03	-.04
Admission criteria emphasized computing work/ volunteer experience	2.66	-.09
Admission criteria emphasized computing experience	3.58	.11
Admission criteria emphasized communications skills	3.84	.20
Admission criteria emphasized area of research interest	3.49	-.08

($r = .40$, $p < .01$; $n = 34$). In other words, there appears to be a point at which effort begins to result in measurable increases in women's representation. Below that point, graduate enrollment in departments exerting little or no effort ranged widely from 16% to 31% women. There was no measurable relationship between effort and women's representation at the low end of the effort spectrum. At the mid to high end of the effort spectrum, however, more effort was associated with greater gender balance.

What does "effort" mean? Both faculty and chairperson responses suggest that recruiting from liberal arts and women's colleges is an effort to recruit women. Even so, in the average department, recruitment from these types of undergraduate programs occurs between "never" and "rarely." At most, faculty reported recruiting from women's colleges or liberal arts colleges "rarely" or "sometimes." Other, less strongly correlated components of effort were indicated by faculty and chairpersons, but none had a significant positive relationship with women's representation.

Why would effort be related to women's representation when none of the practices associated with effort are related to women's representation in the expected manner? There are several possible explanations. It may be that effort refers to something other than the practices we specified. Alternatively, effective effort might require combinations of practices, and the correct combination might vary by department. Another possible explanation is that effort might be expended only by a designated person or group while the average faculty member operates in ways that reinforce the status quo.

The role of effort requires further investigation to untangle its non-linear relationship with women's representation. For the remainder of this chapter, we explore the effects of one type of recruiting practice that had a significant, but unexpected, effect on women's representation.

Although personal recruiting by faculty may be productive, it failed to show the expected positive effect on women's representation. Most faculty members believe that meeting with prospective students and encouraging them to apply is the most effective means for increasing the number of women in their graduate program. Both male and female faculty members endorse this method, but that does not mean that they employ it, nor does it mean that their goal is to promote gender balanced enrollments when they do employ it.

Slightly more than half (54%) of the faculty in the average CSE department frequently meet with prospective students. This action appears to be an effective recruiting practice in that it was strongly associated with graduate student reports about the importance of their "impression of faculty during a campus visit." Table 3 shows that male and female CSE students were more likely to consider the impression they got of faculty to be important in their choice of program if faculty members met with prospective students often. This relationship suggests that faculty members do help recruit graduate students, at least graduate students who consider their impression of faculty members to be important, as women are slightly more likely than men to do.

Not shown in Table 3 is that instead of the expected positive association between women's representation and faculty efforts to recruit students through personal meetings, there was a moderately strong negative correlation between the average frequency of meeting with visiting prospective students and a department's percent of female graduate enrollment ($r = -.50, p < .01$). Similarly, if the average faculty member in a department took an active approach to recruiting and called or mailed prospective students, the program was likely to have low female enrollment ($r = -.51, p < .01$). This finding corroborates results from a nationwide pretest of our survey questions. The pretest showed that meetings between faculty members and prospective graduate students had a statistically significant negative relationship with women's representation in departments that had low National Research Council ratings (Cohoon and Baylor, 2003). Our cur-

Table 3. The importance of meeting faculty.

Correlations between Faculty Meeting Prospectives and Importance of Impression Made by Faculty

	Mean frequency of faculty meeting with prospective students	Male faculty frequency of meeting with prospective students	Female faculty frequency of meeting with prospective students
Mean enrolled student importance of impression made by faculty	.70**	.70**	.43**
Male student importance of impression made by faculty	.69**	.63**	.48**
Female student importance of impression made by faculty	.43**	.53**	.16

n = 42 due to listwise deletion of missing cases. Similar results are obtained with pairwise deletion.

* Correlation is significant at the .05 level (1-tailed).

** Correlation is significant at the .01 level (1-tailed).

rent study indicates that this relationship is also common to the average CSE graduate program, regardless of its rank.

Table 3 indicates similar, but weaker, relationships between recruiting by female faculty and importance of impression. Perhaps the reason for the weaker correlations is that women faculty comprised only 15% of the responding faculty in the average department and so were less available to meet with the similarly scarce women prospective students. This scarcity could also explain why women's enrollment is independent of their impression of women faculty.

Faculty meeting prospective students might negatively affect women's representation for several reasons. It is possible that women comprise a smaller number of applicants in the departments where personal recruiting is often practiced. This situation would look like effective recruiting together with low female representation. An alternative explanation is that meeting prospective students is an effective tool insufficiently applied to recruiting women. Among the faculty members who reported frequently meeting with prospective students, 18 percent indicated that they do not believe their department should actively recruit members of underrepresented groups. This minority could be wielding an effective recruiting tool in a manner that advantages men over women.

Although students generally may be effective recruiters, recruitment by current graduate students failed to show the expected positive effect on

women's representation. Close to one third of graduate students in the average department say they helped out in the recruitment of new graduate
students. In the departments where many current students helped recruit
new students, graduate students generally reported that their impression of
current students was important in the decision to enroll in that program.
This relationship included women; there was a moderately strong correlation ($r = .55$, $p < .01$) between women's rating of how important their
impression of students was and the percent of students in a department
who helped recruit new graduate students.

Our analysis, as shown in Table 4, indicates that recruiting by experienced graduate students was moderately correlated with first-years who
considered their impression of students during a campus visit to be important in their selection of a graduate program. The relationships suggest that
students can help recruit students to their graduate program.

We also see from a comparison of the first and second columns in
Table 4 that women recruiters appealed more than men recruiters to both
men and women applicants. This observation suggests that because they
also attract men, women graduate student recruiters do not improve the
gender balance despite the positive influence they have on prospective
women. These findings may help explain why women students' recruitment efforts had no measurable direct association with women's representation in their departments.

Effective recruiting by men may advantage men. Without data on the
gender composition of program applicants, we cannot examine the ad-hoc
hypothesis that personal recruiting actually yields more gender balanced
enrollments than would otherwise occur. For now, we consider another
explanation for how personal recruiting can be both effective and negatively related to women's representation.

CSE departments are typically majority men among both faculty and graduate students. As these male department members meet with prospective
students, they are more effective at recruiting men than recruiting women.
In departments where male faculty members met often with prospective
students, women's representation was lower than in departments where
this action was seldom taken ($r = -.43$, $p < .01$). Likewise, in departments
where many of the experienced male students actively recruited, women's
representation was lower than in departments where few male students
actively recruited ($r = -.33$, $p < .05$). The stronger positive effect that
recruiting by men faculty has on men students appears to advantage prospective male students over female students.

To accommodate the small number of cases in our data set, we performed a factor analysis and combined recruiting through personal contact

Table 4. The importance of student recruiting.

Correlations between Experienced Student Recruiters and Importance of Student Impressions		
	% of experienced female students who helped recruit	% of experienced male students who helped recruit
female first-year mean importance of student impression	.42**	.32*
male first-year mean importance of student impression	.41**	.36*

n = 38 due to listwise deletion of missing cases.

* Correlation is significant at the .05 level (1-tailed).

** Correlation is significant at the .01 level (1-tailed).

by male faculty with recruiting by experienced male graduate students into one variable that represents personal recruiting by men in the department. This factor score variable had a moderate negative correlation with women's representation (r = −.47, p < .01, factor loading = .65.) We used this combined variable in subsequent analyses.

Predicting the gender composition of enrollment. Based on the preceding analyses, we can suggest some components of a linear model for predicting the gender composition of enrollment in CSE graduate programs. Our model is far from complete, but it is a good initial step toward measuring the effects certain department activities have on women's representation. Of all the recruitment and admission practices and student preferences we considered, it appears that departmental effort to enroll women, program flexibility, and recruiting by men have the strongest influence on gender balance. Results were similar whether limiting analysis to only those cases that put more than a little effort into recruiting women or using the full set of departments. Table 5 summarizes these results. The most notable difference between the two sets of results was that the negative effect of men recruiters is less for departments that put some effort into recruiting women.

Together, these factors account for 29 percent of the variance in women's representation in graduate CSE programs. As Table 5 shows, when all study departments are considered, both flexibility and effort to enroll women have a positive association with a department's percent of graduate students who are women (Beta = .21 and .29, respectively, p < .05), and recruiting by men has a negative association (Beta = −.49, p < .05). When the regression includes only the subset of departments with a linear association with effort, the size of the effects differ somewhat, but all relationships are in the same direction.

Table 5. Regression results.

Regression on Women's Representation in Graduate CSE Programs		
	Beta for all departments	Beta for departments where effort $> = 2.6$
	$n = 46$	$n = 34$
Flexibility in program content	0.21*	0.18
Men recruiters	-0.49**	-0.35*
Effort to enroll women	0.29*	0.36*
Adjusted R^2	0.29**	0.29**

* Significant at .05 level.

**Significant at .01 level.

Discussion and Conclusions

Computer science and computer engineering programs operate under special circumstances. They award credentials attesting to expertise in a field that our culture defines as appropriate for men (Charles & Bradley, 2006). As a result of the gender typing of computing as masculine, practices that may be adequate for gender-balanced enrollment in the graduate programs of most disciplines are insufficient for creating gender balance in CSE. Nevertheless, this study demonstrates that it is possible to overcome the cultural beliefs and stereotypes that promote gender imbalance to some degree.

Our findings about effort suggest that an approach tailored to the conditions in individual departments may be necessary for achieving measurable differences in gender balance. Although reports of more than a little effort were associated with relatively higher women's representation, we could not identify particular efforts that were related to gender balance in the manner expected. Analysis using more sensitive methods might elicit such evidence, but it might also be the case that interventions require multifaceted approaches, that interactions occur between effort and particular practices, or that effort expended by a designated person or subgroup is insufficient to counteract routine practice by the average faculty member in a department.

On the whole, men and women were attracted to computing graduate study and programs by the same features, with both sexes identifying the same conditions as most important. Interest and enjoyment of computing was the top reason both sexes decided to go to graduate school in CSE. Reputation, financial aid, research opportunities, and areas of specialization were the top influencers on choice of graduate program for both sexes. Male-female differences emerged primarily in strength of ratings. But among the factors that were rated differently by men and women, only flexibility in program content was significantly related to women's representation. The meaning and importance of flexibility is being further investigated in analyses currently underway, but it appears that this aspect of CSE graduate programs could contribute to attracting women into particular programs.

Experts and activists recommend particular practices for achieving gender balance in computing, but our research suggests that many recommended practices fail to have the desired effect, and some practices may even work against women's representation. In particular, personal recruiting is a highly recommended practice that our analysis calls into question. The Computing Research Association Best Practices (Cuny & Aspray, 2000) recommends being "proactive in making recruiting contacts" and calls for personalized contacts with prospective students, but our findings point to the critical role that implementation and motive might play. We found a moderately strong negative association between women's representation and recruiting by male faculty and students, so this action, as it is commonly practiced, seems to generally work against gender balance.

The negative relationship between women's representation and recruiting by men does not necessarily imply that we should abandon a behavior that practitioners strongly endorse. Active, personal recruiting was a positive factor that attracted many of the students who are currently enrolled in CSE graduate programs. Furthermore, faculty members have faith in the effectiveness of this practice. These realities should not be ignored by those who wish to create a gender balance in computing.

It is possible that personal recruiting by male faculty members is a powerful and effective tool that only increases women's representation under specific conditions. As is the case with mentoring CS undergraduates (Cohoon, Gonsoulin, & Layman, 2004), action with the intention to promote diversity might be a necessary component for positive effects on women's participation in computing. Even when faculty members are open to recruiting women, they may unconsciously underestimate women prospective students. This process is documented in many evaluation situations, including hiring at law firms (Gorman, 2005) and the peer review process in science (Wenneras & Wold, 1997), and it may be the reason women's representation is not higher when faculty members meet with prospective students. In other words, the purpose and skill with which a tool such as personal recruiting is used affects the results achieved.

Further research is needed to investigate whether personal recruiting yields higher female representation than an applicant pool would otherwise produce. But for now, we should consider a noteworthy implication of our recruitment findings—departments with the goal of adding women to achieve gender balance cannot afford to ignore gender. Being gender blind does not attract women into computing.

Acknowledgments

This material is based on work supported by the National Science Foundation grant EIA-0203127. Any opinions, findings, and conclusions or recommendations expressed in this material are those of the authors and do not necessarily reflect the views of the National Science Foundation.

References

Charles, M., & Bradley, K. (2006). A matter of degrees: Female underrepresentation in computer science programs cross-nationally. In J. M. Cohoon & W. Aspray (Eds.), *Women and information technology: Research on underrepresentation* (pp. 183–204). Cambridge, MA: MIT Press.

Cohoon, J. M. (2006). Just get over it or just get on with it. In J. M. Cohoon & W. Aspray (Eds.), *Women and information technology: Research on underrepresentation* (pp. 205–238). Cambridge, MA: MIT Press.

Cohoon, J. M., & Baylor, K. M. (2003). Female graduate students and program quality. *IEEE Technology and Society, 22*(3), 28–35.

Cohoon, J. M., Gonsoulin, M., & Layman, J. (2004). Mentoring computer science undergraduates. In K. Morgan, J. Sanchez, C. A. Brebbia, & A. Voiskounsky (Eds.), *Human perspectives in the Internet society: Culture, psychology, and gender* (pp. 199–208). Southampton, UK: WIT Press.

Cuny, J. E., & Aspray, W. (2000). Recruitment and retention of women graduate students in computer science and engineering. Washington, DC: Computing Research Association.

Fox, M. F. (2001). Women, science, and academia: Graduate education and careers. *Gender & Society, 15*(5), 654–666.

Gorman, E. H. (2005). Gender stereotypes, same-gender preferences, and organizational variation in the hiring of women: Evidence from law firms. *American Sociological Review, 70*, 702–728.

McPherson, M., Smith-Lovin, L., & Cook, J. M. (2001). Birds of a feather: Homophily in social networks. *Annual Review of Sociology, 27*, 415–444.

Reskin, B. F. (2003). Including mechanisms in our models of ascriptive inequality. *American Sociological Review, 68*, 1–21.

Reskin, B. F., & McBrier, D. B. (2000). Why not ascription? Organizations' employment of male and female managers. *American Sociological Review, 65*(2), 210–233.

Reskin, B. F., McBrier, D. B., & Kmec, J. A. (1999). The determinants and consequences of workplace sex and race composition. *Annual Review of Sociology, 25*, 335–361.

Tillberg, H. K., & Cohoon, J. M. (2005). Attracting women to the CS major. *Frontiers: A Journal of Women Studies, 26*(1), 126–140.

Wenneras, C., & Wold, A. (1997, May 22). Nepotism and sexism in peer-review. *Nature, 387*, 341–343.

Chapter 8

Women's Interest in Information Technology

The Fun Factor

Bettina Bair and Miranda Marcus

Abstract

Using surveys and interviews, we explored factors that influence male and female undergraduate students' choice of academic majors and careers. We collected data from 772 undergraduate male and female students, and also conducted follow-up surveys and interviews with 89 women non-IT majors. We validated some of our results by comparison with other studies, and also by surveying more than 100 current IT professionals. Our study shows that both men and women want interesting, fun work; that women, especially, have misconceptions about what IT careers are available; and that women, especially, don't believe that IT careers would be interesting or enjoyable. Better marketing of potential IT careers and opportunities would help encourage more women to consider computer science as a career.

Introduction

After a peak in the late eighties, women have become significantly underrepresented in engineering and IT, declining from 35.2% in 1990 to 28.4% in 2000 (Lancaster, 2001). Between 1998 and 2004, interest in CS among women fell 80 percent (Vegso, 2005). Although the demand for technology employees grows, fewer women are pursuing degrees that will prepare them for these jobs (Thibodeau & Holohan, 2000). Women are more likely to "fall into" an IT career than to plan for it (Information Technology Association of Canada [ITAC], 2002).

Many women have misconceptions about high-tech careers. The stereotype of the nerdy male hacker is just one factor that seems to be keeping women from disciplines associated with computing. They fear getting stuck forever staring at a computer, writing lines of perplexing code. Women generally want more people interaction, and they don't feel that they can get a lot of human contact in an IT career (Lancaster 2001; Margolis & Fisher, 2002).

Since March, 2002, we have collected data from 772 undergraduate male and female college students, using an electronic survey containing 140 questions. The survey examined factors that influence how students chose their major and career direction. For validation, we also conducted follow-up surveys and interviews with 89 women non-IT majors. We were able to confirm some of our results by comparison with other studies and also by surveying more than 100 current IT professionals.

What's Important to a Student's Choice of Career?

We asked students to consider what was important to their choice of career and to describe their expectations of the life that their selected major might offer them. We gave students a choice of several different adjectives to describe day-to-day life in their chosen profession. Men and women both showed a preference for fun, over other career priorities like income or achievement. However, men and women used different adjectives to describe their future "fun" jobs. Women were more likely to say that a fun job would be influential and socially important, compared to men, who were more likely to find appeal in risk and complexity.

Seventeen representative job titles were selected from a search for information technology jobs on Monster.com. Students were asked to rate, on a scale of 0 to 5, where 5 is the most familiar, how familiar they were with each job. Then they were asked to pick one job as the one they were most familiar with. Although both men and women indicated a moderate or low level of familiarity with most IT jobs, men were more likely to say that programming was the career with which they were most familiar. Women were more likely to think of Web development.

We asked students to characterize their own chosen careers and, for comparison, the life of an IT professional. We gave students the same set of adjectives to describe the day-to-day life of a professional in both areas. They were allowed to pick as many as they thought would apply. Women were more likely to assign negative terms like "difficult" and "tedious" to IT careers than men. Women found positive statements about the programming field to be unbelievable.

The female non-IT majors confirmed that while they enjoy many of their computer activities, their chosen career appears to offer them more social interaction and possible career growth. In our interviews, women students made remarks such as "[computer professionals] stare at a monitor all day ... they don't really need people skills". Many young women do seem to believe in a geek myth of computing—that to be successful in IT, they must possess absolute dedication. As one of our interviewees said, computing "involves too much science, is hard, unattractive, and not of any interest."

Women also tend to feel that they lack the "knack" of computing. They are likely to conclude that any setbacks are due to their lack of a sort of "computer gene" or inborn talent (DiDio, 1997; Margolis & Fisher, 2002).

Seeking Interesting and Fun Work

In order to understand the context of students' decisions to major (or not) in an IT-related field, we asked them to pick what was most important to them in a future career. Students chose between several different priorities for career selection: interest/fun, income, achievement/challenge, quality of work life, social significance, prestige, and other. Students were also offered the opportunity to add other priorities to the list, although only 2% indicated additional priorities, such as stability.

More female students (49%) said that "interest/ fun" was an important career consideration. A fun job was also most important to male students (42%).[1] The second most important quality of their future career was different for men and women. Twenty-one percent of women thought that a career should be "challenging" and have opportunities for "achievement." More males (28%) were motivated by "income" concerns (Figure 1).

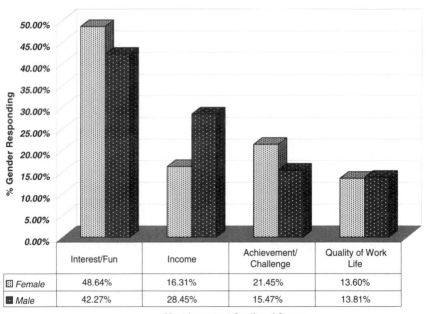

	Interest/Fun	Income	Achievement/ Challenge	Quality of Work Life
▦ Female	48.64%	16.31%	21.45%	13.60%
■ Male	42.27%	28.45%	15.47%	13.81%

Most Important Quality of Career

Figure 1. Both men and women want interesting, fun careers.

Women were more likely to consider a preoccupation with income self-ish or short-sighted. One MFA student stated that she would rather do what she enjoys than choose a career based on money. This way, she rational-izes, if the money ever left the job, she wouldn't be stuck doing something she didn't like.

However, when women IT majors were compared to women majoring in other fields, some interesting distinctions appeared. For example, women IT majors were less likely to be concerned with fun and more likely to consider achievement or income as important to a future career choice (Figure 2).

We asked students to indicate their chosen major and a typical job which might be available to them after graduation. Then they were asked to select adjectives from a list that might apply to that future job. For comparison, the students also selected adjectives for an IT job that they were familiar with. Both men and women selected words such as "exciting," "interest-ing," and "fun" to describe their own career. However, women were more likely to choose words such as "influential" and "socially important" for their future jobs. Many men chose words like "predictable" and "risky" for their own career options.

We compared the adjectives selected for a student's expected future job with those selected for an IT job with which the student was most familiar. When students indicated that a fun and interesting job was important to

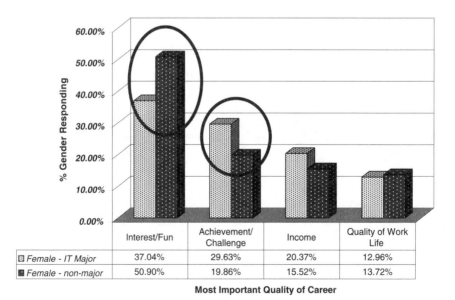

	Interest/Fun	Achievement/ Challenge	Income	Quality of Work Life
⊞ Female - IT Major	37.04%	29.63%	20.37%	12.96%
■ Female - non-major	50.90%	19.86%	15.52%	13.72%

Most Important Quality of Career

Figure 2. Women IT majors less concerned with fun, more concerned with challenge.

them, females were less likely to pick words such as "complex" and "difficult" for their future jobs, and males were more likely to pick words such as "complex" and "difficult" for their future jobs. In interviews, several women remarked that their career path would be less intimidating than a career in an IT-related field.

Lacking Valid Information about Opportunities in IT

Students were asked to rate their level of familiarity with several representative IT job titles. Then they were asked to select one title from the group as the one that they were most familiar with, for further discussion. Initially, male and female students rated their familiarity with most IT jobs about the same (not much). Both sexes gave "word processor" their highest ratings for familiarity.[2] Web developer, programmer, and data entry also got moderately high ratings for familiarity with students (Table 1). The lowest rated job titles were system administrator, systems engineer, systems analyst, quality assurance analyst, technical writer, and test engineer.

The similarities ended when students chose one job to discuss in more detail (Figure 3). Although men and women had originally rated the jobs very similarly, they picked different jobs as their most familiar. Many female students chose Web developer (27%) as the IT job that they were most familiar with; a surprising number (26%) picked data entry or word processing.

Table 1. Average familiarity ratings for IT jobs (out of 5, where 5 is very familiar).

Average Rating (out of 5)	Female	Male
Word processor	3.82	3.94
Web developer/designer	3.72	3.64
Programmer	3.57	3.66
Data entry	3.54	3.48
Computer operator	3.08	3.42
Electrical engineer	3.25	3.24
Data analyst	3.01	3.17
Web administrator	2.93	3.13
Network administrator	2.70	3.07
Internet architect	2.70	2.89
Database administrator	2.73	2.84
System administrator	2.54	2.89
Systems engineer	2.64	2.79
Systems analyst	2.59	2.82
Quality assurance analyst	2.41	2.70
Technical writer	2.41	2.54
Test engineer	2.23	2.50

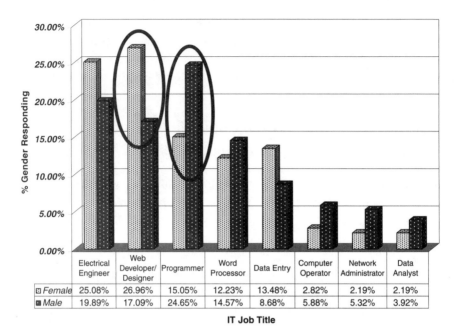

	Electrical Engineer	Web Developer/ Designer	Programmer	Word Processor	Data Entry	Computer Operator	Network Administrator	Data Analyst
▣ Female	25.08%	26.96%	15.05%	12.23%	13.48%	2.82%	2.19%	2.19%
▪ Male	19.89%	17.09%	24.65%	14.57%	8.68%	5.88%	5.32%	3.92%

IT Job Title

Figure 3. Men and women vary on which IT job is *most* familiar.

A high percentage of males (25%) picked programmer as a classic IT job.[3] Only 15% of women picked programmer. When we broke the women students down by major, more differences emerged. Many women majoring in IT (28%) picked programmer as the IT job that they were most familiar with, after electrical engineering (Figure 4). There were no similar distinctions in the male student responses; men non-IT majors were just as likely to pick programming as the IT job they were most familiar with as the men who had IT-related majors.

We asked students to describe their typical computer usage: school, entertainment, work, other. We also asked them to assign adjectives to the day-to-day work life for an IT professional in the job that they were most familiar with. An Educational Testing Service (ETS) study, based on a 1996 College Board report on SAT program test takers, reported several differences among students in their computer-related coursework or experience. Females were slightly more likely than males to have word processing experience[4] and to use a computer in their English courses, and females were less likely than males to use computers to solve mathematics problems or to take courses in computer programming. In our survey, 65% of women respondents indicated that they use their computer primarily for schoolwork (Figure 5).

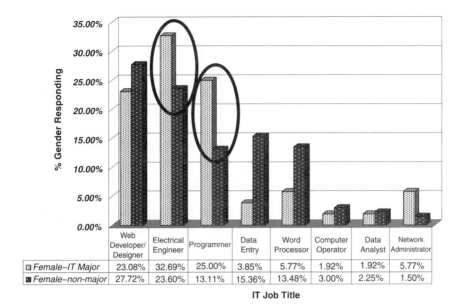

	Web Developer/ Designer	Electrical Engineer	Programmer	Data Entry	Word Processor	Computer Operator	Data Analyst	Network Administrator
Female–IT Major	23.08%	32.69%	25.00%	3.85%	5.77%	1.92%	1.92%	5.77%
Female–non-major	27.72%	23.60%	13.11%	15.36%	13.48%	3.00%	2.25%	1.50%

IT Job Title

Figure 4. Female IT majors more likely to be most familiar with programming and electrical engineering.

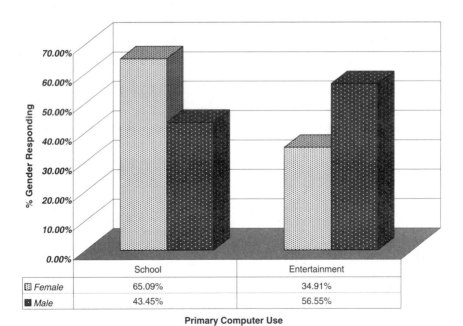

	School	Entertainment
Female	65.09%	34.91%
Male	43.45%	56.55%

Primary Computer Use

Figure 5. Primary computer usage by gender.

Students were asked to select any number of adjectives from a list to describe day-to-day life for a person in the IT job that they were most familiar with. Women were more likely than men to use adjectives such as "difficult" or "challenging" to describe IT jobs. Also, women who did not major in an IT field were more likely to pick words such as "difficult" and "tedious."

When we looked at how men and women described the same job, where the responses differed, the women usually picked a more negatively charged adjective. For example, all students described work as a Web developer as "creative," "interesting," "fun," and "complex"; but female students said that the job would be "challenging," while the male students said that it would be "exciting." Women who picked data entry and word processing as their most familiar IT jobs chose adjectives such as "tedious" and "easy" to describe them. Men also used terms such as "easy" and "tedious" to describe these jobs, but they also selected adjectives like "stable" and "prestigious," where women picked "predictable" and "analytical" (Table 2). Even when students pick programming as their most familiar IT job, there was a difference in the perception. Females picked adjectives like "difficult" and "tedious" more often than males (Table 3).

Because programming was the job title selected by students with the most favorable impression of computer science, we challenged women in

Table 2. Top five adjectives selected for most familiar IT job.

Electrical Engineer is Most Familiar IT Job		Web Development is Most Familiar IT Job		Data Entry/Word Processor is Most Familiar IT Job	
Male	Female	Male	Female	Male	Female
Challenging	Challenging	Creative	Creative	Easy	Tedious
Analytical	Analytical	Interesting	Interesting	Secure	Easy
Interesting	Complex	Fun	Fun	Stable	Predictable
Complex	Difficult	Complex	Complex	Prestigious	Secure
Creative	Interesting	Exciting	Challenging	Tedious	Analytical

Table 3. Top five adjectives selected when programming is most familiar IT job.

Programming is Most Familiar IT Job	
Male	Female
Challenging	Analytical
Interesting	Challenging
Analytical	Complex
Complex	Difficult
Exciting	Tedious

follow-up interviews to consider some positive descriptions of that profession. To pursue this objective, we developed four statements about programming that tested as "credible" to "very credible" among a sample of more than 100 IT professionals and a small set of male undergraduates.

We invited women non-IT majors to consider each of these statements and rate its credibility on a scale of 1 to 5, where a rating of 5 indicates the highest level of credibility. The women non-IT majors' ratings were consistently lower than those of the IT professionals (Figure 6). As the students and professionals were completing the survey, we also collected their comments about the statements and their believability.

1. Programming is a portable skill, which is in high demand by businesses and organizations in both the private and public sector.
2. Good programmers bridge the gap between users and technology. It is not a job for people who are looking for isolation from others.
3. Programming solves human problems and makes customers' and coworkers' lives easier and more enjoyable.
4. Programmers are constantly challenged to use their creativity and intelligence to effectively utilize changing technological advances to their advantage.

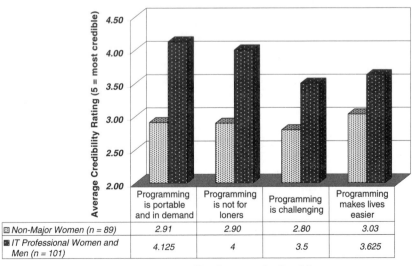

Most Important Quality of Career

Figure 6. Women non-majors don't find statements about programming credible.

Portable and in Demand

While women non-IT majors believed that programming was an important skill and in high demand, they often said that it was too difficult a field to be really portable. At the same time many professionals cautioned that although programming is one of the slower-growing professions in the IT field, they generally agreed that it is portable; for example, one said, "One of the main reasons I took my MS in CS was because I wanted a flexible career where I could get a good job anywhere."

Not for Loners

Women non-IT majors that we interviewed believed that it was important, but very improbable, for a computer programmer to possess people skills. Some IT professionals insisted that it was possible to be a good programmer with no social skills. And some pointed out that this perception has led to unfortunate consequences, saying things such as "This is so true, but programming still seems to attract geeks who only want to interact with the computer. And then we wonder why people claim they don't understand how to use computers. For example, why do we have to click the 'START' button to find the menu to turn OFF the computer? Does that make sense to anybody but a programmer?"

Challenging and Creative

Women non-IT majors typically felt that although CS people were intelligent, they couldn't do anything creative or outside of their "box." In contrast, computer science males and IT professionals felt that programmers must be creative and adaptable. Many commented that there is always something new to learn and that careers in computing should never become routine or boring.

Makes Lives Easier and More Enjoyable

Women non-IT majors felt that there are many human problems that programming cannot solve. Some took special exception to the idea that computers make anyone's life "easy and enjoyable." Computer science males and IT professionals were not much more positive, commenting that "programming should make people's lives easier, but it often does not."

The Fun Factor: Discussion

In studying how men and women choose their career, we found few differences in what students cited as the most important quality in a future job. Most students, regardless of gender, want an interesting, fun job. However, women are generally less likely to see IT jobs as fun or interesting.

The majority of female undergraduates do not have an accurate perception of information technology careers. They tend to be unfamiliar with most IT job titles, except those associated with the Web, data entry, or word processing. The results of our survey suggest that these women characterize IT careers primarily by their own experience using computers for their schoolwork. They see computers as a tool and not as a frontier. Computers don't have the same novelty or create the same interest as they once did. Also, browsing the Web or using a word processor is not the sort of activity that demands creativity or challenges the user's intellect. Even when presented with positive assertions about programming, many women see information technology as tedious, uninteresting work.

The type and degree of misconceptions about IT careers vary. One student, a psychobiology major, felt that in order to get a degree in an IT field, a student needed to know several programming languages before coming to college. Another student, working toward a master's degree in math, with perfect GRE scores, initially chose computer science as her future career, but felt that she would lag behind male students who seemed to know all of the material already.

Show that IT Careers Are Fun

Communicating the realities of computer science careers may require a paradigm shift in emphasis and presentation. Women see computers more as tools than toys. It is inadequate to continue to simply assert the mission of the field; and preaching the "coolness" of technical toys is unpersuasive (Margolis & Fisher, 2002). Women need to see the exciting possibilities of a computer career. We include here some recommendations for programs and marketing strategies that specifically target the concerns that women have. Each of these practices has been shown to have a measurable positive impact on either recruiting or retention of women in information technology.

Many women fear that a career in computing will lead to a socially isolating work life that is confined to a cubicle. In fact, many companies are now looking for IT candidates with strong interpersonal and communication skills, as well as the expected good understanding of technology. For example, one of the fastest growing computing professions is computer systems analyst (Sargent, 2004). Computer systems analysts coordinate user requirements specifications for all of a system's stakeholders throughout the system development life cycle (Bureau of Labor Statistics, 2002). They must be excellent communicators. More information about these emerging professions needs to be made available to high schools students and new freshmen in college.

Another way to illustrate the social possibilities of computing is to encourage and institutionalize pair programming. Pair programming is a style of software development in which coders alternate roles as scribe and navigator. Such collaborative learning environments emphasize the importance of face-to-face meetings and result in increased confidence among women (Berenson, Slaten, Williams, & Ho 2005). Students who pair in their introductory programming course have greater course completion and pass rates and are more likely to persist in computer-related majors. Although pairing helps all students, studies have shown that it is particularly beneficial for women (Werner, Hanks, & McDowell, 2005).

Women often find assignments in computing courses to be esoteric and without real world application. A typical first-year programming task might be to sort an array of integers and find the average value. The pedagogical goals are valid: students need to understand data structures such as arrays and programming structures such as loops. However, a larger context and meaning are absent when the numerical values are selected randomly.

To change this state, education should be made relevant, creative, social, and results-oriented (Margolis & Fisher, 2002; American Association of University Women, 2000). Georgia Institute of Technology has developed an Introduction to Media Computation course in which students learn to program through the manipulation of image and sound files. Students learn about arrays and loops while they reduce red eye, create ticker tape movies of CNN headlines, splice and reverse sounds, create synthesizers, implement chroma key, and put themselves on the moon (Collaborative Software Laboratory at Georgia Institute of Technology, n.d.).

Another strategy to show the impact that computing can have is to integrate student projects with community needs. Research on achievement-related behavior and on women college students studying computing suggests that there are potentially important gender differences in motivations and interests related to computing. Female students are likely to report choosing a major that will make it possible for them to help people (Eccles, 1994). The extra value that women put on contributing to society suggests that recruitment efforts should emphasize the ways that computing allows them to do so.

One example of this is the Engineering Projects in Community Service (EPICS) program at Purdue University. Purdue created the EPICS program to alleviate perceived shortcomings of the engineering program. Teams of undergraduates design, build, and deploy real systems for local community service and education organizations. All participants benefit from the program. Students gain experience and see first-hand the role of the customer in engineering design and the role that engineering can play in the community. Community organizations gain access to technology and expertise that would normally be prohibitively expensive, giving them the potential to improve their quality of service or to provide new services. This program has attracted a disproportionate number of women students (Jamieson, 2001).

While EPICS is a large program that involves students from all engineering disciplines, The Women in Computer Engineering (TWiCE) at the Ohio State University is more modest and focused in scope. Through participation in TWiCE, undergraduate women with an interest in computing are matched with local area community nonprofits. These students help the organizations by training their employees, inventorying and maintaining equipment, and building Web sites. At the same time they serve as role models in their community, demonstrating that computer scientists are not all introverted and nerdy ("TWiCE," 2005). Preliminary analysis of recruiting and retention rates at Ohio State shows that participation in TWiCE has had a strong positive impact. Women students in the program have all been retained in their CS major; and an unusually high proportion are pursuing graduate degrees.

Most popular media channels depend heavily on an unappealing stereotype of computer people as being brilliant but socially awkward. This is doubly negative as women fear that they won't measure up intellectually and that they may be perceived as weird for being interested in computers. An example of this stereotype is the action figure named "Geekman" that actually formalizes—while it epitomizes—these unattractive qualities. In advertising the figure is described as a "tall, bespectacled, pocket-protector-wearing [man] known for his ungodly coding abilities, opposite sex repulsion and less than ideal personal hygiene routine" ("Geekman," 2005). When computer science departments develop marketing material, they do mostly avoid this trap, but often do not show people in their brochures at all, only screen images or panels of colored lights.

Educators and speakers can confront the fallacy of this image directly by showing gender and race diverse pictures of IT professionals in their materials. The Center for Women and Information Technology (CWIT) has developed a music video that portrays a wide variety of women, both past and present, using technology in a variety of fields. The video strongly conveys the message that technology is cool and offers many exciting fields for women as well as men (CWIT, n.d.). For those without the resources to make their own original music video, simple presentation tools can still be used to make a strong point. The Women@SCS Roadshow includes baby pictures of the speakers and shows computer scientists that are white, black, male, female, old, and young. A computer professor is shown riding a unicycle; another is shown wearing a chicken costume ("Women@SCS," 2004).

Our study shows that women who do pick an IT major have a more realistic picture of possible information technology jobs. They think that information technology jobs will be fun, exciting, interesting, challenging, and creative. We need to make sure that all women are educated about the fun and interesting possibilities of a career in IT, so that they can make their career choices based on accurate information.

References

American Association of University Women. (2000). *Tech-savvy: Educating girls in the new computer age.* Retrieved October 3, 2005, from http://www.aauw. org/research/girls_education/techsavvy.cfm

Berenson, S., Slaten, K., Williams, L., & Ho, C. (2005). Voices of women in a software engineering course: Reflections on collaboration. *ACM Journal on Educational Resources in Computing (JERIC), 4*(1), Article 3. Retrieved September 25, 2006, from the ACM Digital Library database: http://portal.acm.org/browse_dl.cfm?linked=1&part=journal&idx=J814&coll=ACM&dl=ACM

Bureau of Labor Statistics (2002). The 2001–2002 occupational outlook handbook. Washington, DC: US Department of Labor

Center for Women and Information Technology (Producer), (n.d.). *You can be anything: A music video to empower girls with technology* [Music Video]. Retrieved September 25, 2006, from CWIT Web site http://www.umbc.edu/be-anything/

Collaborative Software Laboratory at Georgia Institute of Technology. (n.d.). *Learning CS through media computation.* Retrieved October 3, 2005, from http://coweb.cc.gatech.edu/csl/83

DiDio, L. (1997). Boys' club on campus? *Computerworld, 31*(20), *68.*

Eccles, J. S. (1994). Understanding women's educational and occupational choices: Applying the Eccles et al. model of achievement-related choices. *Psychology of Women Quarterly, 18,* 585.

GEEKMAN 6 inch action figure from happy worker geek man. (n.d.). Retrieved October 3, 2005, from http://shop.store.yahoo.com/cmdstore/geacfifrhawo. html

Information Technology Association of Canada. (2002, May 14). *ITAC study reveals IT worker gender gap.* Retrieved September 27, 2006, from http://www.itac.ca/Archive/ITACNewsRelease/NR-ITACStudyRevealsITWorkerGenderGap.htm

Jamieson, L. H. (2001, May). Women, engineering, and community [Expanding the pipeline]. *Computing Research News, 13*(3), pp. 2, 16.

Lancaster, H. (2001, August 14). Career journal: Women try to break tech-glass ceiling. *Wall Street Journal Europe.*

Margolis, J., & Fisher, A. (2002). Unlocking the clubhouse. *SIGCSE Inroads Bulletin, 34*(2), 79–83.

Sargent, J. (2004). An overview of past and projected employment changes in the professional IT occupations. *Computing Research News, 16*(3), pp. 1, 21.

Thibodeau, P., & Holohan, M. (2000, July 24). Congress blasts poor IT diversity record, calls on government, industry to increase women, minorities and disabled workers *Computerworld 34*(30), 38.

TWiCE—The women in computer engineering. (n.d.). Retrieved October 3, 2005, from http://twice.cse.ohio-state.edu

Vegso, J. (2005). Interest in CS as a major drops among incoming freshmen. *Computing Research News, 17*(3). Retrieved September 20, 2006, from http://www.cra.org/CRN/articles/may05/vegso

Werner, L., Hanks, B., & McDowell, C. (2005). Pair-programming helps female computer science students. *ACM Journal on Educational Resources in Computing (JERIC), 4*(1), Article 4. Retrieved September 25, 2006, from the ACM Digital Library database: http://portal.acm.org/browse_dl.cfm?linked=1&part=journal&idx=J814&coll=ACM&dl=ACM

Women@SCS outreach roadshow! (n.d.). Retrieved September 25, 2006, from http://women.cs.cmu.edu/What/Outreach/Roadshow/

Notes

1. Students have varying ideas of fun, as we will see.
2. This is a concern in itself, since few word processing jobs still exist.
3. It is worth noting that although programming may epitomize computer science for many students (especially female IT majors and males), most IT professionals view programming as an entry level position and an outdated term. In fact, two of the fastest growing jobs in IT are computer systems analyst and systems software engineer, both of which were near the bottom of the list of students' familiarity.
4. This may explain why occupations like word processor and Web developer made the top of the women's most familiar IT jobs list.

Part IV

Information Technology Careers

Women and Information Technology Careers

Carol J. Burger and William Aspray

Of the three major topics in this volume—girls in secondary school, women in higher education, and women's careers in information technology—the last of these is the one least covered by the research literature. Some of the research about women's participation in computer science may inform us about information technology, but IT, while including computer skills, is broader than computer science. In addition, the explosion of technology jobs has implications for inclusion of women in the IT workforce. As a discipline, computer science has been present in the academy for over fifty years; information technology, sometimes called information sciences, has a relatively short history. For this reason, it was thought that women would have an easier time entering and staying in this new field.

What is an IT career? IT involves the use of electronic computers and computer software to convert, store, protect, process, transmit, and retrieve information. IT includes all forms of technology used to create, store, exchange, and use information in its various forms: business data, voice conversations, still images, motion pictures, multimedia presentations, and other forms, including those not yet conceived (http://www.whatis. techtarget.com). Some topics and technologies that shape IT-related careers include information security, Web page design and maintenance, digital library, pattern recognition, data management, data processing, data mining, metadata, data storage, database, data networking, technology assessment, cryptography, information technology governance, and telematics (Labor Law Talk, 2006). But these are not fixed because the technologies are changing quickly. An IT employee may or may not be located in the technology industry. In fact, most IT jobs are located in non-IT companies such as banking, retail, insurance, transportation, and education. In other areas, such as library science, the role of IT is still emerging. Any of these positions may be at the managerial, technical, or support levels and may or may not require a computer science degree for success (Roldon, Soe, & Yakura, 2004).

IT can be distinguished from computer science in that it is not just concerned with hardware and software but with using those tools to solve
problems. Newly founded (in the past five years), IT academic programs
include the human element in their courses: team and group problem solving, working with real-world problems, and using computers as a tool
rather than as an end in themselves (see, for example, the Web site for the
Pennsylvania State University College of Information Sciences and Technology at http://ist.psu.edu/).

Since information technology has only recently become a discipline in its
own right, there are few studies about recruitment and retention of women
into IT. We do know that, as in several of the other sciences, women and
minorities are significantly underrepresented in the IT fields. As of 2005,
women constituted 30% of the US IT workforce (Information Technology
Association of America [ITAA], 2005). This does not take into account
those doing hands-on IT work but does include women (one out of every
three) who are in administrative job categories, such as being the manager
of an IT support service or of a network maintenance team (ITAA). Further,
women are overrepresented in lower-level jobs identified as being pink-
collar ghettos (Sumner & Niederman, 2002; Roldon et al., 2004).

The failure of women to take elective computer courses in high school
might limit their IT career options (Crombie, Abarbanel, & Anderson, 2000).
In order to succeed in IT, according to Ullman (1997) and reiterated by
Leventman and Finley (2005), women are required to develop strong technical skills outside the traditional courses taught at the secondary level. The
economic cost of not being IT literate can be high. When young women are
not aware of factors that can lead to their future earning ability, their access
to higher paying career opportunities may be limited. IT careers are high
paying and position young executives for even higher placement (Teague,
2002). Because women are in lower-level positions in IT, their perspectives
and concerns may not be reflected in the design, development, implementation, and assessment of emerging technologies. Further, the lack of a balanced representation of women and minorities in IT careers may lead to
new technologies reflecting male values and male styles of doing IT work
even more.

While the proportion of women in IT careers is 25%–30% of the US-
based IT workforce (US Department of Labor, 2006; ITAA, 2005), only 9%
of the mid- to upper-level computer engineering jobs are held by women
(Gender Advisory Board, 2000).

Why are women, who comprise 47% of the US workforce, involved in
fewer than 20% of the non-administrative careers in IT (ITAA, 2005)? Recent
research suggests fewer females than males choose IT careers because (a)

girls are discouraged from using technology as early as elementary school (Sadker, Sadker, & Klein, 1991); (b) their self-confidence in their abilities related to technology is lower than that of males (Zeldin & Pajares, 2000); (c) technology and its applications are still perceived of as a male domain; and (d) girls are not encouraged to participate in technology use (Pajares, 1996; Zeldin & Pajares). These findings suggest that the low participation of women in IT is historical and cultural and can start to be addressed at the K–12 level.

The detailed literature review of the social science literature on women and IT careers by Bartol and Aspray (2006) can provide a context for understanding the chapters in this section.[1] Many of the assertions in this sparse literature are undertested and may be modified considerably as a result of further research. This literature pertains primarily to the United States; the situation in other countries may well be different.[2]

One of the most studied issues is confidence and self-efficacy. Women report being less confident of their IT technical abilities, even where there is objective evidence that the women are as technically competent as their male peers. Lack of confidence in IT may translate into not choosing an IT career. Various studies at the high school and college level have found that women are generally more anxious about computers than males of the same age, but studies about the workplace are mixed about whether there is a gender differences in computer anxiety. Several studies show that age and computer experience moderate gender difference in computer confidence and anxiety.

The effects of mentoring and role models are frequently researched and discussed. The literature shows that mentoring and having role models are important to all people, but especially to women. Many different kinds of people can serve effectively as mentors in the educational pipeline and on the job. There are claims in the literature that men are more likely than women to receive career advice from mentors and through informal networks and that the advice given to men and women is different. However, there is not strong scholarly evidence to back up these claims at this time. Role models are important to career choice because they represent for the career chooser an example of someone like themselves who has succeeded in that career; so they can see that model as a "possible self." Role models are particularly important, according to theory, for legitimating novel or gender-role-deviant career options. Some of the literature has noted the shortage of women in senior IT technical and managerial positions in industry to serve as role models.

There is gender typing in IT occupations. For reasons not fully understood, women express preference for IT jobs that are less technical. Women end up in IT jobs that are indeed less technical and at lower levels—even among technically prepared populations such as members of the computing professional organization the Association for Computing Machinery (ACM; see http://www.acm.org for reports about women's participation in computer-based careers). Women are underrepresented in management, technical and network support, and jobs involving system operation. They are overrepresented in data entry, systems analysis, programming, and help desk jobs. There is no gender difference among IT workers, as self-reported, in importance to them of autonomy, the service nature of their work, the intellectual challenge of the work, or being entrepreneurial. Women report a higher importance to job security, while men report stronger importance on holding management positions and, somewhat surprisingly, in holding jobs that are geographically secure. There has been no increase over time in ghettoization of certain IT occupations as female. Even with a worker shortage during the late 1990s and early 2000s, there were no IT occupations that became segregated by gender as males fled these jobs and women were hired into them. There has been a precipitous increase in departure rates for women in IT careers, especially from computer operations, where there had been high percentages of women filling those jobs previously. A number of studies show that women perceive IT work as male dominated and not welcoming to women, and that this perception affects women's choice and persistence in an IT career.

The literature on pay issues has good and bad news for women. There is gender difference in pay, even when adjusted for age, experience, education, and work level in the organization. Women earn 88–90% of the salary of men in IT occupations. However, entering professional women do better in IT in terms of pay equity than in many other professional fields, notably business. Men rate pay and having responsibility in their job as more important than women do; women rate work environment, good social relations, and good hours as more important than men do. In companies with lower percentages of women, women in IT jobs are promoted and paid on par with men; in organizations with larger percentages of women, women in IT jobs are paid less, have less experience, and are slightly less well educated.

The literature on satisfaction with and commitment to IT shows that men and women self-report about the same levels of satisfaction with pay, work, supervision, and promotion. There are conflicting results about gender differences in organizational commitment and intention to leave the IT profession. Satisfaction results may be biased because most studies are of women who have remained in the field.

The literature on life-work balance shows that women choose careers where they perceive they can balance work and family responsibilities. If a career is perceived as hostile to this balance, they will either choose another career or alter their lives, for example by deferring marriage or postponing having children. Women take five times as many unpaid leaves as men, and women's leaves last twice as long as those of men, presumably reflecting their roles as caretakers. In a study of ACM members, women were more likely to be unmarried than men and much more likely to be childless. There is a generational change afoot; among younger workers, both men and women have a greater concern for life-work balance than previous generations of workers.

Finally, the literature on career paths and progression shows that there are significantly higher discrimination levels in the workplace for women. Also, even where performance evaluations for men and women were similar on average, managers saw women reporting to them as less qualified for promotion to higher-level occupations in the organization.

Other factors that appear to influence women's IT career choice are common to all professional fields and include workplace climate, actual face-to-face discrimination, sexual harassment, and family-work balancing, especially as related to business travel. The impact of the 2000 "dot.com crash" is another factor suggesting uncertainty in the profession. The rapid rate of change suggests to women that they will have difficulty reestablishing their credibility and reviving their skills if time is taken off of work for family duties (National Research Council, 2004; Roldon et al., 2004; Sonnert, 1995; Xie & Shauman, 2003).

While there are multiple routes to an IT career, and not all paths require high school programming courses or even undergraduate computer science degrees and courses, women without this formal training are often at even greater disadvantage than men without this formal training.

In a survey of IT professionals (Campbell & Perlman, 2005), 27% of men had an undergraduate IT degree versus 17% of women, but, of those who had IT graduate degrees as their first degree, 48% were women and 28% were men. Forty-five percent of men had no IT degree at all, versus 35% of women. This would indicate that women are either more likely to enter, more likely to persist, or more likely to succeed in an IT career if they have some formal training. Because formal IT training has not been in existence for very long, there are no longitudinal studies from which to draw conclusions about how much value prior experience has in college and career success. However, earlier work by Taylor and Mounfield (1994) found that prior programming experience was four times more predictive of computer science success in college for women than it was for men. Moreover, there was a positive correlation, for both males and females, between taking programming in high school and persistence in computer science in college

(Nelson, Weise, & Cooper, 1991). There are no available data to explain whether this formal training is needed to give women the necessary skills and knowledge to succeed or if it simply increases their confidence enough to persist, but if we measure success in terms of the number of women in IT careers, perhaps it is enough to recognize the correlation between formal training and the number of women in IT careers.

Two large-scale studies provide insight into the female IT workforce. The first, *Why Women Choose Information Technology Careers: Educational, Social, and Familial Influences*, examined the educational backgrounds of female IT professionals by surveying members of Systers, an organization for women information technology professionals (Turner, Bernt, & Pecora, 2002). The survey response was low (275 useable responses from about 2500 members), but the authors state: "While their responses cannot be regarded as statistically representative of women's experiences in general, their perceptions and their stories do provide valuable insights about the issues facing women who pursue careers in the IT field. It is possible to garner valuable lessons from their stories" (p. 3). Other studies document the idiosyncratic nature of women's progress through IT careers. Nearly one third of the women currently working in IT fields did not enter by way of a computer science degree but chose IT jobs later because they provided emotional fulfillment and were a good fit for their skills (Turner, Bernt, & Pecora, 2002).

In the second study, *Women in the workforce: The societal context of IT employment and feelings, attitudes, and opinions of IT professionals*, Leventman and Finley (2005) reported that the varied backgrounds of IT professionals prompted researchers to seek stronger indicators of IT career pathway than formal education alone. An analysis of surveys from 432 IT professionals and of interviews with 44 of the survey respondents showed that IT professionals appear to fall into three equal categories: Traditional, Transitional, and Self-directed. The Traditional third decided on and pursued a technical career in high school or college. The Transitional third had nontechnical backgrounds and had to obtain a technical master's degree to enter an IT career. The Self-directed respondents also had nontechnical backgrounds, but they honed their IT skills on the job (Leventman & Finley; Leventman, in this volume).

Women who enter IT fields do so either owing to personal idiosyncrasies, external influence, or both (Trauth, 2002). Those factors account for men's recruitment, too; but, in addition, women want their IT work to be "purposeful" and tied to people and other areas within the organization (Margolis & Fisher, 2002). A negative for married women with children is that IT careers are primarily full time, with considerable "after-hours work" and travel built in to the job (Ahuja, Herring, Ogan, & Robinson, 2004; Webster, 1996).

Several themes cut across the three chapters that appear in this section as well as in a paper on IT technicians presented by Clem Herman and Debbie Ellen from The Open University in the United Kingdom at the Crossing Cultures, Changing Lives conference (Herman & Ellen, 2005).

Many computer scientists talk about the pipeline of women in computing (see, for example, Camp, 1997). The argument goes something like this: if females do not take a set of mathematics and computer science preparatory courses in high school, then they are not prepared to study computing or major in a computer-based discipline in college; if they do not major in computer science or IT in college, they are not prepared for graduate study in computer science or for a good entry-level IT job; and if they do have a good entry into an IT career, then they are not prepared for a higher-level technical or management career in IT. Thus at each stage, the education and career pipeline leaks out a percentage of the women able to succeed in IT, leaving fewer and fewer women in the IT field as one moves along the pipeline.

As powerful and intuitive as this metaphor is, there are serious problems with it. The linear notion of the pipeline does not correspond with the expectation of life-long learning in today's knowledge economy; one does not get all her education first and then work for the rest of her life, but instead goes back and forth between education and work, often doing these simultaneously. One study (Wardell, Rogers, & Sawyer, 2004) shows that one-third of men and one-quarter of women had educational experience in IT after graduation. The pipeline metaphor also does not match well with employment patterns. In the second half of the 1990s, for example, the number of IT jobs in the United States was growing at up to 200,000 jobs per year. However, the educational system was only supplying about 30,000 new computer science baccalaureates each year. What happened was that, unlike in physics, where almost all physicists receive physics degrees, few people who enter IT careers have formal computing degrees. There are many pathways to an IT career, and the majority of people find their path outside this pipeline that is so commonly discussed.

The Leventman chapter understands this point very well. It discusses three different routes to an IT career, only one of which encompasses the traditional pipeline pathway. The other two routes, she finds, are as common in her study group as the traditional route. The Kuhn and Rayman chapter also discusses the multiple pathways to IT careers. It pays attention to the importance of two very different but significant reasons that people choose to enter IT careers: the reward structure and their intrinsic intellectual interest in computing. The Herman and Eller study also understands the importance of alternative pathways. Their study group included people working in, or preparing to work in, certain IT occupations such as technicians, Web designers, and systems administrators. For these occupations, certification is more important than the traditional degree.

The Leventman chapter discusses one recent phenomenon that has not yet made its way into much of the social science literature on women and IT. This is the impact of globalization, and of offshore outsourcing in particular, on people's perceptions about whether to pursue or persist in an IT career in the face of jobs moving to low-wage countries. Ultimately, offshore outsourcing may be beneficial to the IT industries in developed nations. It may create more jobs than it eliminates in these countries, but some individuals and communities are bound to be harmed in the process. Bureau of Labor Statistics data show that there has actually been an increase in the number of IT jobs in the United States between 1999, the height of the dot-com boom, and late 2003, by which time offshore outsourcing was well underway (Patterson, 2005). Unfortunately, the reality is not as important as the perception in making career decisions.

The Warner and Wooller chapter also points to the importance of perceptions in people's decisions and actions about their careers. We do not have the data available to know whether perceptions about offshore outsourcing are having a disproportionately negative effect on IT career decisions by women in developed countries. A few reports suggest that some women are turned off by their perception of IT as a career that is highly technical with little social relevance. Two other common, and important, themes in the literature about women in IT careers are addressed in this chapter: institutional culture and life-work balance. The Kuhn and Rayman chapter also discusses life-work balance, paying attention to issues such as work stress and the decision of many women not to have children. One of the commendable things about their study is the careful and systematic way in which they investigate men as well as women, and nontechnical as well as technical women, giving the reader a basis for comparison.

A topic that is somewhat more unusual in the literature on women and IT is Warner and Wooller's discussion of the interplay between demand, national policy, and representation in the workplace. Most of the analysis in this literature focuses on the individual or the local setting: school, home, or workplace. Very few studies have considered national supply and demand for workers or policy responses to imbalances in supply and demand.

Implications for Recruitment to IT Careers

Present students with a fuller picture of IT work including flexible time schedules, interaction with others, and the positive implications and real world applications of the work.

Recognize and support through programs and training sessions the women who are taking circuitous routes into IT careers. Concentrating only on those with a technical undergraduate degree, i.e., computer science or information technology bachelor's degree, will miss those who have the skills and background to succeed in IT careers.

Institute and enforce policies that create a welcoming, rather than hostile and competitive, work environment.

Implications for Retention in IT Careers

All IT workers were concerned about job security and about their ability to have a healthy lifestyle while working at an IT job. Therefore, companies that allow more part-time work and flexible hours will be able to better retain female workers.

Women were happy in their jobs when they performed satisfying work. Having external positive feedback for their efforts would validate them and make them more confident about their skills.

Future Research Directions

As stated above, there is little research that directly addresses gender issues in IT careers. There is a need for more snapshots, through surveys, of women's views about their relationship to their career in IT. While the data are more difficult to obtain, there is also a need to survey and interview women who have left the IT profession. By comparing these data, we can obtain a better understanding about the factors that contribute to a positive experience as a female IT worker. Current IT professionals are an untapped resource of retrospective information about how they arrived in their current position. As Leventman points out, there are many paths to an IT career. It would be interesting to compare her findings with the paths taken by women in other countries. Ascertaining the pivotal points in women's decision-making process to proceed into IT or to leave that path for another career would be very helpful in developing effective recruitment interventions.

The methodology used by Kuhn and Rayman could be used to collect and analyze data about workforce issues in other countries. Educational institutions are increasing the number of online courses, including IT courses, they can provide to students from anywhere in the world. Knowing the needs and expectations of those students can help mold the IT course content. Industry would also be interested in learning about the most effective ways to recruit and retain female IT employees into their global workforce.

Warner and Wooller emphasize the need for continuous monitoring of the numbers of female IT workers by federal and state agencies, and for the political will to institute policies that will result in changes in hiring practices; work schedules that allow employees to work from home; a humane leave policy that allows time off to deal with family matters including child rearing and elder care; and stronger enforcement of antiharassment policies.

References

Ahuja, M., Herring, S. C., Ogan, C., & Robinson, J. (2004, April). *Exploring antecedents of gender equitable outcomes in IT higher education.* Paper presented at the 2004 SIGMIS conference on computer personnel research, Tucson, AZ. Retrieved September 29, 2006, from http://portal.acm.org/citation. cfm?id=982401

Bartol, K. M., & Aspray, W. (2006). The state of research on transitioning to the workplace for women in IT. In J. M. Cohoon & W. Aspray (Eds.), *Women and information technology: Research on underrepresentation.* Cambridge, MA: MIT Press.

Camp, T. (1997). The incredible shrinking pipeline. *Communications of the ACM, 40*(10), 103–110.

Campbell, P., & Perlman, L. (2005). *What brings workers to information and why do they stay?* Retrieved November 30, 2005, from http://www.campbell-kibler.com

Crombie, G., Abarbanel, T., & Anderson, C. (2000). All-female computer science. *Science Teacher, 67*(3), 40–43.

Gender Advisory Board. (2000). *Increasing the participation of women in computer science and engineering (CSE): Recommendations to the World Summit on the Information Society.* Retrieved April 15, 2006, from http://gab.wigsat.org/wsis. html

Herman, C., & Ellen, D. (2005, August). Women IT technicians: Moving through the glass partition. Paper presented at the Crossing Cultures, Changing Lives Conference, Oxford, England.

Information Technology Association of America (2005). *Building the 21st century information technology workforce: Groups underrepresented in the IT workforce* [Task Force Report]. Retrieved October 10, 2005, from http://www.itaa.org/ workforce/studies.recruit.htm

Labor Law Talk. (2006). Information science or informatics. In *Labor Law Talk dictionary.* Retrieved June 22, 2006, from http://encyclopedia.laborlawtalk. com/Information_science

Leventman, P., & Finley, M (2005). *Women in the workforce: The societal context of IT employment and feelings, attitudes and opinions of IT professionals.* Retrieved August 30, 2005, from http://www.campbell-kibler.com/SocialContextIT.doc

Margolis, J., & Fisher, A. (2002). *Unlocking the clubhouse: Women in computing.* Cambridge, MA: MIT Press.

National Research Council (2004). *On evaluating program effectiveness: Judging the quality of K–12 mathematics evaluations.* Washington, DC: National Academy Press.

Nelson, L. J., Weise, G. M., & Cooper, J. (1991). Getting started with computers: Experience, anxiety, and relational style. *Computers in Human Behavior, 7,* 185–202.

Pajares, F. (1996). Self-efficacy beliefs in academic settings. *Review of Educational Research, 66*(4), 543–578.

Patterson, D. (2005, September). Restoring the popularity of computer science [President's Letter], *Communications of the ACM, 48*(9), 25–28.

Roldon, M., Soe, L., & Yakura, E. K. (2004, April). *Perceptions of chilly IT organizational contexts and their effect on the retention and promotion of women in IT.* Paper presented at the 2004 SIGMIS conference on Computer Personnel Research. Tucson, AZ. Retrieved September 29, 2006, from http://portal.acm.org/citation.cfm?id=982399

Sadker, M., Sadker, D., & Klein, S. (1991). The issue of gender in elementary and secondary education. In G. Grant (Ed.), *Review of research in education* (pp. 269–334). Washington, DC: American Educational Research Association.

Sonnert, G. (1995). *Who succeeds in science? The gender dimension.* New Brunswick, NJ: Rutgers University Press.

Sumner, M., & Niederman, F. (2002, May). *The impact of gender differences on job satisfaction, job turnover, and career experiences of information systems professionals.* Paper presented at the 2002 ACM SIGCPR conference on Computer Personnel Research. Retrieved September 29, 2006 from http://portal.acm.org/citation.cfm?id=512395

Taylor, H. G., & Mounfield, L. (1994). Exploration of the relationship between prior computing experience and gender on success in college computer science. *Journal of Educational Computing Research, 11*(4), 291–306.

Teague, J. (2002). Women in computing: What brings them to it, what keeps them in it? *Women and Computing, 34*(2), 147–158.

Trauth, E. M. (2002). Odd girl out: An individual differences perspective on women in the IT profession. *Information Technology & People, 15*(2), 98–118.

Turner, S. V., Bernt, P. W., & Pecora, N. (2002, April). *Why women choose information technology careers: Educational, social, and familial influences.* Paper presented at the annual meeting of the American Educational Research Association, New Orleans, LA.

Ullman, E. (1997). *Close to the machine: Technophilia and its discontents.* San Francisco: City Lights Publishers.

US Department of Labor. (2006). *Women in the labor force in 2005.* Retrieved June 5, 2006, from http://www.dol.gov/wb/factsheets/Qf-laborforce-05.htm

Wardell, M., Rogers, J., & Sawyer, S. (2004, October). *Women in the IT workforce: How level the playing field?* Paper presented at the IT Workforce Principal Investigators Meeting of National Science Foundation, Philadelphia, PA.

Webster, J. (1996). *Shaping women's work: Gender, employment, and information technology.* London: Longman.

Xie, Y., & Shauman, K. A. (2003). *Women in science: Career processes and outcomes.* Cambridge, MA: Harvard University Press.

Zeldin, A. L., & Pajares, F. (2000). Against the odds: Self-efficacy beliefs of women in mathematical, scientific, and technological careers. American Educational Research Journal, 37(1), 215–246.

Notes

1. See Bartol & Aspray (2006) for references to studies in this section.
2. It should be remembered that the results cited here are statistical and do not apply uniformly to all women.

Chapter 9

Women on the Edge of Change

Employees in United States Information Technology Companies

Sarah Kuhn and Paula Rayman

Abstract

To better understand the workplace experiences of women in IT careers, we present results from a study of women and men in the software and Internet industry. Drawing on over 1600 survey responses and 200 semistructured interviews, we find challenges balancing work and family, widespread reports of stress, and a majority of women with no children. Security, when it is found at all, is in an employee's skill set and in the social capital of relationships and community ties. For women there are many pathways into IT work, and although pay is the primary attraction for women and men, both groups also show a strong intrinsic interest in their work. In order to attract and retain women in IT work, we recommend policies that support employees' ability to work and have a life; building security and social capital by strengthening networks; and changing, where appropriate, the conditions or the perceptions of IT work.

Introduction

Efforts to address the underrepresentation of women in IT careers in the United States have met with limited success. To the extent that women's decisions not to enter IT occupations and workplaces are based on notions about the nature of the work and the workplace in IT (Margolis & Fisher, 2002), it is important to understand what the experiences of women in IT have been, and what motivates them to continue in or to leave the IT field. A deeper understanding will allow us to assess the advantages of IT careers for women and to better support women who seek the benefits that IT careers can offer. In so doing, we hope to create the conditions for satisfying and effective contributions by US women to the national and international economy.

In this chapter we take a close look at the experiences of women working in the software and Internet industry in Massachusetts. Our data, both qualitative and quantitative, include responses from women and men in technical and nontechnical occupations, allowing us to compare technical women with other groups in the same industry.

Methods

Our research used a multimethod approach, combining survey, interview, and focus groups. Our Internet-based survey was created with input from our research partner, the Massachusetts Software & Internet Council (MSIC), and from focus groups of Women in Technology International (WITI) members. We sent electronic mail to representatives of companies listed in the MSIC database of approximately 3,400 software and Internet companies, asking that they distribute the link for our survey Web page to their employees. We also distributed a link to the survey to the members of the Boston chapter of WITI, enabling us to oversample women. We received 1,690 responses during the six weeks our survey was posted, beginning in late March and ending in early May 2002.

Beginning in May 2002 and continuing through the summer, we interviewed 100 women and 100 men using a semistructured interview protocol. Interviews lasted from one to two hours and were conducted at a location chosen by the interviewee, typically at their workplace, home, or a local coffee shop. The majority of interview participants were drawn from survey respondents who volunteered and the rest by snowball sampling from names suggested by interviewees.

When cross-tabulations of survey data were available from the survey firm that created the Web site and collected the responses, we met in focus groups with WITI members and members of the MSIC Board to discuss our findings, reviewing in particular any puzzling or seemingly contradictory results.

Survey respondents were 40% female, with a median age of 40. Most (87%) were US citizens, and only 13% identified themselves as racial minorities. Three quarters of the men and more than half of the women (57%) identified themselves as being in technical jobs when asked about their job category. Nearly one quarter had a computer science degree (see Tables 1 and 2).

Our focus on the workforce in Massachusetts allows us to take an in-depth look at IT employees, while at the same time placing some limits on generalizability. The Massachusetts economy, like those in other IT-intensive states, was hit by the "dot-com bust" that was in full swing when we

Table 1. Selected characteristics of survey respondents.

Total Number of Respondents		1690
Gender	male	60%
	female	40%
Median age	men	40
	women	39
Citizenship	US Citizen	87%
	Green Card holder	4%
	Non-US Citizen with temporary visa	4%
Racial/ethnic background	White/European	87%
	East/Southeast Asian	4%
	South Asian	3%
	Hispanic/Latino(a)/Chicano(a)	2%
	Black/African American	1%
Highest level of education	Doctorate	6%
	Master's	30%
	Bachelor's	49%
	Less than Bachelor's	15%
Most commonly held technical degrees	Computer Science	25%
	Mathematics	13%
	Chemical Engineering	12%
	Information Science	9%

Job category	Women	Technical	57%
		Nontechnical	43%
	Men	Technical	77%
		Nontechnical	23%

Table 2. Technical degrees most commonly held by survey respondents, by field and age.

Age	Computer Science	Mathematics	Chemical Engineering	Info. Science
18–24	33%	11%	4%	7%
25–34	22%	20%	9%	8%
35–44	19%	9%	12%	9%
45–54	8%	26%	12%	3%
55 and up	31%	9%	13%	12%

Note. More than 90% of respondents reported having a post-secondary degree; 5% were associate's degrees, 49% bachelor's degrees, and 30% master's and other professional degrees.

conducted our survey. Massachusetts was particularly affected by the drop in demand for networking equipment, but at the same time the resilience and diversity of the region's economy, and its orientation toward producers and capital goods, also provides some protection from the irrational exuberance of Silicon Valley. While Massachusetts' IT sector may not be typical, it is nevertheless diversified and resilient, and can give some strong indications of what researchers are likely to find in other regions in the United States.

Work and Family

An issue of concern to many women, and increasingly to many men as well, is the ability to combine work with a satisfying family and nonwork life. An idealized picture of new economy workplaces suggests that the flexibility offered to employees enables them to meet some of the challenges of integrating work-family demands (Kuhn & Rayman, 2005). Our Project TechForce data, however, document a more complex picture, highlighting the many hours worked by IT professionals and the uneven experiences with arranging work flexibility.

Work Hours, Stress, Sleep

A key factor in an IT employee's ability to meet both family and work responsibilities is hours worked. Almost all of our respondents, 96%, worked full-time (among the few who worked part-time, two thirds were women). Fifty-six percent reported working between 41 and 50 hours per week, another 25% worked 51–70 hours per week, and a small percentage reported working even more hours. These data are consistent with self-reported work hours for IT professionals from other studies, although they significantly exceed the work hour data from the US Bureau of Labor Statistics Current Population Survey (CPS), probably because the CPS includes a much higher percentage of programmers doing relatively routine work in other, non-IT industries (National Research Council, 2001).

In addition to long work hours in their primary employment, 12% of respondents—slightly more men than women—reported other sources of employment income in addition to their primary jobs. Compounding the problem, many employees commented in interviews on the long commute times necessary to reach their jobs, and several said that the long commute was the one thing they would most like to change about their jobs. Long work hours and commute times necessarily cut into time that would otherwise be available for family, leisure, and community pursuits. Two thirds of men, and nearly as high a percentage of women, agree that "I often work during what is supposed to be family or after-work hours." The flexibility available to many, although not all, IT employees can mitigate somewhat the impact of long work hours, but in the final analysis, long work hours are a serious impediment to combining work and family.

More than two fifths of our survey respondents told us that they did not get enough sleep, with women more likely than men to strongly agree that they got too little sleep. Furthermore, a whopping 78% of men and 71% of women agreed that "I have a lot of stress in my life," with more than one third of men and almost one quarter of women strongly agreeing. Bailey (2005) summarizes the research on the negative health effects of stress and of long work hours, and points to these as contributors to the problem of worker burnout among IT employees in Massachusetts. With such a significant proportion of the workforce reporting high stress, sleep deprivation, and the intrusion of work into family and leisure time, there seems ample reason to make this area a focus of further study by those seeking to recruit and retain talented IT workers, both female and male.

Flexibility

In the social science literature regarding balancing work and family, there has been much discussion of the issue of flexible work schedules and which employees are most likely to have "flex time." In their study of biotechnology workers, Eaton and Bailyn observed that the structure of work organization seemed to create the potential for flexibility in scheduling (Radcliffe Public Policy Institute, 1999). However, they noted that there was often a variance between potential and actual use of flex time, with a number of factors playing a role, such as size and culture of firm, occupational tasks, and unequal distribution of time arrangements by managers. They also found that, due to differences in work tasks, senior scientists engaged in research and discovery had more flexibility than those at the lower end of the occupational ladder (Eaton & Bailyn, 2000).

In IT work, flexibility has two components: the ability to shift place and the ability to shift time. Shifting place is generally referred to as "telecommuting," and more than two thirds of our survey respondents reported that their company has a policy permitting telecommuting. However, only one third of the respondents in those companies actually telecommute, despite the fact that two thirds of this group say that telecommuting provides a satisfying work experience. Of those whose companies do not allow telecommuting, a strong 70% of respondents, both women and men, say that they would like to telecommute. Furthermore, three quarters of respondents say that their place of work is solely or primarily the employer's premises, but only a minority (47%) prefer this arrangement. Telecommuting offers the chance to better integrate work and family by offering more flexibility but also contributes to the blurring of boundaries between work and family of which some interviewees complained.

The second component of flexibility in IT, the ability to shift time, is also valued by employees, according to evidence from interviews. Sixty-three percent of survey respondents said that their companies offered "flex-time," with slightly more men than women having access to this option. However, for many, the ability to time shift is limited because schedules must be coordinated with coworkers, managers, and overall project schedules.

The Project TechForce findings tell a slightly different story than that told by Eaton and Bailyn (2000) about work in the biotechnology industry. While qualitative data from interviews confirm that indeed there is a discrepancy between the potential for flexibility and actual experiences, we found that men and women workers on both the top and bottom rungs of the occupational ladder have less flexibility than those in the middle. Those at the top were in charge, had more responsibility and numerous meetings, and felt they had to be exemplars and show up for "face-time" at their workplaces. Those on the bottom rungs also had to put in a lot of face time since they reported to others and many of their tasks required them to be at the workplace. Those in the middle seem to have the most flexibility, because they can more often perform their work asynchronously with others. The requirements of their jobs demand fewer meetings and can, through the use of technology, be performed remotely from their primary place of work in some situations. Those who did have flexibility often commented, in interviews, about how much they valued it.

Women and Mothers at Work

Slightly more than half of women in our survey agreed that their gender played an important role in their work experiences, but 83% of women also agreed that their firm provided equal opportunities for women. In interviews, women who worked in companies headed by older men and with a more traditional work culture were most likely to complain of tensions or even harassment. Women were far more likely than men to believe that "the world of IT was more 'male' than 'female,'" with more than one third of women strongly agreeing with this statement, compared with a percentage of men that was half as large. In interesting contrast, however, more than three quarters of both men and women agreed that they "fit well into the culture of the company." Funk (2000) found that "fit with company culture" was the best single predictor of an IT employee's intention to stay with his or her current employer, although our findings do not confirm this as a strong result.

Women with children generally maintained in interviews that being a mother had considerably more effect on their job prospects than being female. Among other things, mothering made it more difficult to compete for participation in the time-consuming, cutting-edge projects that would give them high visibility in the company and help them develop the new, state-of-the-art skills that are necessary for advancement and for continued employability.

Women in our interview group reported a wide variety of strategies for combining work and mothering, including having a husband or partner who became the primary caretaker; opting for work that was less interesting and challenging but had a more predictable schedule; and working part-time rather than full-time. No single strategy emerged from the group of mothers we interviewed; instead, each woman—each family—seemed to make a decision based on their own very specific circumstances and preferences.

Well over half (56%) of the women responding to our survey had no children or stepchildren (compared to 35% of men, see Table 3). By contrast, the US Census Bureau reports that the overall US percentage of women of childbearing age who are childless is 44% (Downs, 2003). The discrepancy between women in our sample and women in the US as a whole, although large, is understated, because the census data include women as young as 15, and more than 90% of 15–19 year olds have no children. Removing this group of younger women, who do not appear in our survey sample, would further lower the percentage of US women without children. Also, the census data do not include stepchildren, making the 56% of women IT workers without either children or stepchildren even more striking.

We believe that the toll on mothers who work in IT shows up in the very high number of women who remain childless, as well as in the reasons women give for why they would leave the software and Internet field. While men report that they would be most likely to leave for better pay,

Table 3. Children and stepchildren among survey respondents, by gender and age.

Percentage of men and women with no children or stepchildren	Women	56%
	Men	35%
Percentage with no children, by age	18–24	93%
	25–34	24%
	35–44	74%
	45–54	12%
	55 and up	35%

women give "too many hours of work" as the most likely reason for a voluntary departure. "Unfavorable work environment or workplace culture" and "stressful industry" are also among the top five reasons given by women for why they would depart (Table 2). Men also are bothered by these features of IT work, but do not give them as high a priority in making a decision about whether to leave the IT field.

Creating Security in an Insecure World

We asked our interviewees what advice they would give to someone considering a job in the software and Internet industry. Typical comments were "be prepared for a lot of change," "if you are looking for stability, it's not for you," and "have a plan B." This advice spotlights the necessary qualities for successful long-term employment in the industry. Eighty-five percent of our survey respondents agreed that "I am comfortable dealing with constant change," suggesting that most who responded had the resilience needed to survive in a fast-paced environment.

Like the professionals studied in the biotech industry (Radcliffe Public Policy Institute, 1999), both women and men in IT reported, "The security is in the industry, not the job." More specifically, the Project TechForce data suggest that workers in the IT industry "hopscotch" from one job to another, carrying around their skill sets in their own metaphorical backpacks as they move around. Because the fortunes of firms rise and fall, and because projects come to completion or are cancelled, workers leave either voluntarily or involuntarily. "If you want a guaranteed job, be a nurse," and "You are as secure as your skill set," said our interviewees.

Skills as a Source of Security

One traditional source of security in technical professions is a technical degree. Nearly one quarter of respondents reports having a computer science (CS) degree, with men more likely than women to have a CS degree (26% of men and 18% of women). The second most popular degree is mathematics, held by 13% of respondents, with chemical engineering a very close third. These relatively low numbers highlight the fact that the software and Internet industry is distinct from some other technology-intensive industries such as biotechnology in that a technical degree is not a requirement for significant participation in the professional ranks. We wondered whether the ability to enter IT without a CS degree was a characteristic of the industry in its infancy, and whether with increasing industry maturation, a CS or other technical degree became a necessity. A look at the data by age of respondent, however, is puzzling, because the largest proportions of CS degree holders are at the two extremes of the age spectrum: 18–24 year olds, one third of whom have degrees, and those 55 and older, 31% of whom have degrees. Only 8% of 45–54 year olds have CS degrees (Table 2). This may reflect the existence of different "eras" in the life of the industry, when hiring was relatively more, or less, open to those without degrees. Alternatively, because we did not ask survey respondents when they acquired their degree, these data could also suggest an increased propensity of older workers to go back to school for a degree in order to increase their employability.

Skills are a very important source of employment security in the software and Internet industry, and in IT work in general. Skills may be obtained on the job, through self-study, or through formal education or training. One quarter of men and 18% of women strongly agreed that they had "up-to-date technical (programming or other) skills." (The gender difference could simply reflect the fact that men are more likely than women to be in technical positions, and men are far more likely than women to be programmers.) Most (81%) agree that "I worry about keeping my skills current," with 41% strongly agreeing. The concern expressed underscores the importance of skills to employability, the worry caused by the prospect of falling behind, and the time commitment sometimes needed from workers who want to keep their skills up to date.

Interviewees' advice to those who would enter the industry focused on the importance of continuous learning as a necessity for those who sought long-term employment. Working on cutting-edge projects and learning on the job are primary strategies, but self-directed study is also important, as is seeking jobs with companies using high-demand technology. Overall, developing some breadth in technology, combined with depth in a specific area, seemed to be the consensus advice.

Social Capital as a Source of Security

As the nature of work evolves from one of loyal employer–employee long-term contracts to a less secure, more contingent arrangement, the role of an employee's social capital—sustainable formal and informal networks and relationships—becomes increasingly significant. Project TechForce data suggest that on two important social capital dimensions women experience more relational and network ties.

Mentoring relationships. Women respondents to the survey were more likely to report having mentors in their educational and work pathways—in college and in their careers. Looking back at their college years, 17% of women and 14% of men reported having a mentor. Once at work, 25% of women and only 16% of men reported currently having a mentor. The social science literature has previously documented the significance of mentorship for the attraction, recruitment, and retention of women and minorities in STEM fields (Rayman & Brett, 1993; Ambrose, Dunkle, Lazarus, Nair & Harkus, 1997). However, while these data provide evidence that women were more likely then men to have mentors, women still report that in college they were significantly less likely than men to receive encouragement to major in STEM fields (half of men and about one third of women received such encouragement).[1]

A recent study by Malcom, Teich, Jesse, Campbell, Babco, and Bell (2005) states that the lack of diversity among IT/CS faculty may play a role in the lack of interplay between faculty and students. Mentorship, then, does not automatically translate into encouragement to enter or remain in IT and related disciplines. Furthermore, the vast majority of both women and men reported not having a mentor at any time during their IT pathway journey.

Broader job searches. When facing job loss, equal numbers of male and female respondents, 56%, reported that "friends" were the most helpful source during a job search. All other methods, including Internet job postings, classified ads, and employment agencies, were more frequently mentioned by women than men. This suggests that women cast a wider net in their job searches than men in the industry. About half of all respondents are members of formal or informal professional associations or networks, but qualitative interview data suggest that women are more comfortable forming help networks than men during job loss times. This confirms earlier studies of job loss, which document the isolation felt by unemployed men in the aircraft and engineering occupations (Rayman & Bluestone, 1982). The roles of networks and relational social capital formation deserve more attention in future studies of the IT and other STEM industries.

Community ties. The high level of mobility common in the new global economy has its costs, especially in terms of the important community attachments which support working parents and others who have caregiving responsibilities. A study of biotech professionals and community attachment (Bookman, 2004) reported that while only a small percentage of workers were engaged in civic affairs (defined as participating in electoral politics or government affairs), many were involved in activities linking them to community based services and institutions. These included child care and senior care centers, team sport leagues, local health clubs, adult education classes, public school organizations, and other volunteer activities. More than half of the biotech workers were involved with faith-based institutions.

In our interviews with IT workers, these same community-based affiliations were referred to as a way of accommodating the need to build security in the midst of an insecure economy. When Project TechForce began in 2000, there was a boom still going on in the industry. By the time we were doing interview field work in 2002, decline of industry employment had set in and some of our initial survey respondents had experienced job loss. What often made a difference in swimming rather than sinking were both the social capital networks mentioned earlier and the community links which helped sustain individual households and family units. Our interview data seem to indicate that men remained more socially isolated, and that may reflect the reality that women handle more of the caregiving responsibilities in most families—the estimate is that women in the United States do 90% of informal and formal caregiving (Rayman, 2001). Women are more likely to be connected to community care institutions and also more likely to be community volunteers.

The issue of community links for IT workers deserves further research as it offers another view of their lives that is in contrast to the often held public perception that IT workers are young, nerdy, and socially disconnected. The women and men studied offer a more complex picture. In many ways these employees fit into a more universal picture, at this time of our nation's economic history, of workers struggling to survive an insecure economy and to live balanced work and family lives.

Attracting, Recruiting, and Retaining Women in IT

Many Pathways to IT Work

Although women and men gave similar answers to many of the questions we asked in our survey, there was, not surprisingly, a large gender difference in how men and women responded to the item, "When graduating high school, I considered a career in the technology field." Forty-one percent of men, but only 16% of women, considered it "very seriously," yielding one of the largest gender disparities in our survey (see Table 4). Many studies have documented this "gender gap" between young men and women.

Because we were studying those who ended up in the IT workforce, we could look retrospectively at reported attitudes at the time of high school graduation. Interestingly, if we look just at the women who became technical employees in the software and Internet industry in Massachusetts, more than half (53%) said that on high school graduation, they did not consider a technical career seriously at all. This finding has two important implications: first, it has become conventional wisdom that female students should be reached in middle school (or, at the latest, high school) in order to attract

Table 4. Survey respondents' intentions to pursue a technology career on high school graduation, by gender and age.

When graduating High School, I considered a career in the technology field:		Very seriously	Somewhat seriously	Not very seriously	Not seriously at all
Gender	Men	41%	16%	16%	21%
	Women	16%	12%	18%	43%
Age	18–24	26%	19%	24%	24%
	25–34	24%	9%	18%	39%
	35–44	33%	17%	17%	28%
	45–54	36%	14%	9%	26%
	55 and up	33%	16%	18%	27%

them to technology careers, and many programs have been established to accomplish this goal (National Science Foundation, 2004). However, our findings show that women can and do enter careers in IT despite having no interest in a technology career at the time of secondary school completion. Our data show no trend by age of respondent, so we believe that our findings hold true even today and that we should be recognizing and supporting multiple pathways, at all levels of schooling as well as beyond, to support women who wish to enter IT careers.

The second implication of this finding is that women may enter IT less well prepared than they might otherwise be. If men develop an earlier interest in IT than women, they will have more opportunity to make educational and career decisions based on their interest and thus have better credentials for leadership in the IT workforce. Early intervention programs designed to attract girls to technology careers therefore continue to be a good idea. On the other hand, Margolis and Fisher (2002), in their study of undergraduate women and men in computer science at Carnegie Mellon University, observed that many women caught up with and even surpassed their male peers in undergraduate CS programs, despite weaker initial preparation—in particular, less hands-on experience with computers. From a policy point of view, a "both/and" strategy is most valuable—work to attract girls and women at all levels, recognizing that it is possible to enter and succeed at IT careers at different stages of the life cycle.

One would expect an age effect in the extent to which men and women considered technology careers at high school graduation, and that this gender discrepancy would narrow and perhaps disappear among younger workers, as the national consensus about encouraging women to enter technical fields grew. Interestingly, however, the 25- to 34-year-olds in our survey were by a wide margin (10% or more) least likely of any age group to agree that they had considered a technology career seriously when graduating high school. The fact that this age cohort ended up in a technology-based industry could reflect high demand during their college and early professional years, and/or the success of post-secondary programs to recruit young women to technical careers. These workers, typified by an interviewee who said, "I never thought I would be in this field," were drawn into the industry, pulled by the presence of many well-paying jobs and pushed by the lack of similar opportunities in other fields. At times of high demand, IT employers have sometimes pursued a conscious strategy of hiring capable workers who were not planning to pursue computing, exemplified by the information systems manager at a large commercial bank in the mid-1980s who said that she sought out bright graduates from "starvation majors" and trained them to be information systems professionals (Kuhn, 1989). We can conjecture that those who are thus "pulled in" might also be those with the greatest propensity to leave, since their presence in the industry does not grow out of an intrinsic interest, but it is also possible that those who find themselves in the industry "accidentally," as it were, could discover that it is very much to their liking.

The assertion that there is no real "IT pipeline," beginning in grade school and diminishing with each advancing stage, is confirmed by the number of women in our study who had not contemplated an IT career when leaving high school, nor had a technical degree, yet ended up in a technical position in the software and Internet industry. Perhaps the IT labor market is more like a "sponge" than a "pipeline," with employees pulled in when the economy is good and the market for IT talent tight, and squeezed out when employment sags.

Motivation

When survey respondents selected the top three reasons they would remain in the software/Internet field, they listed good pay most often. Three quarters of both men and women specified good pay as a top attraction, and men gave "better pay elsewhere" as the top reason why they would leave the field (for women, this reason ranked third.) Almost 80% of respondents reported being the primary income earners in their households (89% of men and 63% of women), and because 61% of our female respondents report either being married or living with a partner, women living alone are not the only women who are the primary earners in their households.

Fifty-six percent of survey respondents had an individual pretax income of more than $75,000 in 2001, with 10% reporting over $150,000. Men were two and a half times more likely than women to be in this top 10%. Because these income figures are significantly higher than average, it is clear why employees seeking good pay find this industry very attractive.

Beyond the extrinsic motivator of high pay, there is also ample evidence of the intrinsic appeal of this work to those employed in the industry. "Exciting or challenging work," "always opportunities to learn something new," and "opportunities to use my skills" were the three most popular reasons, after good pay, for staying in the industry (Tables 5 and 6). In interviews, participants said, "Be sure you like this kind of work"; "you can't just be in it for the money." These statements highlight the importance of having an intrinsic interest in the work, to counterbalance the very real stresses involved in working in the industry.

Clearly, the content of the work they do is second only to pay as a motivator for this workforce, and challenging work, a chance to learn something new, and a chance to use skills are collectively more important than even good pay as reasons for remaining in the industry (see also Davis & Kuhn, 2003). This emphasis on variety, challenge, and skill acquisition is a signature characteristic of the IT employees whom we studied.

Several of our interviewees mentioned, without any prompting from us, that "puzzle solving"—in these very words—was an important attraction of work in the industry. "It's like getting paid to do the crossword puzzle," said one. Senior men in top management positions were most likely to see puzzles as real-world problems whose solutions could benefit the business community or society as a whole, and to emphasize IT's importance to the economy and to society, perhaps because of entrepreneurial fervor, and the wider view and deeper commitment associated with their leadership positions in the industry. When others, particularly women, spoke of puzzle solving, they were referring to an intellectual challenge detached from the "real world" of social and business significance. Overall, the interest this group of employees had in solving puzzles, and the ability to see their work as a puzzle, was one of the most striking findings to emerge from our interviews.

In his 1988 book, *Why Work?*, Michael Maccoby asserts that the workforce is undergoing a transition from a predominance of "organization" men to a newer generation of "self-developers." Self-developers find their primary satisfaction in holding a variety of positions, sometimes involving lateral rather than upward organizational moves, that use and enhance their skills. Unlike their parents' generation, they do not seek or assume that they will have lifelong careers in a single large organization. "Brought up in an environment of change, they have learned to adapt to new people and situations, and to trust their own abilities rather than parents or institutions. They value independence, and they accept responsibility for themselves"

Table 5. Top three reasons why survey respondents would remain in the software/Internet field.

	Female (%)	Male (%)	Total (%)
Good pay	73.7	74.3	74.1
Exciting or challenging work	50.3	57.0	54.4
Always opportunities to learn something new	49.9	42.3	45.3
Opportunities to use my skills	39.1	48.7	45.0
Favorable work environment or workplace culture	22.3	16.8	18.9
Scheduling flexibility	18.8	14.2	16.1
My colleagues	10.9	10.3	10.5
Benefits and/or stock options	8.9	9.2	9.0
Opportunity to travel	7.8	7.0	7.3
Promotion opportunities	4.3	5.0	4.7
Other	0.6	2.5	1.8

Note. 483 women and 736 men responded.

Table 6. The top three reasons survey respondents would leave the software/Internet field.

	Female (%)	Male (%)	Total (%)
Laid off/involuntary departure	39.8	34.9	36.7
Better pay elsewhere	27.8	36.6	33.0
Too many hours of work	31.5	26.5	28.4
Work is boring or lacks challenge	24.6	26.6	25.9
Unfavorable work environment or workplace culture	25.1	22.2	23.3
Stressful industry	22.2	19.3	20.5
Lack of promotion opportunities	19.7	17.9	18.7
Retirement	12.0	20.3	17.0
Poor match with my value system	16.3	12.9	14.3
Too much required travel	10.7	15.1	13.9
Limited opportunities to use my skills	11.8	13.9	13.2
Limited opportunities to learn something new	12.6	12.0	12.3
Too little scheduling flexibility	13.4	6.9	9.5
Return to school	9.3	8.1	8.6
Other	6.2	5.3	5.7

Note. 483 women and 736 men responded.

(Maccoby, 1988, p. 167). Lazonick, writing about what he calls the "New Economy Business Model," defines it in part as "the end of organization man" (Lazonick, 2005, p. 2). These theories about work and motivation in the twenty-first century are entirely consistent with the characteristics we found in our interviewees and survey respondents.

Women, IT, and the Future of Work

How can we shape a future for women, their families, and their communities, recognizing the attractions and strengths of IT careers while reducing the negative aspects of work in this industry? Based on the findings from our study of the Massachusetts software and Internet workforce, we offer these thoughts.

Support Employees' Ability to Work and Have a Life

Many factors make it difficult for members of this workforce to combine work with other pursuits, and policies and practices that address these challenges and support women and their families will make work in this industry more attractive.

The very high levels of stress reported by this workforce—women and men alike—are cause for concern, as are the long work hours, the lack of sleep, and the intrusion of work on family and nonwork time. Studies of the causes of this stress, along with employer policies designed to make more efficient use of the workday and increased encouragement to make use of telecommuting and flextime, will help to address these problems.

A sense of stability and security among IT workers can be encouraged by such measures as support for lifelong learning, provision of high-quality part-time jobs with benefits, ensuring the portability of employee benefits, and universal health insurance so that no family goes without health care, including during the period of transition between jobs.

The number of childless women in the workforce, and the compromises and career sacrifices made by women with children, speak to the challenges faced by mothers in IT. When educated and well-paid working women must forego motherhood because of the demands of their jobs, both individuals and the society may suffer. While some women are childless by choice, the high incidence of childlessness in this workforce is unlikely to simply reflect personal preference, absent job pressures. Policies that support mothers, not just women in general, can help relieve the burden. Policies to support fathers could also ease the impact on women. Today more fathers, particularly younger fathers, seek work that allows them to be involved with family.

Build Security and Social Capital by Creating and Enhancing Networks

"Networks" are both a literal and a metaphorical fact of life for IT professionals. The literal network, the Internet, is a model and a vehicle for the metaphorical networks maintained by IT workers and others in the twenty-first century.

Professional networks can be more or less formal. Among the more formal are professional associations like the Association for Computing Machinery and the Institute of Electrical and Electronics Engineers, or interest groups for women such as our collaborator WITI and the Systers network for women in computing. Less formal networks include groups formed by alumni of firms like Data General and Interleaf, who stay in touch through listservers even after the company goes out of business. These networks may support job searches and even personal activities like political debates and classified ads. These can create both increased job security and build social capital. Support for these networks—whether from companies, government, or private donors—might particularly aid women, who, as we noted, are more likely than men to make a broad-based job search and to be involved in community institutions. Getting men more involved in these might also ease some of the burden on women, if men's job searches become more effective and if they become more involved in caregiving.

International networks could increase international understanding and may have the potential to address the insecurity and anxiety created for US workers with the growth of IT outsourcing. At present, some of the stress and insecurity felt by IT professionals in the US comes from the threat of outsourcing and offshoring of IT work. Building international networks, particularly of women in IT, can help IT workers around the globe to see one another not just as threats but as colleagues, and could help to raise labor standards and prevent abuses worldwide.

Change Perceptions or Change the Reality

As we know, many US women choose not to pursue IT careers. In some cases, women's decisions to avoid IT careers are based on stereotypes that do not conform to the reality we found in our study (Ambrose et al., 1997). In cases where women are uninformed or misinformed, programs that provide better information, or exposure to the realities of IT careers, could help counter decisions made based on faulty information. Many programs exist to introduce women to IT and to build their confidence and skills. Providing women with such programs, and with more accurate information on the range of possibilities in IT careers, can help address the problem of inaccurate perception.

In other cases, women's decisions not to pursue IT careers are based on accurate perceptions of job content, a hostile work or school culture, job insecurity, or other factors. In these situations, it is our job, and many have already undertaken this effort, to change the reality of the schools and workplaces that women find unattractive. When women's decisions to avoid IT careers are rational, we must focus our attention, as many are already doing (Margolis & Fisher, 2002; Perlow, 1997), on changing the school or the job rather than on changing the woman.

Acknowledgments

This article is based on work supported by the National Science Foundation under grant EIA-0089965. Project Tech Force, based at the University of Massachusetts Lowell, in partnership with the Massachusetts Software & Internet Council, is an interdisciplinary study of the work experiences of women and men in the software and Internet industry. Data collection and preliminary analysis are the result of the collective efforts of the Project Tech Force research team. The authors wish to thank the National Science Foundation and the Center for Women and Work for their support, and the Massachusetts Software & Internet Council and the Boston chapter of Women in Technology International for their collaboration. Particular thanks to Joyce Davis, Research Director, for her important contributions to our research. We dedicate this article to the memory of Barbara Lazarus, pioneer in the support of women in science and technology.

References

Ambrose, S., Dunkle, K., Lazarus, B., Nair, I., & Harkus, D. (1997). *Journeys of women in science and engineering: No universal constants.* Philadelphia: Temple University Press.

Bailey, K. (2005). *A study of worker burnout in the Massachusetts high technology sector.* Unpublished master's thesis, University of Massachusetts Lowell.

Best, M., Paquin, A., & Xie, H. (2004). Discovering regional competitive advantage: Massachusetts high-tech [Electronic Version]. *Business and Economic History On-line.* Retrieved February 16, 2006, from http://www.thebhc.org/publications/BEHonline/2004/beh2004.html.

Bookman, A. (2004). *Starting in our own backyards: How working families can build community and survive the new economy.* New York: Routledge.

Davis, J. & Kuhn, S. (2003, April). *What makes Dick and Jane run? Examining the retention of women and men in the software and Internet industry.* Paper presented at the Association for Computing Machinery Special Interest Group on Management Information Systems and Computer Personnel Research Conference. Philadelphia, PA.

Downs, B. (2003). *Fertility of American women: June 2002* [Electronic Version]. US Census Bureau (P20-548). Retrieved February 21, 2006, from http://www.census.gov/prod/2003pubs/p20-548.pdf

Eaton, S. C., & Bailyn, L. (2000). Career as life path: Tracing work and life strategies of biotech professionals. In M. Peiperl & M. Arthur (Eds.), *Conversations in career theory* (pp. 177–198). London: Oxford University Press.

Funk, S. A. (2000). *Summary of findings from employee research.* PowerPoint report on results of a major international survey of employees in several large IT firms.

Kuhn, S. (1989). The limits to industrialization: Computer software development in a large commercial bank. In S. Wood (Ed.), *The transformation of work?* (pp.266–278). London: Unwin Hyman.

Kuhn, S., & Rayman, P. (2005). Software and Internet industry workers in Massachusetts: Findings and implications for the Future of Work. Retrieved September 12, 2006, from http://www.umass.edu/lrrc/futureofwork/research_and_book/pdfs/Kuhn%20and%20Rayman.pdf

Lazonick, W. (2005). *Evolution of the new economy business model.* Retrieved September 13, 2006, from http://www.uml.edu/centers/CIC/Lazonick%20NEBM%20October%202005.pdf

Maccoby, M. (1988). *Why work? Leading the new generation.* New York: Simon and Schuster.

Malcom, S., Teich, A. H., Jesse, J. K., Campbell, L. A., Babco, E. L., & Bell, N. E. (2005). *Preparing women and minorities for the IT workforce: The role of nontraditional educational pathways.* Washington D.C.: American Association for the Advanced Science.

Margolis, J., & Fisher, A. (2002). *Unlocking the clubhouse: Women in computing.* Cambridge, MA: MIT Press.

National Research Council. (2001). *Building a workforce for the information economy.* Washington, D.C.: National Academy Press.

National Science Foundation. (2004). *New formulas for America's workforce: Girls in science and engineering* (NSF 03-207). Retrieved September 12, 2006, from http://www.nsf.gov/pubs/2003/nsf03207/start.htm

Perlow, L. (1997). *Finding time: How corporations, individuals, and families can benefit from new work practices.* Ithaca, NY: Cornell University Press.

Radcliffe Public Policy Institute. (1999). Professional pathways: Examining work, family and community in the biotechnology industry. Cambridge, MA: Radcliffe College.

Rayman, P. (2001). *Beyond the bottom line: The search for dignity at work.* New York: St. Martin's Press.

Rayman, P., & Bluestone, B. (1982). *Out of work: Job loss in the aircraft industry.* Washington D.C.: National Institutes of Mental Health.

Rayman, P., & Brett, B. (1993). *Pathways for women in the sciences.* Wellesley, MA: Wellesley Centers for Women.

Notes

1. While there are differences among STEM fields—for example, biotechnology generally requires an advanced degree and has a distinct career "pipeline," neither of which is true in IT—all STEM fields exhibit some barriers to entry by women, making many findings on women in other STEM fields relevant to the study of women in IT.

Chapter 10

Multiple Pathways toward Gender Equity in the United States Information Technology Workforce

Paula G. Leventman

Abstract

The Northeastern University IT Workforce Study summarized in this chapter identifies three pathways that men and women took toward their IT careers: Traditional, Transitional, Self-directed. The application of this typology to survey findings and qualitative interview transcripts explains how career pathways relate to experience in technical skill-set areas, time-on-task, levels of job satisfaction and salary differentials. The Northeastern University IT Workforce Study examined sex similarities and differences in how and why women and men come to IT, what jobs and tasks they do in IT, and their feelings about IT careers. Findings revealed few significant differences between the sexes: women and men are both highly satisfied with their careers, perform the same kinds of tasks at work, and are apt to feel that gender did not influence IT career development. Overwhelmingly, women had positive experiences in IT careers. Initial expectations were far exceeded by career realizations for those in Transitional and Self-directed pathways. Most women felt relatively equal to men in terms of salary and organizational position. However, the recruitment of increasing numbers of women to IT careers is jeopardized by labor market instability and the increased outsourcing of IT work.

Introduction

Authorities agree that an abundant supply of skilled IT professionals is essential to US competitiveness in the global economy of the twenty-first century (Joy & Kennedy, 1999). During the 1980s and 1990s, there was an explosion of jobs in the IT sector (including mathematical and computer scientists, computer systems analysts, and computer programmers). Numbers of IT positions increased dramatically, from 1,182,000 in 1983 to 2,999,000 in 1996 (See table No. 645, US Census Bureau, 1997). The

Bureau of Labor Statistics (BLS) estimated the number of IT professionals at 3,104,000 in 2003 (BLS, 2004).

Women have always been under represented in the IT workforce. Instead of increasing with the size of the IT workforce, the percentage of women in these positions trends downward, from 33.4% in 1999 to 30.1% in 2001 (Commission on Professionals in Science and Technology, 2002). BLS household data shows a continuation of the declining percentage of professional women in IT from 30% in 2001, to 28% in both 2002 and 2003 (Bureau of Labor Statistics, 2004).

Multiple Pathways Perspective

People have taken many educational and occupational routes into professional careers in information technology. Rapidly expanding job opportunities beginning in the early 1980s and lasting into 2001 resulted in a large bubble of job opportunities for people who could prepare for or slip into these positions, in one way or another. The National Science Foundation concluded that:

> People enter IT careers in a variety of ways. IT workers include people who majored in IT-related disciplines at the associate, bachelor's, master's, and doctoral degree levels; people from other science, engineering and business fields; and people from nontechnical disciplines who have taken some courses in IT subjects. (National Science Board, 2002)

The US Department of Commerce affirms that "[t]here is no single path to prepare for a professional IT job. There is no 'one size fits all.'" However, the report finds that two thirds of IT professionals have a four-year degree or higher. It also notes that while these degrees are in a diversity of fields, a majority are in science, math, or engineering (US Department of Commerce, 2003).

The goal of the research reported in this chapter is to contribute to a growing knowledge base required to increase the representation of women in the IT workforce. The research focuses on the values, attitudes, and decision-making criteria of computer professionals. A major objective of the research was to identify and assess the efficacy of various routes into professional information technology careers. The central research task was to collect sufficient quantitative and qualitative data to identify the education pathways and workplace conditions that promote gender equity in the IT workplace.

Methods

An extensive survey instrument was developed from the literature and pilot tested. It was completed by 432 IT professionals distributed throughout several high technology and computer applications organizations in 2002. Once data was collected and analyzed, a qualitative protocol was developed and used in face-to-face interviews in 2004.

The sample of IT technical professionals came from two sources. One included graduates of the Northeastern University Master of Science in Information Systems (MSIS) program, a career transition program, from the years 1986–2001 (186 of 416, 45% response rate). The other source was IT professionals recruited from four corporations. One organization, a large nonprofit health care company, had a higher level of participation (205 of 541, 38% response rate) than the remaining three for-profit corporations ($n = 41$).

Statistical analysis was conducted on survey data. Cross-tabs, t-tests, and one-way and two-way analysis of variance (ANOVA) explored the distribution, comparison of means, and significant relationships within the data.

During spring and summer 2004, 44 face-to-face interviews were conducted with 29 women and 15 men. Interviews lasted from 45 minutes to one hour or longer. They were conducted in private areas at the respondents' places of work or in their homes. The interviews were audiotaped and professionally transcribed.

Sample Demographics

Respondents were predominately United States citizens (92%, 399); most were native-born (85%, 366) and white or Asian American (85%, 365). Two thirds of the sample was female (67%, 289) and one third male (33%, 142). Women and men were about the same age (women: mean = 40, SD = 9.1; men: mean = 41; SD = 8.6). Men were more apt to live with a spouse or partner (81%, 115 versus 66%, 190; $p = .002$) and to have children (66%, 93 versus 45%, 128; $p = .0001$).

Multiple Pathways to IT Careers: Typology and Analysis

A major thrust of the 2002 survey and 2004 follow-up interviews conducted for the Northeastern University IT Workforce Study was the creation and substantiation of a typology to help explain how education, training, occupational experiences, and other life history factors combine to form the pathways leading to careers in the IT workforce. The typology is described and analyzed below. Our respondents were grouped into three major pathway patterns that appear in the US IT workforce and in our data. The criteria used for this classification were degree field, career history, when the decision to go for an IT career was made, and how IT skills were acquired.

Traditional Pathway

- *Bachelor's degree:* IT or highly technical field
- *Career arc:* Jobs in IT or highly technical field
- *When decided for IT:* During high school or undergraduate education

We classified 31% (126 people) who responded to the 2002 survey as Traditional because they had technical undergraduate degrees. They decided to go for a technical career when they were in high school or during their undergraduate education, and the jobs they held were all in technical fields.

People on the Traditional pathway majored in technical subjects in college: math, physics, chemistry, and engineering. Depending, of course, on when they were undergraduates, computer science or information technology may not have been an option. They took jobs in IT because jobs in the sciences were not available without a doctorate and because salaries in IT were very attractive. They had no trouble getting IT jobs in the 1980s and 1990s. They found they could do the work. Some really liked it. Others liked the salary. People on the Traditional pathway appear to have greater job stability through tough times than others. They are generally satisfied with their jobs but voice lower satisfaction ratings than others.

Career Profile of a Female in the Traditional Pathway

Job 1: "I started off as software engineer on the product team and I was in charge of enhancing and obtaining the core product code. I did that for three and a half years. Towards the end it was more of a technical lead type job where I oversaw some other engineers within my group. My job was to oversee the work of other engineers in my group for a specific project and be the liaison between the business users and the technical team.

"I left in the middle of the whole dot-com boom and there were other companies out there doing very exciting things, working with Java, and they had the free soda machines and pinball machines. It seemed like a younger, funner culture and so I went out there. That was just what the second job was like. Also, I did quite a bit of product work that I felt never left the door. Like, I wrote a lot of code, that was an emergency at the time that I was writing it, and it never seemed to get utilized out in the field. So I felt that my work wasn't really adding to the company.

"They had a CRM [Customer Relationship Management] application and my job was really to maintain the infrastructure around it. We did failover work for the product to make sure the product stays up in a 24/7 environment. We were in charge of all of the core applications and features.

"The essential system is based on what they call system rules. You can create a whole bunch of rules to customize the application of the system for major users. These can be used by call center reps to track and to process customer activities. For example, if I have a problem with my Fleet account, I call a Fleet customer rep. They use the customized system to open up an item that's recording the fact that I called them, and they use our product to manage that whole interaction.

"When a product is out in the market, there are certain things the customer may want enhanced or changed. The company had a tendency to bow to these changes from certain customers if they barked about them enough. There were many times when we would go and make the change and then the company would forget that they'd wanted it, so it never left the door. That happened quite a few times. It was frustrating for me."

Job 2: "My second job was high growth computer developer. I started in November of 2000 as a Consulting Engineer in the Services Department. I was really using the product to build Web sites for customers. I started off as a software engineer working on projects for customers, building Web sites, using the company's product, and I eventually was promoted. My responsibilities increased while I was there to be another kind of tech lead similar to my role in my first job. I was in charge of maintaining a group of engineers designing the application, assigning resources to build the application and I was also the technical interface to the customer.

"I was there three years. I left when I got pregnant and had a baby. That job is not a mommy job. It requires travel. It requires many long hours and I was not willing to do that."

Job 3: "I was on maternity leave for about five months. I quit my second job after four months and then I was out of the workforce for about a month. Then my first employer called me back. I had always kept in contact with the people there. One of the engineers contacted me about a project that they were working on. They were wondering if I wanted to come in and work as a consultant. And I've been back, it's been four months. It's really a software engineering function. I'm in charge of certain features that they're looking to add to their product, so I'm writing code to support those features."

Transitional Pathway
- *Bachelor's degree:* In non-IT field
- *Career arc:* Included nontechnical and non-IT jobs
- *How acquired IT skills:* Graduate career transition program
- *When decided for IT:* Prior to grad degree, during non-IT work

These people did not start out with technical degrees. We classified 38 % (152 people) who responded to the 2002 survey as Transitional because they had non-IT jobs and took a formal graduate program to change the direction of their careers. The Northeastern University Master of Science in Information Systems program (NU MSIS) is the prototype Transitional. A small percentage of MSIS alumni had technical bachelor's degrees and were classified as on the Traditional pathway.

Most of the women on the Transitional pathway had undergraduate degrees in nontechnical subjects such as history, sociology, psychology, business, art history, and others. They were teachers, social workers, attorneys, and nurses, among other careers. They were attracted to a master's level career change program where they were taught basic and essential technology skills and how to learn on the job. The program featured career counseling services, job placement assistance, and peer group support. MSIS program completers doubled or tripled their preprogram salaries, achieved high organizational positions, and expressed relatively high job satisfaction. As for the men, some used the MSIS program to change careers, but many used it as a stepping stone. These were men on the way up who took the MSIS degree part-time in order to move into management positions. They achieved high organizational positions, high salaries, and expressed high job satisfaction.

Career Profile of a Female in the Transitional Pathway

Job 1: "When I graduated from Northeastern in 1990 with my master's, I started out as a programmer. It was very much like a typing pool, it was a programming pool. The company was a software vendor that produced accounting software. I worked on modifying what they call their standard package and the projects that we got were usually a year or longer.

"We were purchased by a larger company. I was moved into a consulting department and ultimately had to travel a lot. They started to have some difficulty financially, they expanded very fast, went public, and in the position that I ended up with I had to travel a lot. It was literally living places for a number of months and just coming home on weekends. I was a single parent, and I had two, not really young children at home, but just felt that it was a lot of effort. I wasn't learning a lot. I stayed there for about five years."

Job 2: "A colleague from my first job moved to a position with a nonprofit doing asset management. He was working on a conversion of their portfolio management system from one vendor to another. He brought me on board to work with him. On that, I made my foray into financial services. I was doing all the integration programming so I was pulling trading system data into the portfolio management system. I was working around a vendor package, and I ultimately became assistant manager of that department. Then I became director and vice president of systems and technology. Ultimately that piece was purchased by a large international financial firm."

Job 3: "At that point I went to another large financial investment firm. I thought that it was a very good company, very focused on technology and they would never outsource their IT. Well, they never will, but the environment was just a very intense environment. I went over there as director of software engineering for the business of bringing in market data. The company was so large that it took an entire department just to deal with this piece. We were basically feeding all the trading rooms with their pricing data, and the Web. I did a lot of interfacing with the various users. I realized it wasn't the kind of environment that I was used to. I was used to investments and dealing with economists. They're not businessmen, for the most part, they're laid back.

"Ultimately I gave it about two years and then moved on. At this point the economy was getting very bad so I ended up negotiating for a layoff and so I was able to leverage for a severance package."

Job 4 (Financial Services Consultant): "I really have been pigeonholed, so to speak, in the financial services. I started to look for contacts in financial services. They've outsourced considerably, to overseas, bringing people in from overseas to a very large degree and I'm saying entire departments, and I was able to get a short contract just with a manufacturing company, for a while, but that kind of got me on my feet.

"I pulled another contract in financial services. I went in and actually did the same thing. They had asked me to come in to work on their market timing, their after hours trading and to integrate into their software checks and balances so that those particular issues wouldn't happen. Then I got this contract at my present company which hopefully will last for a while longer.

"Again, I'm actually in regulatory affairs, which is under legal and compliance but I'm on the IT side, so I'm taking all the regulations, they are literally rebuilding, they're being very proactive, rebuilding all their trading systems. Our system is a compliance system that literally won't just look for problems, but is going to evaluate every trade coming in against the FCC regulation, any regulations that's out there now, that's coming down the pike, we're actually programming the rules and right now my job is to work in between the business and the outsourcers to actually provide the English interpretation. So that's kind of the loophole. There had been some problems in the understanding, so luckily I was kind of able to get in between that and as I can speak both technical and some of the legalese. We translate that into rules, regulations and ultimately plug it into this compliance application.

"I'm working on my own. It feels scary, in terms of pension, in terms of health insurance, but I'm making into the six figures, although I don't know how long it will last, that's the thing."

Self-Directed Pathway

- *Bachelor's degree:* In non-IT field
- *Career arc:* Included non-technical jobs, or non-IT jobs in an IT organization
- *How acquired IT skills:* Classes, trainings, on their own (without structured MS program)
- *When decided for IT:* During non-IT employment

We classified 31% (126 people) who responded to the 2002 survey as Self-directed. These individuals had a non-IT bachelor's degree and a career arc with non-IT and IT employment. Typically, they decided to pursue an IT career during non-IT employment. They used a combination of classes, internal and external trainings, and on the job training to enable the evolution into IT positions.

Career Profile of a Female in the Self-Directed Pathway

"I was a nursing major in college, and then I went into the nursing field. I left to help a computer vendor develop some nursing applications. It was very interesting at the time. It was something that involved traveling and meeting with end users. At that time, around 1996, in the nursing industry, nurses were scarce. It was long hours, tedious hours, so it was a way to get out, instead of doing weekends and holidays and so forth and so on. So, it was kind of a nice alternative and I had no computer background, but they just wanted someone with clinical background, so it was a nice change."

Job 1: "My first IT job was with a medical software company. I got that through a family friend who was the director there, and he just said that they were looking for clinical people with background and I said, 'Great.' I was an application consultant, they called it. I was in charge of building dictionaries, training end users. My focus was on order entry nursing and the result was viewer application. And from there our client was Columbia HCA. And we traveled around to their hospitals and helped implement the nursing application—the order entry application and the result viewer application. I started there in January of 1997 until May of

1998, so a year and five months. I changed jobs because I needed more money."

Job 2: "My second job was with an insurance company. I started there in June of 1998. The market was very high. There was like a sign-on bonus and the pay was really good. I was just a consultant. I started in June of 1998. The second day after I started, they had me in a project here with a major healthcare organization. I was on an MGH [Massachusetts General Hospital] order entry project from June of 1998 until May of 2000.... We implemented medical and surgical floors at MGH on the order entry application. So it was everything from the beginning of the project—designing, testing, then all the way through implementation. And then once the implementation was done, I rolled off to a new project here with the major healthcare organization. And that happened about June of 2000, and I went to a project at another hospital under the same umbrella. It was under the same director. At that point, I helped do the EMAR [Electronic Medication Administration Record] project pilot. And I did the Brigham Emergency Department order entry system. And that was until October. And the from October of 2000 until December of 2000, I worked on the chemotherapy order entry team, and so after I did that for two months, I decided to apply for a permanent position with the major healthcare organization."

Job 3: "I started here as an employee in January of 2001 as Corporate Team Lead. I have staff unto myself. I am responsible for the adult chemotherapy order entry. The application spans across most of the Partners entities, MGH, Dana-Farber, Partners, Faulkner, and Brigham."

The multiple pathways typology was constructed from a specific set of items in the 2002 survey data: bachelor's degree and master's degree fields, IT and non-IT career history, and point at which decision was made to go for an IT career. The multiple pathways typology was then applied to other 2002 survey findings. We examined the typology in terms of experience in technical skill-set areas, time-on-task, annual salary, and job satisfaction ratings. The 2004 interview transcripts were used to provide career profiles of women from each of the three pathways.[1]

Pathways and Experience Level in IT Skill Set Areas

Respondents were asked to rate their level of experience in eight IT skill-set areas as listed in Table 1. There are no significant differences between the sexes in five of the eight skill-set areas. However, men rate their level of experience significantly higher than women in three areas: other program languages, operating systems, and networking.

Table 1. Skill set area means by career pathways and sex.

EXPERIENCE		Traditional	Transitional	Self-Directed	p	Total #
Object oriented languages	FEMALE	**2.56**	**2.32**	**1.64**	**.000**	387
	MALE	**2.77**	**2.63**	**1.82**	**.001**	
Other programming languages	FEMALE	**3.04**	**2.95**	**1.80**	**.000**	386
	MALE	**3.38**	**3.21**	**2.38**	**.001**	
Operating systems	FEMALE	**3.48**	**3.27**	**2.56**	**.000**	392
	MALE	**3.70**	**3.44**	**3.00**	**.013**	
Databases	FEMALE	**3.21**	**3.12**	**2.51**	**.001**	391
	MALE	3.10	3.21	2.67	.098	
Graphics	FEMALE	1.92	1.98	1.81	.540	379
	MALE	2.09	2.22	1.89	.379	
Web authoring tools	FEMALE	**1.78**	**2.09**	**1.71**	**.050**	385
	MALE	**2.29**	**2.54**	**1.80**	**.023**	
Web languages	FEMALE	**2.59**	**2.58**	**2.03**	**.008**	388
	MALE	**2.69**	**2.83**	**2.16**	**.043**	
Networking	FEMALE	2.08	2.12	1.76	.092	383
	MALE	2.63	3.00	2.18	.058	

Note. Bolded numbers are statistically significant.

When experience level is examined within the pathways, filtered by sex, there are highly significant differences between the pathways. Within almost every skill-set area (with the single exception of graphics); women and men on Traditional pathways provided the highest experience ratings, followed closely by women and men on Transitional pathways. Self-directed men and women provided lower mean experience ratings in all skill-set areas.

Overall, men gave their technical skills somewhat higher ratings (using a five-point scale where 5 = high and 1 = low) than did the women. People on the Self-directed pathway gave their technical skills low ratings, and the lowest set of ratings was found among the Self-directed women. What these findings show is that people with technical educational backgrounds feel most comfortable about their IT skills. Findings also show that technical deficiencies at the bachelor's degree level can be compensated for through formal training at the master's degree level, if then directly applied in professional IT positions. People without degrees in technical fields are apt to be unsure of their technical skill set.

Pathways and Job Tasks

In order to understand the type of work our respondents were doing, they were asked to explain the relative time they spent on a series of 21 IT job-related tasks. Specifically, they were asked to indicate which of the tasks they spend 20% or more of their time doing. Multiple responses were encouraged. In general, women and men are doing the same job tasks, although more men are doing programming and software development and more women are doing project management.

When time-on-task is examined within the pathways, filtered by sex, as shown in Table 2, we found significant differences between the pathways among the women. Those on the Traditional pathway are more likely to spend 20% or more of their time doing programming, networking, and Web design; those on the Self-directed pathway are more likely to spend 20% or more of their time doing customer service, documentation, teaching and training, and technical support (softer technical skill-set areas) than others.

Pathways and Salary

Overall, men in the 2002 Northeastern University IT Workforce Study sample were apt to earn higher annual salaries than women. Among the women, 26% earned $60,000 or less, compared with 13% of the men. Among the women, 48% earned more than $75,000, compared with 63% of the men ($p = .027$).

However, when the multiple pathways typology is introduced, as shown in Table 3, it is apparent that there are no significant differences between the salaries of men and women in the Transitional and Self-directed pathways. The differences between the sexes in terms of salary are accounted for by men and women in the Traditional pathway. People in the Traditional pathway held only technical jobs in which a male-dominated infrastructure may be may be a historical holdover. High tech companies and some of the computer application industries are "newer" and may reflect a greater degree of gender equity.

Pathways and Job Satisfaction

We have found time and again that IT professionals are highly satisfied with many dimensions of their careers. Respondents were asked to rate their degree of satisfaction on a scale of 1 = low to 5 = high. Satisfaction ratings were medium-high to high (4 and 5), approaching 80%. There were no significant differences between the sexes. However, as shown in Table 4, there are significant differences in satisfaction ratings between the career

Table 2. Career pathway by time-on-task and sex.

TIME ON TASK	WOMEN				MEN			
	Traditional	Transitional	Self-Directed	p	Traditional	Transitional	Self-Directed	p
Accounting	.04	.07	.11	.283	.03	.08	.04	.666
Customer service	**.24**	**.17**	**.38**	**.003**	.17	.28	.15	.397
Database administration	.12	.09	.13	.637	.09	.16	.22	.172
Design equipment	.15	.10	.10	.589	.21	.12	.15	.582
Documentation	**.29**	**.24**	**.41**	**.026**	.34	.16	.33	.225
E-commerce	.06	.04	.06	.721	.10	.04	.09	.642
Managing & supervising	.37	.33	.41	.493	.33	.32	.37	.880
Networking	**.03**	**.00**	**.00**	**.047**	.02	.04	.09	.246
Programming	**.38**	**.32**	**.15**	**.004**	.45	.24	.41	.199
Project management	.47	.45	.59	.137	.34	.32	.41	.683
Quality assurance	.19	.18	.25	.470	**.03**	**.20**	**.20**	**.020**
Recruiting	.09	.03	.06	.236	.00	.08	.04	.131
Research	.22	.17	.11	.209	.16	.20	.13	.746
Sales	.07	.06	.01	.188	.05	.12	.00	.070
Security	.07	.03	.01	.132	.03	.04	.07	.754
Software development	.24	.22	.20	.872	.40	.36	.39	.951
Systems analysis	**.34**	**.24**	**.45**	**.008**	.36	.28	.41	.544
Teaching & training	**.18**	**.12**	**.28**	**.016**	.09	.04	.15	.292
Technical writing	.07	.06	.05	.838	.14	.08	.15	.685
Technical support	.21	.27	.38	.065	.26	.32	.30	.811
Web design	**.19**	**.13**	**.05**	**.030**	.16	.20	.15	.857

Note. Bolded numbers are statistically significant.

Table 3. Percentage distribution of current salary by sex and career pathway.

CURRENT JOB SALARY	TRADITIONAL		TRANSITIONAL		SELF-DIRECTED		TOTAL
	Women	Men	Women	Men	Women	Men	
< $45,000	5%	0%	12%	4%	8%	2%	23
$45,001–$60,000	16	6	16	9	20	13	52
$60,001–$75,000	28	14	21	35	29	27	88
$75,001–$90,000	20	38	24	13	21	33	90
> $90,001	31	42	27	39	23	24	106
TOTAL	100%	100%	100%	100%	100%	100%	100%
	(64)	(50)	(100)	(23)	(77)	(45)	(359)

$p = .024$

pathways on three dimensions of career satisfaction: overall satisfaction, satisfaction with career advancement opportunities, and satisfaction with benefits. We see the same pattern in these areas; people on Self-directed pathways are apt to provide the highest satisfaction ratings, followed by people on Transitional pathways. People on Traditional pathways tend to provide the lowest satisfaction ratings.

Self-directed women and men spend less time and money in formal preparation for IT careers than others. Self-directed women tend to do the "softer" jobs and provide the lowest rating of their experience in the more technical skill-set areas. The relatively higher job satisfaction expressed by the Self-directed than by others is perhaps explained by the fact that they are well rewarded in terms of salary and position, at a lower cost in terms of time and money, than people on the other pathways.

Most of the Self-directed sample in the Northeastern University IT Workforce Study consisted of employees from our health care systems partner, a large not-for-profit organization. There were no layoffs in this organization from 2001–2004, as there were in most other companies. Some people changed jobs to this nonprofit, and employees tried hard to remain there because of job stability and working conditions. Job security was a major factor in the higher satisfaction ratings provided by these professionals than by people on the Transitional or Traditional pathways. This is an organization with a high percentage of female managers who are liked by most men and women. The work may be less challenging than in other types of organizations. Systems procedures do not seem to change as rapidly here, and training is available when they do. With job stability, good working conditions, and family-friendly policies, it is not surprising that people on the Self-directed pathway are highly satisfied with their information technology jobs (see Table 4).

Table 4. Mean distribution of job satisfaction by career pathway.

		Mean	Number	Significance
Overall job satisfaction	*Traditional*	3.78	124	.031
	Transitional	3.99	149	
	Self-Directed	4.06	126	
	Total		399	
Opportunities for career advancement	*Traditional*	3.16	123	.023
	Transitional	3.21	148	
	Self-Directed	3.51	126	
	Total		395	
Degree of satisfaction with benefits	*Traditional*	3.53	122	.044
	Transitional	3.72	134	
	Self-Directed	3.87	122	
	Total		378	

Experiencing IT Careers

Transcripts of the face-to-face interviews conducted in 2004 provided North-eastern University IT Workforce Study researchers with qualitative data for an exploration of how women and men feel about and experience their IT careers, in several areas.

Success and Satisfaction

Professionals who work in IT are "highly satisfied" with their jobs. Most respondents felt successful (at least before 2002). There were no gender differences in these response patterns. Both women and men defined success in terms of income, challenge and recognition. Many men, as well as women, described satisfaction in terms of love for work and personal happiness.

Gender and Career Development

All of the men and two thirds of the women said gender did not make a difference in their career development. Approximately 15% of the women said their gender helped and 15% said gender hindered their career development. When asked if women still had to "prove themselves" in the workplace, all of the men said "no." While most women also said "no," a minority said "yes" or even "absolutely."

Technical and Supervisory Responsibilities

Most of the people interviewed in 2004 were in managerial or high technical content positions. Most managers interviewed liked the supervisory responsibilities they described. However, they also talked about their technical interests, the technical aspects of their work, and the interactions between the technical and the managerial in information technology workplaces.

The men and women in high technical content positions typically had few people, if any, reporting to them directly. They were technical experts who really liked their work. Organizationally, they were people in the middle. They described interactions between the technical and the managerial aspects of what they did on the job. Both women and men were divided almost equally between people who wanted more managerial responsibility and those who absolutely did not.

Mentoring

The importance of mentoring for career development, especially for women and racial minorities, is well established in the literature. The Catalyst research organization advises women to "find someone to teach you the rules of the game ... as well as for guidance and advice at critical junctures" (Catalyst, Inc., p. 25). Other descriptions of "mentoring" are summarized by Wadia-Fascetti and Leventman (2000):

- "A mentor guides a protégé in the direction which will best assist the protégé in learning" (Brown, 1993).
- "Mentoring consists of a unique and personal relationship between two people, with an effective mentor providing the mentee with a true sense of what it feels like to be in her position" (Caravalho & Maus, 1996).
- "Mentoring is defined as offering practical academic help, explaining the customs, secrets, and myths of the profession; and, sometimes, offering emotional support" (Garner, 1994).
- "Mentoring provides career benefits as well as psychological benefits for both mentors and their students, and can facilitate a working environment that encourages individual growth" (Vallone & Smith, 1996).

Respondents to the Northeastern University IT Workforce Study 2002 survey were asked to rate the degree to which they experienced "little or no mentoring on the job." The item was used as an indicator of job dissatisfaction. There were no statistically significant differences between the mean ratings of female and male respondents. In 2004, we asked those we interviewed personally, "How much mentoring have you experienced during your IT career?" Four conceptions of "mentoring" were spread throughout the interview transcripts: (1) mentoring as "helping," (2) mentoring as "teaching," (3) mentoring as socialization into company culture, (4) mentoring as career guidance.

IT professionals reported several kinds of experiences with mentoring. Informal mentoring is prevalent across IT employer companies. A few respondents had direct experience with formal mentor programs. There were few overall differences in the prevalence of mentoring experiences described by the women, as compared with the men we interviewed. The difference between the sexes was entirely in the intensity of the experience described. Men tended to describe mentoring in terms of teaching and training. Women were more likely to describe positive and effective career-building mentoring experiences.

Networking

Almost all respondents said that networking was "very important" or "important" to IT career development. Conceptions of networking ranged from mainly socializing, to socializing with technical content, to mostly job-related technical knowledge exchange. A minority said that networking was "not very important." The only gender difference was in the proportion of men (approximately two thirds) saying networking was very important, as compared with women (about half). There was only one reference to an "old boys' network."

Keeping Skills Current

By far, the most frequently mentioned source of "positive feelings," mentioned in open-ended response to the 2002 survey, was the stimulation and challenge provided by the work itself. The difficulty of keeping skills up-to-date in view of the pace of technological change was by far the most frequently mentioned source of "reservations" about an IT career. Response patterns did not vary with sex.

Respondents in 2004 were asked to describe how they kept technical skills current. Approximately one third of the women and men talked about keeping up-to-date in terms of the challenge and stimulation and said they were always learning and training. Almost everyone mentioned the importance of on-the-job training. Although keeping up with change is normative in high tech companies, project deadline pressures can conflict with time allowed for employee professional development. Keeping technical skills current is difficult, if not impossible, for those who choose to move into higher management positions.

Tough Times: Layoffs, Mergers, Downsizing, Outsourcing

Layoffs

The Northeastern University IT Workforce Study was funded in the period just before the economic downturn in IT. The focus of the research was increasing gender equity in IT in what was then predicted to be an expanding workforce. To some extent, technical professional job markets tend to be somewhat cyclical but the depth of the problem was unanticipated. Layoffs began in 2001 and intensified during 2003 and 2004.

Evidence of an economic recession in the high technology industries was clearly visible by late 2001. The highest unemployment rates in Massachusetts were found in the suburban communities surrounding the Route 128–Route 495 ring. This is the high technology belt surrounding the greater Boston area (Harrington, Sum, & MacCready, 2001). The same companies that offered signing bonuses, high salary offers, and augmented benefit packages to lure computer professionals as recently as 2000–2001 were beginning a pattern of layoffs that continued through 2004.[2] The IT Workforce Data Project estimated that approximately 150,000 core IT positions (computer scientists, systems analysts, software engineers and programmers) were lost in 2001 and 2002 (Ellis & Lowell, 2003). Layoffs continued through 2004 with fierce competition for every job (Gavin, 2004).

The Northeastern University IT Workforce Study did not randomly sample IT professionals who were laid off, as compared to those who were not. What we do have are descriptions of layoff experiences and effects on IT careers from the women and men who responded to our 2002 survey and from the 2004 follow-up interviews. Ninety-two people (21%) of the total survey sample of 432 experienced layoff at some point during their IT careers.

Layoff Criteria

Survey respondents were asked if they knew how decisions about layoffs were made in the organizations where they worked. In open-ended responses, a majority identified layoff criteria used by management that resulted in their job loss. Seventy-five percent of the survey sample mentioned economic factors unrelated to the quality of their job performance. Response patterns were further detailed by women and men interviewed in 2004. Among the specifically mentioned economic criteria were events such as company closure, project discontinuation, contract cancellation, division closure, and product line or project termination. Frequently, layoff criteria were related to business cost-cutting practices including mergers, reorganization and downsizing. Respondents made statements such as "The company was sold and then downsized," "The division was sold and all employees within it were terminated," "The company was bought out, reorganized, and my job was eliminated."

Factors other than economic were mentioned by the remaining 25% of the 2002 survey and explained in greater detail during the 2004 interviews.

Formal or informal seniority rules, rather than an individual's contribution to the organization in terms of productivity, were criteria mentioned by a few of the men. Internal company politics and disagreements with management were discussed by several others. The 2002 Northeastern University IT Workforce Study found virtually no difference between the percentage of women (21%) and men (23%) who experienced layoffs. During the qualitative interviews in 2004, none of the men and only a few of the women mentioned gender as a layoff criterion.

Impact of Layoffs on Information Technology Careers

2002 survey respondents were asked to describe the impact of being laid off on their subsequent IT careers. We had 35 open-ended responses in 2002, amplified by the ten qualitative interviews with people who were laid off by 2004. A few of those laid off in the years before 2000 indicated that the layoff spurred them to get better jobs. However, layoffs after 2001 were problematic and sometimes very painful for those involved.

After varying lengths of time (months to years) out of work, 26% changed the emphasis of their IT career—"from development to business," "from straight IT to liaison between IT and finance," "from software development to QA." In addition, 17% said they took positions below their skill and experience levels to secure reemployment in information technology—"no longer team a leader," "lower pay," "regression in skills." Some of these people were self-employed as "consultants," and sometimes they became "consultants" at the same companies they had worked for in the past but now without employment benefits.

Many people tried to use time out of work to acquire new IT skills. Some employers didn't want developers to take time away from deadline pressures to learn the newest technologies. So time out-of-work seemed opportune for upgrading technical skill-sets. Yet being out of work brought other difficulties. For one thing, people are no longer in position to learn on the job. Even worse, it's difficult to know how to train for which skills in a shifting IT job market. Even so, about 10% went for more training or another graduate degree. They took time out for retraining—"studying for certification exams," "taking more technical courses to be more marketable, "taught myself new languages," "went back to school to work for my PhD."

A few of our respondents spoke of the impact of layoff on career in terms the presence or absence of a "layoff stigma" when looking for reemployment. In the period before 2001, several people said that the first round of layoffs at a company may have been used for cleaning out "deadwood," or people with marginal skill-sets. So the concern about being so considered persisted for some. As the numbers of jobless professionals increased after 2001, many people, especially young people, saw layoff as less of a stigma in the job market.

Sometimes, after one or more layoffs, people left or considered leaving careers in IT (17% left IT entirely, and another 11% considered leaving). They said things such as "I used benefits after layoff to pursue a non-IT degree," "Left after third lay-off, took early retirement package," "I decided to go back to teaching," "I'm re-evaluating whether or not to stay in IT," and "I decided it wasn't worth going back and also I have two young children. After a year and a half, I'm coming to a point where I'm looking into a work position again for financial reasons, but I'm not sure I will look into IT again. I'm looking at career change again."

Impact of Tough Times on People Not Laid Off

Many of the people who retained their jobs despite the recession in information technology nonetheless felt pressured and stressed in new ways during this period. They talked about changed working conditions as the result of mergers and downsizing to increase profit margins, resulting in layoffs. They spoke of changed company culture, tighter management controls, and greater corporate focus on meeting roll-out dates than assuring the quality of products.

As further examples of how corporate culture and organizational practices changed in the years from 2002 to 2004, we quote from the interview transcripts of two women employed by the same company before and during this period. The company had been a middle-sized Boston area software company with the reputation of being a great place to work and with a female-friendly corporate culture. It was purchased by and merged with a very large international IT company. The first is from the perspective of a female software developer and technical manager, age 50, with 15 years of experience in IT. The second is from the perspective of a female software engineer, age 30, who is upwardly mobile and seeking new career opportunities.

Female, experienced, retained: "This is a large global organization where cost and profit determine everything. Things have gotten worse all over these industries, as companies worry about survival. Upper level managers set the goals and deadlines. We are all very understaffed and have far fewer resources than we need. Everyone I know in other companies who are in positions like mine are in the same situation. Upper managers can request anything they want immediately, or on very short notice. So it is impossible to control your own time. My work used to be very creative, very exciting. Not so anymore, although I do have two good projects now. We had two cycles of layoffs in the last two years. Absolutely the hardest thing I've ever had to do. Upper management told me how many people I could keep, the rest had to be laid off. I had to decide who stayed and who went. It was really terrible. The second time, I worked very, very hard and got most of the people I had to cut placed in other positions somewhere else in the company.

"Two years ago, I managed the development of one of five related products that was being produced in my department. I knew the product extremely well, and was the technical lead as well as manager. I managed five direct reports. We worked very well together in a cooperative atmosphere. We also formed close working relationships with other teams involved with our product, such as the testers, technical writers, and support personnel. We had a great deal of input in the planning process and ensured that the deadlines for our deliverables were achievable. We were very serious about putting out a quality product. Yet, at the same time we had fun. We enjoyed our jobs and enjoyed working with each other.

"I now manage five software products and have 15 direct reports. I manage both development and testing of the products. My workload as well as the workload of my direct reports more than doubled. I am also responsible for a great deal more administrative work. We use to have dedicated personnel help us with software licensing issues, support logistics, expense reporting, asset management and other administrative tasks. Most of these support jobs have been eliminated. I now put in between 55–60 hour work weeks, even more when deadlines approach. Even when on vacation, I spend between 1/4 and 1/2 of that time working so that I do not miss a deadline.

"The stress level has greatly increased. Missing a deadline can have serious consequences ranging from poor performance reviews, little to no salary increase, to separation of employment. As a consequence, product quality has decreased. Also unhealthy competition has increased. People do not share information as readily or are as willing to help others. Establishing and maintaining relationships with other teams is more difficult as most people are too busy to deal with any issues outside their immediate realm of responsibility. The perception of technical savvy, individual contribution and visibility are more highly valued than team work and cooperation. Unlike two years ago, I am no longer content with my job or the company that I work for and I am no longer proud of the work that I do."

Female, upwardly mobile, retained: "Our integration with this much larger company has had many positive impacts. Our group has grown as has our workload so I have had more opportunities to take on different roles. This has helped me to distinguish myself as a leader within my team. I have definitely been rewarded for my efforts but lately I am beginning to feel bored and frustrated in my current role. I have been told repeatedly that I have 'executive potential' but I am not getting very much feedback on how to turn that potential into the skills I need to actually be an executive. It is frustrating because I know there must be opportunities within this company for growth but it is more difficult to identify what they are or to get help finding them given the size of the company and our ever increasing workload. My previous job was with a small company compared to this one so it was much easier to keep up with what was going on within it and it seemed easier to identify new opportunities. I also think there was more time available to focus on career growth at the small software company. The good news is that I recently started working with a mentor through a leadership development program so I am hoping he will be able to help me figure out my next move."

Outsourcing

An increasing trend for firms to send core IT jobs (computer scientists, systems analysts, software engineers, and programmers) overseas accompanied layoffs, mergers, and downsizing in the early years of the twenty-first century. Outsourcing of IT work to locations in other countries is rising rapidly; ... About 150,000 of these positions were lost in 2001 and 2002, almost two thirds of them in programming (Ellis & Lowell, 2003). Estimates of the extent of off-shoring vary, as do forecasts and predictions. Forrester Research forecasts that, at the present rate of growth, the number of jobs moved overseas will be 472,000 by 2015 (Konrad, 2003). Gartner, Inc., an IT research firm, describes outsourcing as the fastest growing segment in the IT industry, including companies such as Apple, Motorola, EDS, IBM, Hewlett Packard, Microsoft, Oracle, and Sun Microsystems (Ellis & Lowell, 2003). Bardhan and Kroll (2003) analyzed US Bureau of Labor Statistics data to show that from the first economic quarter 2001 through the second quarter 2003 (27 months), employment in computer systems design and related professional positions fell from 1,341,200 to 1,148,100, a decline of 15.5%. The US government does not require firms to report the numbers and extent of jobs sent overseas, and accurate data do not exist.

As IT companies tried to cut costs and increase profits, they were attracted by the comparatively low salaries paid to IT professionals overseas. In 2002, the average annual salary for a systems programmer in the US was $63,331, compared with $5,880 in India, $5,000–$7,500 in the Russian Federation, $8,982 in China, and $7,200 in Malaysia (CIO Magazine, 2003). In addition to cost advantages, Bardhan and Kroll (2003) describe several other factors enabling the outsourcing trend: the use of the English language as the accepted standard in education and business, a time differential created by geographic location resulting in the capacity for 24/7 service and overnight turn-around time, and the availability of an abundant supply of young and well-educated technical professionals.

At the same time that increasing chunks of IT work are being shipped out, large numbers of foreign "specialized knowledge" workers are being moved into the US economy. In the aftermath of September 11, 2001, the number of new H-IB visa applications approved decreased by 68% (from 115,800 before fiscal year 2001 to 36,500 in fiscal year 2002) (Office of Immigration Statistics, 2003). However, the numbers of foreign technical professionals doing IT work in the US remained high. Globalization trends brought large numbers of foreign "high tech specialists" into the US to train for managerial and technical positions in the global economy on temporary work visas (NAFTA (North American Free Trade Agreement) authorized L-1 visas). L-1 visas were intended to help multinational corporations by allowing for the transfer of managers for up to seven years and for "specialized knowledge" workers for up to five years. L-1 visas are attractive to employers because they have no caps and no requirements to match salaries to local prevailing wages. The number of L-1 visas issued to foreigners increased from 70,000 in 1996 to 120,000 in 2002 (Ellis & Lowell, 2003).

2003 research conducted by the Fisher Center at University of California at Berkeley reported a growing concern in many sectors that the US could be experiencing the "largest out-migration of nonmanufacturing jobs in the history of the US economy" (Bardhan & Kroll, 2003). Firms announced layoffs in the US at almost the same time as they announced 25,000 to 30,000 jobs in Indian newspapers and business journals for the month of July, 2003.

The Northeastern University Information Technology Workforce Study does not have a random sample of views and opinions about the issue of outsourcing. The 2002 survey did not include questions about the subject. However, we do have substantial qualitative data. During the 2004 follow-up interviews, respondents were asked several questions about job-related feelings and experiences. Thirty percent (13 of the 44 people interviewed) voluntarily introduced "outsourcing," usually as part of an open-ended response to questions about career expectations, achievement of success, feelings of satisfaction, and others.

Female, laid off twice: "They were starting to outsource QA. I actually had a wonderful two-week trip to Singapore to train people to do my job. So I had been testing Powerbuilder, and then all of the Powerbuilder testing went overseas; it was done from an office in Singapore, but the testers were actually in India."

Female, laid off: "The company has changed now with off-shoring and the devaluing of the IT skills, and now a whole lot of people are just worried about survival....The off-shoring thing really upsets me. I don't think we're addressing it. I think it's becoming a trend. I think we are forgetting what's going to happen because there are fewer knowledge workers here in this country. What I worry about is, what we are going to evolve into?"

Female, not laid off: "Everything that I worked so hard for could be taken away from me very quickly because of the economy and outsourcing. A lot of groups are being outsourced in support. We are all right now, but I feel like it is only a matter of time before I lose my job."

Female, not laid off: "I went on a site visit to Mexico. All these people were employed, very happy, making a good wage. The people we contracted with that ran it were two men from Utah and this was their mission. to bring jobs to underemployed and impoverished populations. They had set up in Mexico and these were people who had a clean environment to work in, were treated well, were well paid, well respected, set hours. So that was kind of nice."

In recognition of the importance of outsourcing to US high tech firms, the Northeastern University Master of Science in Information Systems (MSIS) program offered a new course in Fall 2004, team taught by faculty of the College of Business Administration, Global Outsourcing Technology. The course description is quoted below.

> Today, large numbers of white collar and highly technical jobs, including software development and research activities, are increasingly being performed offshore. This practice could become even more pervasive and perhaps a standard feature of all business in the US. This course examines the critical issues in global outsourcing of technology—why outsource, what can be outsourced, criteria for identifying elements for outsourcing, organizing for outsourcing, managing the outsourcing operation and finally the impact of outsourcing on the image of a US firm and how to manage it.

It is ironic that the program that trained the people classified in our sample as on the Transitional pathway is now teaching students how to survive in a corporate environment where the technical work that once brought them success and satisfaction is moving overseas. One guest lecturer in this course, a senior vice president from a major Boston area financial institution, objected to the word outsourcing in the course title. "We call it 'Global Resource Management,'" he said.

Conclusions and Implications

The varied backgrounds of IT professionals prompted Northeastern University IT Workforce Study researchers to seek a stronger indicator of IT career pathway than formal education alone. The Multiple Pathways Typology is a composite of several variables: level of education, field of degree or degrees, career history, and IT career decision points. The constructed pathways— Traditional, Transitional and Self-directed—provide good descriptions of the types of people in the IT workforce and how they got there. The application of the typology to the survey findings and the qualitative interview transcripts enhanced our understanding of experience in technical skill-set areas, levels of job satisfaction, and salary differentials. It is helpful to cluster several relevant variables into a single indicator when studying emergent and rapidly expanding workforce sectors. This type of analysis will become increasingly important as new fields emerge in the postmodern society of the twenty-first century.

Northeastern University IT Workforce Study research findings must be viewed within the context of the explosive growth in the high technology and computer applications industries during the last generation of the twentieth century. Many respondents were upwardly mobile and took advantage of the expanding job opportunity structure for IT professionals. Many moved up into professional IT positions and then moved up again during the course of their careers into higher level supervisory and technical content positions, and at higher salaries. The economic bubble burst for these industries by 2002, but not before large numbers of women were actively recruited and welcomed into all levels of professional employment in IT.

In the boom years, the IT workforce appeared as an open frontier of professional job opportunities and attracted people with technical and nontechnical educational and occupational backgrounds. It attracted people directly from college. It attracted people whose first post college job was not leading to an interesting career path, even some who were not enjoying entry-level jobs in science and engineering. It attracted dissatisfied professionals at midcareer looking for jobs with better pay and challenging experiences.

While men took advantage of the expanding IT job market, prospects were particularly attractive to women with the ability but not the desire to pursue technical careers previously. The market attracted women experiencing burnout in the traditionally female fields of nursing and teaching. It attracted single women and single moms who sought the means of supporting themselves and their children. Obviously, a prime requisite for attracting women to careers in information technology is simply an abundance of jobs.

The presence of greater numbers of women in many computer companies and computer applications organizations influenced corporate culture and working conditions. This is indicated by the lack of differences between the sexes in responses to most work-related items. As noted throughout this chapter, women and men expressed the same high levels of job satisfaction. Women and men described job satisfaction to the same degree and in the same affective terms: love for work, personal happiness, and feelings of accomplishment. Also considered important to both sexes equally are quality of work environment and the ability to balance work and family responsibilities.

For the most part, women and men performed the same kinds of tasks at work. We found the same percentage of men and women in high technical content positions, and a lower percentage of women than men in low technical content positions. Overall, the salaries of men are somewhat higher than the salaries of women, but this depends on career pathway. Men and women on the Traditional pathway account for all of the measured difference. There are no differences between the salaries of women and men on the Transitional and Self-directed pathways.

All of the men and most of the women said that gender did not influence their IT career development. A few women said that females still had to "prove themselves" in the technical workplace, and a few said that mothers were treated differently by employers. Some study respondents had 15 years of experience in the IT workforce and noted that conditions for women were improving.

It's difficult to determine the extent to which gains made by women in the IT workforce prior to 2002 persisted through tough times. It does not appear that female IT professionals were more impacted by layoffs, mergers, downsizing, and outsourcing than males. Once conditions and cultural expectations shift, they are not usually reversed. However, the disappearance of an open IT opportunity structure after 2002 means that the Transitional and Self-directed pathways used by so many women to enter IT were virtually cut off. People will not change careers and train for jobs that do not exist. There are few openings into which people can slide. The Traditional pathway has reemerged as the route to high technical content positions. Companies are now hiring technical professionals and consultants with training and experience in specific niche areas. There are also openings for computer scientists with PhD degrees to design new generations of programs and products. This means that efforts to increase the numbers and percentages of women in the IT workforce are once again dependent on the progress made in the precollege and college years.

The Northeastern University IT Workforce Study provided evidence that IT organizations are good places for women to work. These are places where technical skills and communication skills are equally important for men and women. Requisite conditions for attaining gender equity in any company include these goals: (1) the same proportion of women and men hold high positions in the organizational structure, and (2) the same proportion of women and men receive the highest financial rewards. For the most part, these conditions were met within the large nonprofit healthcare organization that participated fully in this research. An atypical set of circumstances combined to help this organization approach gender equity. Half of the IT professionals are female. Equity in terms of numbers influences corporate culture. Both men and women talked about the importance of family-friendly policies, good benefits, and flex-time. There are high percentages of women in project management and corporate management positions. The Chief Information Officer (CIO) is a female with a stay-at-home husband. She explained how she uses the annual merit and salary review to make sure that salary scales are in fact comparable for women and men. These conditions are not easily met in higher pressure for-profit organizations. However, we might look to information technology to model gender equity in the postmodern workplace of the twenty-first century.

Acknowledgments

This study was funded by the National Science Foundation (0119839) and was conducted by the Northeastern University Women's Project team and Campbell–Kibler Associates, Inc. Assisting Dr. Paula G. Leventman, Principal Investigator, at Northeastern University, were research associates Meghan K. Finley (PhD candidate) and Ellie Tetreault-Mah (MSIS). Dr. Patricia B. Campbell and Lesley K. Perlman of Campbell–Kibler Associates, Inc. conducted an advanced quantitative analysis of the survey data.

References

Bardhan, A. D., & Kroll, C. A. (2003, November 2). *The new wave of outsourcing* (Fisher Center Research Report No. 1103). Berkeley, CA: University of California at Berkeley, Fisher Center for Real Estate & Urban Economics. Retrieved September 14, 2006, from http://repositories.cdlib.org/iber/fcreue/reports/1103

Bartley, S. R., & Kunda, G. (2004). *Gurus, hired guns, and warm bodies: Itinerant experts in a knowledge economy.* Princeton, NJ: Princeton University Press.

Brown, C. D. (1993, December). Male/female mentoring: Turning potential risks into rewards. *IEEE Transactions on Professional Communication, 36*(4), 197–200.

Bureau of Labor Statistics (2003). *The 2002-2003 occupational outlook handbook*. Washington, DC: US Department of Labor.

Bureau of Labor Statistics (2004). The 2003-2004 *occupational outlook handbook*. Washington, DC: US Department of Labor.

Caravalho, G., & Maus, T. (1996). Mentoring: Philosophy and practice. *Public Management, 78*(6), 17–20.

Catalyst, Inc. (2001). Leadership careers in high tech: Wired for success. New York: Author.

CIO Magazine. (2003, April 28). Salary comparison. *Computerworld*. Retrieved September 14, 2006, from http://www.computerworld.com/managementtopics/outsourcing/story/0,10801,80675,00.html

Commission on Professionals in Science and Technology (2002). *Professional women and minorities: A total human resource data compendium*. Washington, DC: Commission on Professionals in Science and Technology

Ellis, R., & Lowell, L. (2003, September). *The outlook in 2003 for information technology workers in the USA*. Paper presented at a Congressional "Breakfast Bytes" briefing, Capitol Hill, Washington, DC. Retrieved September 14, 2006, from http://www.international.ucla.edu/cms/files/lowell-ITrpt.pdf

Garner, S. N. (1994, Spring/Summer). Mentoring lessons. *Women's Studies Quarterly, 22*, 6–13.

Gavin, R. (2004, March 20). Job losses mount in bay state: Payrolls shed 9,500 in Feb. as Mass. lags US. *The Boston Globe*, pp. A1, A4.

Harrington, P. E., Sum, A. M., & MacCready, R. (2001, December 13). *Rising unemployment and worker dislocation during the current economic recession in Massachusetts*. Boston, MA: Northeastern University, Center for Labor Market Studies. Retrieved September 13, 2006, from http://www.nupr.neu.edu/12-01/recession.pdf#search=%22Rising%20Unemployment%20and%20Worker%20Dislocation%20During%20the%20Current%20Economic%20Recession%09in%20Massachusetts%22

Joy, B., & Kennedy, K. (1999, February). *Information technology research investing in our future* (US President's Information Technology Advisory Committee Report to the President). Darby, PA: DIANE Publishing.

Kirby, C. (2003, July 30). More and more tech jobs moving overseas consultant calls trend permanent, irreversible. *San Francisco Chronicle*, B1. Retrieved September 14, 2006, from http://www.sfgate.com/cgi-bin/article.cgi?f=/c/a/2003/07/30/BU272273.DTL

Konrad, R. (2003, July 11). Export of core tech jobs could imperil the American programmer. CRN. Retrieved September 14, 2006, from http://www.crn.com/sections/breakingnews/dailyarchives.jhtml?articleId=18839547

Leventman, P. G. (1981). *Professionals out of work*. New York: The Free Press.

National Science Board (2002). *Science and engineering indicators—2002* (NSB-02-01). Arlington, VA: National Science Foundation, Division of Science Resources Statistics. Retrieved September 14, 2006, from http://www.nsf.gov/statistics/seind02/

Office of Immigration Statistics. (2003, September). *Characteristics of specialty occupation workers (H-1B): Fiscal Year 2002*. Washington, DC: US Department of Homeland Security. Retrieved September 14, 2006, from http://www.uscis. gov/graphics/aboutus/repsstudies/h1b/FY2002Charact.pdf

US Census Bureau. (1997). Section 13.Labor force, employment, and earnings. *The 1997 statistical abstract of the United States*. Retrieved September 14, 2006, from http://www.census.gov/prod/3/97pubs/97statab/labor.pdf

US Department of Commerce (2003, April). *Education and training for the information technology workforce* (Report to Congress from the Secretary of Commerce). Retrieved September 14, 2006, from http://www.technology.gov/ reports/ITWorkForce/ITWF2003.pdf

Vallone, T. J., & Smith, C. (1996, May). *Mentoring: Providing profession and organizational benefits*. Paper presented at the Society for Technical Communication Annual Conference, Arlington, VA.

Wadia-Fascetti, S., & Leventman, P. G. (2000). E-mentoring: A longitudinal approach to mentoring relationships for women pursuing technical careers. *Journal of Engineering Education*, *89*(3), 295–296.

Notes

1. The total 2002 Northeastern University IT Workforce Study survey sample consisted of 432 IT professionals, 289 women and 143 men. There was sufficient data from the responses of 404 for classification into career pathways. A higher percentage of men (45%) than women (25%) are classified as Traditional. A higher percentage of women (46%) than men (19%) are classified as Transitional. A higher percentage of men (36%) than women (29%) are classified as Self-directed. These numbers reflect a sampling bias toward MSIS women. Although there were always some male students in MSIS program, it was specifically designed to help women change careers. Many more women than men responded to the 2002 survey, and many more women than men agreed to be contacted for follow-up interviews. MSIS alumni without technical bachelor's degrees were classified as Transitional. MSIS alumni with technical bachelor's degrees were classified as Traditional. In 2004, we conducted a total of 44 complete face-to-face interviews with 29 women and 15 men. Twenty-five percent of the qualitative transcripts were of people classified as Traditional (five women and six men); 45% were of people classified as Transitional (15 women and five men); and 30% were of people classified as Self-directed (seven women and six men).

2. During the first five years of the twenty-first century, layoffs and outsourcing characterized the US IT job market. In these same years, not surprisingly and amidst a complex of social and cultural factors, indicators showed decreased numbers of women and men entering Traditional pathways toward careers in science, engineering, and IT. By 2005, there were widespread concerns about the eroding competitive position of the US in the increasingly knowledge intensive global economy, supported by advancing information technologies. Alarm bells were sounded by the highly touted report *Rising above the Gathering Storm: Energizing and Employing America for a Brighter Economic Future*, The National Academies Press, 2006. Once again, another cycle in US technical professional job markets appears to be underway, albeit with more restraint and less optimism than those in earlier decades.

Chapter 11

Barriers to Women in Science

A Cautionary Tale for the Information Technology Community

Lesley Warner and Judith Wooller

Abstract

In Australia Equal Employment Opportunity for Women legislation was proclaimed in 1986. Women in science and academia waited hopefully for improvements in career opportunities that did not appear. Although more girls than boys, across the developed world, complete high school and more women than men undertake undergraduate degree programs, women and men scientists still do not achieve equivalent successes in their career paths. Since that time, while governments in North America and Europe have been concerned about full work force participation, the Australian Government has not. In this presentation we use data from Europe, the United Kingdom, North America, and Australia to support our qualitative survey of the experiences of a group of North American women scientists that illustrate influences on their career development. We found no significant improvements in the employment patterns of women over the last 15 years. The barriers to opportunity for women continue to include elements of covert discrimination at personal and institutional levels as well as widespread systematic discrimination. Family relationships and life/work balance concerns remain problematic for women. The information technology industry needs to be aware of the need to support girls and women beyond higher education and into the work place.

Introduction

In Australia in the 1960s and 1970s young women had to be incredibly naive, or lucky, or thick-skinned, or stubborn, or a combination of all four to carve out a career in science. By the early 1980s the resurgent women's movement had raised sufficiently the consciousness of politicians and managers alike for them to accept the principles of gender equality in the work place and to begin preparing for changes in the work place. The Affirmative

Action (Equal Employment Opportunity for Women) Act was proclaimed in the Australian Parliament in 1986. At Central Queensland University, where one of us had gained a tenured position ten years after completing a PhD, we developed a half-day workshop called *The Greater Half*. This workshop contained segments of information and role-playing to allow all staff to explore the implications of the legislation and what it would mean for gender balance in the academic community. At this time the strategies deemed most useful to support women through the changing work place environment were focussed around role modelling and mentoring. Women were optimistic that there would be change.

The Decade 1986–1996

In the years that followed, considerable progress was made but there was still a long way to go. Data from the Australian Bureau of Statistics for 1994, for example, showed that in the Commonwealth Science and Industrial Research Organization (CSIRO) none of 42 Division Chiefs were female. In the University sector only 7% of full professors were female although the majority (53.1%) of undergraduate enrollments in science were female.

The assumption was that increased participation rates at the undergraduate level would automatically translate into improved career paths as the larger cohorts of female students moved into the work force. Again we sat back and waited for the career benefits to flow. Strangely, however, whenever and wherever participation rates were examined, the increased proportion of women enrolled in science and engineering disciplines in higher education was not translating into increased participation at higher levels along the career paths of academia and industry.

Researchers such as Eileen Byrne (1993), however, had warned that participation rates would not improve until critical mass (the numbers of women entering careers in science being sufficient for it to be considered a normal career option) was reached. She also argued that systemic and political changes in the workplace were needed to support women in academia in general and science in particular. She further argued against models that blamed the victims, in these circumstances women, for their lack of progress and for models that focused on systemic discrimination. That is that any discrimination against women continuing to occur was, among other things, a result of the differential application of the principles of merit by which university and other appointments were made.

By 1996, ten years after the Affirmative Action (Equal Employment Opportunity for Women) Act was proclaimed, the expectations of women were still optimistic. We felt that significant change must have begun, and it was just a matter of collecting the data to show the improved participation rates at senior levels. Such studies as were available, however, did not support an optimistic outlook. Castleman, Allen, Bastalich, and Wright (1995), for example, reported the pace of change so slow as to be imperceptible, with instances of direct and indirect discrimination being reported by managers. Women were seen as being disadvantaged because they were less likely to be able to meet apparently neutral, but actually gender-biased selection criteria for promotion and appointment. Their analysis of higher education was that men were more likely to secure rewards from the system and to consolidate their position over time (Castleman et al.). Importantly, they noted that, if family responsibilities were significant factors affecting women's status in higher education, then they needed to be addressed by policies that were consistent with Australia's commitment to The International Labor Organization's Convention 156 (Castleman et al.). Research by the Cross University Research in Engineering and Science Group (1996), based in the US, showed far too many women are in entry level positions: far too few are in the most highly compensated and powerful ranks. Warner (1998) noted that we still did not understand what may or may not have been effective equity policies and programs, although it was becoming apparent that systemic change was needed.

Into the New Millennium 1998–2004

By the end of the century, governments in the developed world had begun to consider their workforce needs for the new millennium. Such considerations were informed by the effects of declining birth rates in most developed countries, coupled with the need for increasing available expertise in science and technology (S&T). This is in the context of society's increasing dependence on S&T, reflecting the need to balance future workforce demands with future supply. Consequently, significant studies were commissioned to obtain both statistical and qualitative data on education, training, and career paths in the sciences and technologies. Particular emphasis in these studies was based on gender balance and the outcomes for women, not only because of considerations of equity for all but also because of the probable need to increase the total of pool scientists, engineers, and technologists available in the workplace.

Simultaneously the trend (illustrated here in the Australian context) was towards the further compounding factors of declining higher education enrolments in science nationwide (Dobson, 2003) such that academic staffing entitlements in science faculties either stabilized or decreased. In small regional universities, for example, those universities serving communities outside the influence of the state and commonwealth capital cities, the decline has been more problematic. Central Queensland University is one such regional institution. With campuses in rural towns across Queensland, separated by 300–400 kilometers, our university provides educational opportunities to both on-campus and external students. The number of students enrolled in the sciences and engineering has continued to decline over the past ten years, although the trend for a greater proportion of female students has reflected the national trend. The number of academic staff has declined, in parallel with the falling demand, but the proportion of female staff has also declined during this period.

The effects of these trends—declining interest in science overall but a proportionate increase in female participation at the undergraduate level and a lack of women pursuing careers in science after graduation—have been noted world wide, as the demand for trained scientists and technologists continued to increase (see for example European Commission, 2000; Sears, 2003). This paradox has fostered the need for workforce planners to understand why some women do not continue beyond their undergraduate science experience and what happens to those who do. Consequently, an important series of in-depth studies have emerged, from a variety of sources, to describe unequivocally the circumstances of woman training for or pursuing a career in S&T; for example, national analyses from the US (Nelson & Rogers, 2004; Trower & Bleak, 2004), the UK (Greenfield, 2002), Australia (Dobson, 2003), and the European Union (European Commission, 2000, 2003) have provided the hard data on women's participation, highlighting the consequences of women's exclusion. Past gains have been reported and present barriers documented.

An example of such data extracted from *Set Fair* (Greenfield, 2002, p. 64) is summarized in Table 1. The message is clear and unequivocal. Even in the biological sciences, where women's enrollments at PhD level were close to 50% of the total by 1996, no improvement at higher levels in the career path had been achieved. A similar pattern, described as a scissors diagram, based on aggregated data from 13 countries of the European Union in 1999, has been demonstrated (Koch-Miramond, 2003). In this case women represented nearly 50% of the PhD students and about 12% of the full professors.

Further, in an age-matched study, the careers of a group of 1088 senior Italian scientists (78% male, 22% female) were monitored from 1988. It was found that 26% of the men but only 12.8% of the women made it through to senior positions and that the disparity between the sexes was greater the higher the level achieved (European Commission, 2000). This study in particular highlights the failure of women to progress up the career ladder in the same proportions as men.

Similarly, concerns about workplace culture were being expressed. Between 1995 and 1999 women faculty in science at the Massachusetts

Table 1. Percentage comparison of the attrition rates for men and women along career paths in the biosciences in the United Kingdom in 1996 and 2000. Source: Greenfield, 2002.

	1996		2000	
	Men	Women	Men	Women
PhD students	58%	42%	52%	48%
Researchers	58%	42%	55%	45%
Lecturers	75%	25%	70%	30%
Senior researchers/lecturers	88%	12%	85%	15%
Professors	92%	8%	92%	8%

Institute of Technology (MIT) comprehensively documented details of the overt and covert discrimination to which they were subjected. Their study was acknowledged and then responded to by the dean of the School of Science. He commented that, although the discrimination experienced by the women was unconscious and unknowing, it did nevertheless lead to real consequences for them. Further, the chair of the MIT faculty responded that in the 1990s gender discrimination was subtle and pervasive, stemming largely from ways of thinking that had been socialized into men and women alike.

Unfortunately these scenarios, resulting in women's failure to progress along career paths, have been neither recognized nor understood by the Australian government. Their policies appear to be predicated on the assumption that, since women are participating equally in higher education, nothing more needs to be done.

2004–2005

In 2004 we decided to go beyond watching and lamenting this lack of progress of women in science and to explore the reality for women working as scientists in the new millennium. In the absence of current documented information on Australian women's career paths and the lack of local women scientists, and given previous interview data collected in 1996 (Warner, 1998), a group of 12 women scientists, at all levels along the career path and predominately from the University of Colorado, were interviewed in depth. The aim was to determine what, if any, were the key factors that shaped their careers. The group included women from the University of Colorado, Boulder Campus, who had been interviewed in 1996 (Warner), as well as other North American women scientists. A qualitative methodology, a semistructured interview technique using open-ended questions, was used. This technique was selected because of the nature of the topic, the lived world of the subjects, and their relation to it (Kvale, 1996). This methodology gave the interviewer the tools to reveal the women's perceptions of their career pathways and to try to determine the causal factors that were molding women's career choices, resulting in some instances in the loss of senior women from science. Each of the 12 women interviewed was asked the same questions, but not always in the same order (Morse & Richards, 2002), in a casual context so that the interviewer could facilitate rather than direct the responses. For the women who had been interviewed in 1996 the focus of the questions was the continuing progression, or lack of it, in their own careers during the previous eight years, and to examine their perceptions of any change.

Overall the questions to this new cohort were informed by the themes that arose from the earlier interview set, and the set of open-ended questions was designed to cover the themes of interest. Although each of the participants was asked the same questions, the order of the questioning reflected the flow of the participant responses. The interviewer took on the role of facilitator, not director, gently encouraging the women and probing them to provide in-depth responses. This approach is deemed appropriate when the interviewer is aware of the issues that could arise during the interview (Morse & Richards, 2002).

The completed case study does not claim to be universal, but rather a snapshot in time. More comprehensive reports of the study are being prepared, with this chapter focusing only on those aspects emerging from our analysis of the interviews that seem relevant to the theme of career and professional development for women in information technology.

Case Study Findings

During analysis two relevant themes predominated: problems with life/work balance, especially in relation to child bearing and child rearing, and institutional culture.

Life/Work Balance

Some of the 12 women interviewed had already made life/work decisions predicated on their needs, wants, and aspirations, taking into account the expectations of their partners and employers. Those women who wished to have children needed a supportive partner, a sympathetic supervisor, and a flexible work environment. If even one of these was missing, the career path became difficult to negotiate. As one of the women said, "The life/work balance is all wrong for women." For the younger women the major concern was when or whether to have children. If they did opt for children, what effect would that have on their careers? Men do not have to make these decisions. Comments such as "women with children are seen as a liability, likely to be unreliable" make it difficult for women to fulfill their biologically determined role of reproducing the species. More than one of the women interviewed commented that "if a man has a family he is seen as stable and an asset to the work team and so he does not suffer." Paradoxically, then, having children is an asset for male and a liability for female scientists. Family planning for women in science is fraught with questions about making satisfactory child care arrangements that will allow at least some opportunity to maintain their professional standing in their discipline.

Institutional Culture

Most of the twelve women had stayed on their career path because of their love of science rather than because of workplace satisfaction. For them, this was not a positive environment, being at best neutral, at worst negative. Three of the women interviewed were no longer in mainstream science; one indicated that she regretted her choice of an academic career in science; two were in the process of negotiating solutions to balancing their career imperatives and family aspirations; three had achieved mid-career success; and three mature scientists had had outstanding careers in senior management, research, and academia. As these women reflected on their life experiences as scientists, all were concerned about the difficulty of career pathways for women in science. Most reported that while there was little or no overt discrimination, they had to work harder than men to prove their worth, as is documented in the EU (European Commission, 2003), and UK (Greenfield, 2002) reports. As one woman suggested, "It is not good enough that only good women get on and develop satisfactory careers but average women should have the same chances as average men." While they acknowledged that the University of Colorado was perceived to be more politically sensitive than most other institutions, in reality little had changed since 1996. Women scientists still were forced to come to terms with the predominantly masculine institutional culture, regardless of the university or research facility they worked in. As Castleman et al. (1995, p. 59) noted in the Australian context, "What's blocking them? They're not men." Even at MIT where the reforms suggested in the 1999 report had been implemented, covert discrimination was still a problem, according to one of the senior women interviewed. While more female appointments had been made and policy changes had been implemented, these had not changed the basic culture. As found at MIT (1999) and by Trower & Bleak (2004), the academic workplace in the US (and we would argue in other countries) is neither as inviting to or as supportive of women as it is of

men. Another of the women interviewed said that young women notic-
ing the lack of women pursuing careers in science, as well as the covert
discrimination experienced by those women who do enter science, may
consequently make career choices other than science.

Discussion

It is not surprising that career paths for women continue to be problematic.
In Australia our peak research organization, the CSIRO, has let its equity
programs decline since the 1980s. This is despite only a marginal improvement of from 7% to 13% of senior managerial positions (three chiefs of
division and three managers) being held by women (Foley, 2005). Further, Foley writes, "In government research laboratories and in the minds
of science leaders, the paucity of women in science has disappeared off
the radar" (p. 43). Consequently, laboratories with few women miss out
on their talent and diversity (Browne, 2004) and on their opportunity to
develop a cooperative and collaborative culture (Foley). Since teamwork is
a prerequisite for addressing national priorities and big goals for science in
Australia, Australia is in a perilous situation (Foley).

Ferguson (2002) found that, given the present rate of change across all
disciplines in Australian universities, it would take at least 33 years before
women gain equality of representation with men at appointment levels D
and E (associate professor and professor). She further noted that given the
slowing growth in the sector, this was an optimistic appraisal. For the disciplines of the sciences, with the original imbalance even more marked, and
the slowdown in the sector greater, Ferguson's appraisal is even more optimistic than for academia in general. In the EU there appears to be no particular bias towards a more inclusive, gender-balanced S&T culture in any
single country but rather considerable variation across the member states.
An examination of "She Figures 2003" would suggest, however, that Ger-
man women were overall the most disadvantaged (see for example European Commission, 2003, p 29). Calculations by Marschke and others from
the University of Colorado (unpublished observations) suggest that unless
positive and radical interventions are undertaken, faculty populations will
never achieve more than the present proportions of female PhD graduates
(37% in their model), and that would take at least 93 years.

These analyses support both the qualitative information we gathered
from the women we interviewed, as well as our own perceptions from the
literature and our home institution of the present circumstances.

In Australia the situation is exacerbated by the present political climate.
The key goal areas of the Office of Status of Women (2003) do not include

any components related to equity of participation in science and technology. Recommendations aimed at changing Australian institutional cultures, in a report commissioned by the Department of Employment Education and Training (Burton, 1997), have not been implemented. Chesterman, Ross-Smith, and Petess (2004), in exploring whether the dominance of men and masculinism in organizations is particularly resistant to change in the Australian university sector, found that some transformation of cultures had taken place. This had occurred where there was support from male chief executives and where there were already women in senior positions. They also reported ambiguities in attitudes, however, especially relating to the acceptance of women at more senior levels. Some men were described as feeling threatened by capable women rather then accepting or valuing their contributions. Women are judged more harshly because they are not seen as legitimate leaders. One woman commented: "You have to assert your authority. You are not given authority. You had to take it. Men are given it. It's a very significant difference" (Chesterman et al., p. 11). And again some senior men denigrated women's capacities by suggesting that "women favor soft, fluffy, cuddly decision-making" (Chesterman et al., p. 9). Chesterman et al. concluded that we are in a critical time in relation to gender and the university culture.

Our analysis therefore is that the political climate in Australia remains unsympathetic. and consequently institutional change is unlikely to happen any time soon. In the EU and the UK ambitious agendas to facilitate change have been put forward, although there is no evidence to suggest that they are being implemented or that the situation for women is improving. In the US the issues have been analyzed; but strategies to facilitate change, where promulgated, have either been implemented in a fragmented, case-by-case basis (MIT, 1999; Trower & Bleak, 2004) or disregarded.

To put it succinctly, institutions need to change hiring and work practices (Nelson & Rogers, 2004). Because, as Byrne (1993, p. 6) wrote, "the problem with girls and women is boys and men"; and until the powerful men who dominate science are convinced that it is necessary to change, it will not happen. As one very successful senior Australian academic said, in commenting on the glass ceiling between women and career success, "Women's feet are firmly stuck to the higher education floor, let alone reach the ceiling. When they do reach it, it remains thick enough to hurt your head when you bump against it" (Egron-Polak, 2003, p. 3).

Moreover the culture of "blame the victim" as described by authors such as Byrne (1993) still seems to be pervasive. In particular women seem to be being blamed for wanting to have children as well as an intellectually satisfying career in science. As long as the biological differences of being genetically female continue to be translated as biological differences in intellectual capacity—as happened in the context of a Harvard president's conference address in 2005—then the potential for change remains limited.

Conclusions

The data unequivocally demonstrate that women continue to be disadvantaged in developing career paths in S&T, despite the achievement of critical mass in some disciplines. The pace of change is so slow as to be ineffective. The reasons for this are known. The solutions are, for the most part, outside the control of women. There is no reason to suppose that the problems for women who choose careers in IT are any different. They too have to contend with the culture of the workplace they have chosen and juggle as best they can the conflicting demands of family, child care, and a life outside the demands of IT. It is necessary to look beyond the need to encourage girls into continuing with computer and IT studies in high school and beyond the need to support girls in their higher education choices that will lead to careers in IT and to be concerned about the need for change within the industry itself. Such change will allow women to make choices about their careers without denying them equality of opportunity.

References

Browne, J. (2004, October 2). It's a woman's world. *New Scientist, 2467,* 42–45. Retrieved September 13, 2006, from http://www.newscientist.com/article/mg18424676.400-its-a-womans-world.html9/

Burton, C. (1997). Gender equity in Australian university staffing. Canberra, Australia: Department of Employment Education Training and Youth Affairs.

Byrne, E. M. (1993). *Women and science: The snark syndrome.* London: The Falmer Press.

Castleman, T., Allen, M., Bastalich, W., & Wright, P. (1995). *Limited access: women's disadvantage in higher education employment.* Melbourne, Australia: National Tertiary Education Union.

Chesterman, C., Ross-Smith, A., & Peters, M. (2004). Changing the landscape? Women in academic leadership in Australia. *McGill Journal of Education, Fall,* 2004. Retrieved September 13, 2006, from http://www.uts.edu.au/oth/wexdev/pdfs/changing_the_landscape.pdf

Cross University Research in Engineering and Science Group (1996). *The equity agenda: Women in science, mathematics and engineering.* Ann Arbor, MI: University of Michigan.

Dobson, I. R. (2003). Science at the crossroads? A study of trends in university science from Dawkins to now 1989–2002. Clayton, Vic: Monash University.

Ergon-Polak, E. (2003, October 20-24). *Addressing the gender divide*. Paper presented at Securing the Future for International Education: Managing Growth and Diversity, the 17th IDP Australian International Education Conference, Melbourne, Australia.

European Commission. (2000). *Science policies in the European Union: Promoting excellence through mainstreaming gender equity*. Belgium: Office for Official Publications of the European Communities.

European Commission. (2003). *She figures 2003: Women and science statistics and indicators*. Belgium: Office for Official Publications of the European Communities.

Ferguson, K. (2002). *Locating women in the higher education sector*. Retrieved September 13, 2006, from http://www.avcc.edu.au

Foley, C. (2005, March). Science needs the female factor. *Australian Science, 43*.

Greenfield, B. S. (2002). *Set fair: A report on women in science, engineering, and technology*. London, UK: Department of Trade and Industry.

Koch-Miramond, L. (2003). Women and science: Moving away from discrimination in Europe. *Euroscience News, 24*, 4-5.

Kvale, S. (1996). Interviews: An introduction to qualitative research interviewing. London: Sage Publications.

Morse, J. M., & Richards L. (2002). *Read me first for a user's guide to qualitative methods*. London: Sage Publications.

Nelson, D. J., & Rogers, D. C. (2004). *A national analysis of diversity in science and engineering faculties at research universities*. Retrieved September 13, 2006, from http://www.now.org/issues/diverse/diversity-report.pdf

Office of Status of Women. (2003). *Women 2003*. Canberra, Australia: Department of Prime Minister and Cabinet.

Trower, A., & Bleak, J. L. (2004). Gender: Statistical report. *The study of new scholars: Tenure-track faculty job satisfaction survey*. Harvard Graduate School of Education. Cambridge, MA. Retrieved September 13, 2006, from http://www.gse.harvard.edu/~newscholars/newscholars/downloads/genderreport.pdf

Warner, L. (1998). Role models, mentors and sheer perseverance: Careers for women in science. *WISENET Journal, 46*, 3–6. Retrieved September 13, 2006, from http://www.wisenet-australia.org/ISSUE46/mentors.htm

Part V

Conclusion

Refocusing Our Lens to Reconfigure the Firewall

Peggy S. Meszaros, Elizabeth G. Creamer, Carol J. Burger, and Anne Laughlin

The primary goals of this book, as stated in the introduction, were to synthesize key research findings and conference discussions that cross the secondary, post-secondary, and professional settings in different countries; disseminate results of global research conducted about women's participation in information technology and education; and establish an agenda of critical areas for future research about women and IT. The purpose at the heart of this book was to uncover the factors that influence a girl's interest in and choice of IT as a career field, and how this varies across race and culture. What is our assessment of achieving these goals through chapters in this book?

It is clear as one reviews findings in each section of the book that in order to reconfigure the firewall surrounding female entry to IT interest and choice as a career field, we must refocus our lens from what Jane Butler Kahle calls the characteristic lens, which views differences related to girls' motivational patterns that are maladaptive, to a response lens that sees girls' underachievement and lack of participation as a response to cultural patterns and environment. This approach would avoid having the burden of change placed on the girls and encourage change in society and culture. A number of participants at the international conference and authors of chapters in this volume agree with Kahle's assessment and the need for a changed lens as they raise questions about the utility of continuing to conduct research and consider practices that reinforce gender differences in issues such as attitudes, skills, and confidence. Their arguments against this framework, like Kahle's, are that it implicitly places the blame on young women for their underrepresentation in IT and other SET fields for what is a systemic problem involving cultural messages and an educational system that reinforces compliance rather than problem solving.

Authors in this volume have demonstrated the utility of considering gender differences by casting them within a nonindividualistic sociocultural perspective. Their studies point to elements of the environment that reinforce stereotypical views, without dismissing the importance of their differential impact by gender. Years of using the characteristic lens and individualistic framework have failed to achieve significant change in removing the barriers for female entry into IT careers. Virtually every chapter in this book reviews the stagnation in achieving the goal of more female IT professionals, regardless of the level of analysis, from secondary through post-secondary to the IT professional arena. We reason that our efforts may have failed due to the lens we have used to understand the firewall that surrounds this career field. By incorporating an international perspective, we have learned that the firewall operates in different forms in different countries and that cultural and environmental factors can play a role in building the firewall or finding openings. We conclude that our emphasis for the future must be on promoting what Blum et al. call "change in the microculture" and "change in public perceptions," and Kahle calls the "response lens." This perspective moves us in a different direction as we view recommendations for recruitment and retention strategies and future research. This chapter will review recommendations for change in recruitment and policy formulation using a response lens, posit next steps for crafting a research agenda, and revisit Carla, introduced at the beginning of this book, with a different future and outcome due to our new lens.

Each of the integrative chapters reviewed specific recommendations for recruitment strategies, changes in policies, and suggestions for future research in secondary, post-secondary, and IT career fields. The following summary recommendations are drawn from the chapters and are organized by target populations that must be reached for the broader cultural and environmental changes that are needed, including public perceptions and misconceptions of IT, with the aim of opening the IT career field to more females.

Recommendations for Parents and High School Teachers

Moving from a focus on female deficiencies due to gender, the following recommendations from the three high school chapters bring our attention to the wider lens of changing cultural patterns and the environments among the most influential supporters of female career choice—their parents and teachers. Further, recommendations are made for changing misconceptions about the career field of IT and those who choose it, through educating parents and teachers and producing up-to-date career materials.

To present a more accurate and up-to-date picture of IT careers, it is important to provide parents, teachers, and school counselors with IT career information for females and strategies for talking with and presenting this information in creative ways (Meszaros, Lee, & Laughlin).

To present maximum opportunities for female IT career interest and choice, it is essential to provide professional development workshops, seminars, and other experiences for high school teachers, counselors, and administrators that emphasize changing the high school culture and curriculum to feature the importance of IT courses and career pathways for females (Howe, Berenson, & Vouk).

Parents and teachers can educate themselves and support girls by seeking and providing IT career information that emphasizes flexible work schedules, independent decision-making, and the opportunity to combine career with family (Berenson, Williams, Michael, & Vouk).

Recommendations for College Faculty and Advisors

For many young women, the college years are a time when they begin to consciously explore options and make decisions about a future career. The choice of academic major, as well as decisions about whether to take courses related to math and computing technology, directly impact the IT-related opportunities available after graduation. The following recommendations, directed at college faculty and advisors, encourage a reshaping of the cultures and environments in our institutions of higher education.

Recruiting women to IT is not simply a matter of providing ready access to engaging materials. It requires helping students to become acquainted with the strategies required to make complex decisions, to consider individual interests, skill, and values, and to become familiar with the criteria that can be used to weigh the credibility of different sources of information (Creamer, Lee, & Meszaros).

A commitment to recruit more women to undergraduate majors in computing fields is not likely to be successful if only one or two people are responsible for changing the profile of incoming students. It requires the involvement and commitment of anyone who engages with incoming students, including on an informal basis (Cohoon & Lord).

Supportive microclimates can offset cultural stereotypes of IT as a masculine field that is unsuitable for women (Blum, Frieze, Hazzan, & Dias).

Exposure to creative computer applications is essential to compensate for high school course work that often only involves the most pedestrian uses of computers (e.g., keyboarding) (Bair & Marcus).

Linking IT to the potential for economic development has been instrumental to recruiting women to IT fields in South Africa (Marsh).

Recommendations for IT Professionals

The themes that arise from the chapters about women in the IT workforce are ones that can be addressed through policies that take into account the microculture of women's roles in their families and environmental changes that encourage collegial work relationships based on mutual respect.

Recruiting women into IT careers is inextricably bound to retention because the same factors that motivate women to remain in their positions are ones that can draw women into the IT workplace. These factors include sensible policies that help women balance their work and home life, such as flex-time positions and on-site daycare; support for the maintenance of professional and international networks, which can include professional organizations and less formal online communities; and efforts to change the perception of IT as being hostile to women while at the same time addressing climate issues by instituting strict policies about gender harassment (Kuhn & Rayman).

Understanding the pathways by which women enter the IT field can help pinpoint the important transition points where recruitment interventions could be most effective. The most successful changes for gender equity were made at institutions where both women and men held high (e.g., policymaking) positions and both women and men were equally rewarded for their skills (Leventman).

Barriers to full participation of women in the Australian IT workforce still remain. The barriers that must be addressed include a lack of enforcement of job equity and harassment policies by the Australian government; a perceived hostile climate for women in the IT workplace as well as in educational settings; and a lack of understanding about the needs of women, including attention to family life issues (Warner & Wooller).

Future Directions

The combination of the changing nature of the field of gender and science and the wider social-cultural perspective we have offered in this volume generates multiple ideas for research about women's interest, choice, and success in IT fields, as well ideas about policy implications and an agenda for future funding.

Before moving to an itemized list of specific suggestions, there are several broad challenges we would put forward to guide future research and policy. The first imperative is to acknowledge that the field of gender and science has grown to the point that it no longer conceptually sound to merge the SET disciplines, much less to overlook differences among disciplines in broad groupings such as "engineering" or "science." Second, the state of knowledge in the field is such that there are vibrant theoretical frameworks that should be used to frame future research. Third, rigorous, outcome-based evidence is required to support continued funding in programs directed at involving women in creative, energizing experiences related to IT.

Unlike the fields of biology and math that have proven somewhat permeable, almost no progress has been made in changing the gender balance in the IT field in the US. As dour as this forecast seems, this conclusion gives rise to many suggestions for ways to advance global competitiveness through a creative agenda of policy and research agendas. Some of these ideas are listed in the following sections. Others appear in the integrative chapters that introduce each of the three majors sections of the book, as well as in the individual chapters that appear in those sections. All of the suggestions are directed at advancing a cross-cultural view of IT worldwide.

Research about Policy and Potential Funding Priorities

- Compare the requirements for computer-related coursework at the primary and secondary level across countries.
- Develop in-depth case studies of the common elements of microclimates that have compiled demonstrable evidence of creating environments that are successful in overcoming stereotypes and fostering the view of computing fields as places where women can be successful.
- Survey large government agencies, large industries, and small private employers to identify workers who move into professional positions with a strong academic backgrounds. Compile a listing of colleges and universities with IT programs that provide a direct pathway to the IT world.
- Through additional surveys of IT professionals employers, add to the literature about major alternative pathways to IT careers, including, in the US, from community colleges.
- Create structures to link regionally based informal education programs and community college programs to college- and university-based IT undergraduate and graduate programs in the same region.

Agenda for Future Research about IT

- A better understanding is needed about how messages from family, friends, teachers, and the popular media impact the perception individuals have about the culture of IT and the type of people who work with IT. Qualitative work would be required to get beyond cliché descriptions such as "geek" or "intelligent eccentric" and discover the more nuanced impressions females have about IT work and IT culture.

- More work is needed that will examine the experiences of successful women in IT. Research that considers the experiences of individuals as well as the environmental context would be most useful. These kinds of studies need to be ongoing because academic and professional cultures change over time and because the needs and perceptions of females change across time and generation.

- Research is needed to learn more about academic experiences and environments that foster intellectual maturity and self-knowledge together with the capacity to make complex decisions about questions that have no right answer, such as choice of an academic major or career field.

- Further study is needed to help clarify the role of personal communication and recruiting practices in drawing females toward IT. Recent research has produced the counterintuitive findings that more information about the field and personal recruiting by males may actually decrease the likelihood of females entering the field. Additional studies could address these prior findings directly.

Conclusion

Our purpose was to uncover the factors that influence a girl's career interest and choice of IT as a career field and how this varies across race and culture. We conclude that we have done this successfully through the voices of researchers around the world. We adopt and advocate a new way of viewing the advancement of women using a response lens and cultural perspective, promoting change in the microcultures surrounding women and a change in public perceptions of a career in IT. Using this perspective we have presented new ways to think about recruitment strategies and needed policy changes. We have identified new research using the broader lens, and now we conclude with a hopeful reprising of our character, Carla. We left her as a high-achieving female with interest and abilities in IT and family support to have a good career. She did not, however, make the connection from interest and ability in IT to a career choice in IT. Writing a different ending for her life, assuming changes in the microculture and public perceptions of IT as a career field, here is the optimistic forecast for Carla.

Reprising Carla

When we last saw Carla, she was gathering information, with the help and support of her high school counselor and her parents, about computer-based careers. Carla and her mother had the opportunity to participate in a summer program designed to expose young women to creative ways to use a computer that are not only fun but socially responsible. Before that camp, Carla's mother attended a workshop that used the DVD and Facilitator's Guide developed by the VT WIT team.[1] Carla's mother was able to interact with other parents and began to see how her daughter's skills and interests could match a number of different fields, including IT. She also had access to books and brochures describing the full range of IT career opportunities, including applications that serve society, offer positions with companies that pay good salaries, and offer flexible work hours. Carla took an introductory computer class in high school, but while she learned to type faster and could use a whole array of office software, the only part of the class she enjoyed was when students were able to construct their own Web sites.

During college, Carla had a few negative experiences as she discussed her career interests with others. Some suggested that IT was way too intense and competitive for someone with a personality like hers, while others supported her interest and described IT as dynamic and growing field where demand was so high that workers often had the option of flexible schedules and working at home. By this time, Carla had learned to be comfortable with hearing many different points of view, knowing that in the end it was her job to consider the input and weigh the credentials of the person offering the advice.

Carla graduated from college with a major in IT and a minor in creative writing. Carla now has a job she enjoys as a network administrator for a large, international IT company. She works with a number of other women who came into the field from different routes. Carla chose to follow an IT career path and has a long-term goal to work for policies worldwide that open the doors to an IT career to females in all corners of the world, effectively reconfiguring the firewalls that are coming down for countless young women internationally.

Notes

1. Information about obtaining this resource can be found at http://www.witvideo.org.vt.edu.

Appendix A

Material for Chapter 1, "Predicting Women's Interest in and Choice of a Career in Information Technology: A Statistical Model"

Tables A1-A4. Demographic characteristics of the respondents to the third version of the questionnaire ($n = 777$).

Table A1. Enrollment status of respondents by gender.

Group	Females	Males	Total (%)
High school	293	263	556 (71.6)
College	80	141	221 (28.4)
Total (%)	373 (48.0)	404 (52.0)	777 (100)

Table A2. Respondents' race by enrollment status and gender.

	Females ($n = 369$)		Males ($n = 388$)		
Race	High School	College	High School	College	Total (%)
Caucasian American	92	63	104	114	373 (49.3)
African American	122	3	74	5	204 (26.9)
Asian American	37	9	29	7	82 (10.8)
Hispanic American	11	2	15	3	31 (4.1)
Others	27	3	27	10	67 (8.9)
Total (%)	289 (38.2)	80 (10.6)	249 32.9)	139 (18.4)	757 (100)

Table A3. Respondents' age by enrollment status and gender.

Age	Females (*n* = 373)		Males (*n* = 399)		Total (%)
	High School	College	High School	College	
14 yrs or younger	22	0	15	0	373 (49.3)
15–19 yrs	271	55	239	76	204 (26.9)
20–24 yrs	0	23	4	62	82 (10.8)
25 yrs or older	0	2	0	3	31 (4.1)
Total (%)	293 (38.0)	80 (10.4)	258 (33.4)	141 (18.3)	772 (100)

Table A4. Mother's and father's level of education by respondents' gender and enrollment status.

Level of Mother's Education	Females (*n* = 343)		Males (*n* = 386)		Total (%)
	High School	College	High School	College	
High school or less	114	23	94	41	272 (37.3)
College degree	125	40	110	69	344 (47.2)
Master's or more	26	15	42	30	113 (15.5)
Total (%)	265 (36.4)	78 (10.7)	246 (33.7)	140 (19.2)	729 (100)

Level of Father's Education	Females (*n* = 338)		Males (*n* = 387)		Total (%)
	High School	College	High School	College	
High school or less	132	22	94	28	276 (38.1)
College degree	81	31	98	69	279 (38.5)
Master's or more	49	23	56	42	170 (23.4)
Total (%)	262 (36.1)	76 (10.5)	248 (34.2)	139 (19.2)	725 (100)

Appendix B

Material for Chapter 1, "Predicting Women's Interest in and Choice of a Career in Information Technology: A Statistical Model"

Questionnaire Items in Each Factor

Table B1. IT career interest and choice (dependent variable).

Cronbach's alpha = 0.709 (n = 7)

1. I have a good idea about what people in computer-related fields do in their jobs.
2. I feel a sense of satisfaction when I am able to use a computer to solve a problem.
3. If I chose to, I probably have the ability to be successful in a job in a computer-related field.
4. I have family, friends, and/or acquaintances who work in information technology or a computer-related job.
5. I would be comfortable working in a male-dominated occupation.
6. Working in a computer-related field is one of the career options I am considering.
7. My parents would probably consider a career in a computer-related field a good choice for me.

Table B2. Parental support.

Cronbach's alpha = 0.692 (n = 9)

1. It is important to my mother/female guardian that I have a career.
2. It is important to my father/male guardian that I have a career.
3. My mother/female guardian has a clear idea about careers that would suit me.
4. My father/male guardian has a clear idea about careers that would suit me.
5. My parents/guardians encourage me to make my own decisions about my future career.
6. I would like my parents to approve of my choice of career.
7. My parents have encouraged me to talk to others about career options.
8. My parents have encouraged me to explore a variety of career options.
9. When we disagree, my parents listen to my point of view.

Table B3. Computer use.

Cronbach's alpha = 0.669 (n = 7)

How often do you use a computer for the following activities?

1. Communication (such as email, instant messages, or chat rooms)

2. Games (any computer-based game)

3. General entertainment (such as Internet surfing or music downloads)

4. News and current events (news sites, online magazines)

5. General tasks (such as word processing or creation of databases or spread sheets)

6. Development or design (such as creating web pages or graphics, programming)

7. Educational purposes (such as to conduct research or complete a homework assignment)

Table B4. Attitudes about the attributes of IT workers.

Cronbach's alpha = 0.603 (n = 7)

I think people who chose careers in computers are:

Negative Attitude

1. Geeks (Recoded)

2. Likely to be male (Recoded)

4. Loners/antisocial (Recoded)

Positive Attitude

3. Interesting

5. Hard-working

6. Smart

7. Creative

Table B5a. Decision orientation.

Cronbach's alpha = 0.674 (n = 12)

---

1. I have given a good deal of thought to choosing a career that is compatible with my values, interests, and abilities.

2. I have a plan for what I would like to do as a career.

3. When it comes to choice of a career, my parents know what is best for me so I am inclined to go with what they suggest. (Recoded)

4. I am confident about my ability to set my own priorities about schoolwork.

5. I am confident about my ability to set my own priorities about my personal life.

Table B5a. Decision orientation (continued).

6.	I am confident about my ability to choose a career.
7.	I am unsure about my ability to make my own decisions about a future job. (Recoded)
8.	I am unsure about my ability to make my own decisions about my personal life. (Recoded)
9.	If my parents disagree with a decision I have made, I am likely to change my decision. (Recoded)
10.	If my close friends disagree with a decision I have made, I am likely to change my decision. (Recoded)
11.	I am most likely to trust the advice of people who know me best. (Recoded)
12.	There are times when even authorities are uncertain about the truth.

Table B5b. Receptivity.

Cronbach's alpha = 0.704 (n = 5)

1.	I like to have my parents' input before I make a big decision.
2.	Even when the advice is contradictory, I try to synthesize the information people give me before I make a big decision.
3.	I find it helpful to listen to the input of others before I make an important decision.
4.	When I make an important decision, I often seek the input of members of my family.
5.	When I make an important decision, I often seek the input of my friends.

Table B5c. Information sources.

Cronbach's alpha = 0.784 (n = 10)

How often have you discussed your career options or plans with others?
1. Mother/female guardian
2. Father/male guardian
3. Teacher or professor
4. Counselor or advisor
5. Other family members
6. Male friends
7 Female friends
8. Significant other
9. Employer or boss
10. Family friends

Table B5d. Information credibility.

Cronbach's alpha = 0.842 (n = 10)

How likely are you to consider career advice when these people offer it?

1. Mother/female guardian
2. Father/male guardian
3. Other family members
4. Teacher or professor
5. Counselor or advisor
6. Male friends
7. Female friends
8. Significant other
9. Employer or boss
10. Family friends

Appendix C

Material for Chapter 7, "Women's Entry to Graduate Study in Computer Science and Computer Engineering in the United States"

Program Choice Factors Investigated

1. **Institutional factors:**
a. Expense
b. Availability of financial aid
c. Geographic preferences or constraints
d. Availability of course offerings during the academic year
e. Courses offered at convenient times of day
f. Flexibility in program content
g. Reputation of institution
h. Reputation of program or professor(s)
i. Ability to pursue a particular computing specialization
j. Teaching opportunities
k. Research opportunities
l. Facilities and equipment
m. Departmental recruitment literature or Web page
n. Size of institution
o. Number of faculty in the program
p. Employer tuition reimbursement program
q. Earned prior degree from same institution
r. Minimal academic or bureaucratic obstacles
s. *Please specify other important institutional factor(s):*

2. **Interpersonal factors:**
t. Opportunity to work with a particular research advisor
u. Your impression of students during a campus visit
v. Your impression of faculty during a campus visit
w. Departmental culture

x. Social atmosphere of the campus
y. Presence of women students
z. Presence of women faculty
aa. Prior enrollment of family or friend(s)
bb. Recommendation of faculty or mentor
cc. Faculty member's visit at your undergraduate department
dd. Phone call or mail from graduate faculty member(s)
ee. *Please specify other important interpersonal factor(s):*

Contributors

William Aspray, Rudy Professor of Informatics, Indiana University, USA, invited advisor to the volume. He has prepared several reports on IT workforce issues. Current studies include one on offshore outsourcing and a study on recruiting and retaining women graduate students. Aspray is the co-chair of the Social Science Network of the National Center for Women in Information Technology and studies the policies and history of information technology.

Bettina Bair, Senior Lecturer and Director of Diversity for the CSE Department, Ohio State University, USA. She directs the TWiCE (The Women In Computer Engineering) program, is a faculty sponsor of the student chapter of the Association for Computing Machinery Committee on Women (ACM-W), and is a member of the University President's Council on Women's Issues. She is a recipient of the Mary Ann Williams Leadership award as well as the Ohio State University Distinguished Diversity Enhancement Award. She is also a member of the ACM-W working committee.

Sarah Berenson, Director of the Center for Mathematics and Science Education and Professor of Math Education, North Carolina State University, USA. She built a nationally and internationally recognized mathematics education program. Known for her creative approaches to investigating educational problems, her work focuses on the preparation of teachers and the under-representation of women minorities in science, technology, engineering and mathematics careers.

Lenore Blum, Distinguished Career Professor of CS, Carnegie Mellon University, USA. She is the co-Director of the NSF ALADDIN Center for ALgorithm ADaptation, Dissemination and INtegration. Blum is well known for her work in increasing the participation of girls and women in mathematics and scientific fields. She was instrumental in founding the Association for Women in Mathematics (serving as its third president from 1975 to 1978), the Math/Science Network and its Expanding Your Horizons conferences for high school girls (serving as co-Director from 1975 to 1981) and served as co-PI for the Mills Summer Mathematics Institute for undergraduate women. At Carnegie Mellon she has been faculty advisor to the Women@SCS.

Carol J. Burger, Associate Professor, Department of Interdisciplinary Studies, Virginia Tech, USA. She is the coordinator for the Science and Gender Equity Program at Virginia Tech. She is the founder and editor of the *Journal of Women and Minori-*

ties in Science and Engineering, now in its 10th year of publication. She served as Senior Program Director, Program for Women and Girls, National Science Foundation in 1996. She has published over 50 immunology and SET equity research papers, book chapters, and monographs, and she is the co-investigator on several NSF-funded projects.

Elizabeth G. Creamer, Professor, Educational Policy and Leadership, Virginia Tech, USA. Dr. Creamer has expertise in the areas of qualitative research methodology, most specifically case study, grounded in teaching graduate courses and employing qualitative research methodologies in various settings. She is co-PI on several NSF funding projects related to women's interest and choice in careers in information technology. Creamer has an extensive publication record, including three authored and co-authored books and 45 refereed journal articles and book chapters.

Joanne McGrath Cohoon, Assistant Professor, Department of Science, Technology, and Society; Senior Research Scientist, National Center for Women in IT, University of Virginia, USA. Her research interests include technology and gender; gender and education; higher education; and organizational structures.

M. Bernardine Dias, Research Scientist, Robotics Institute, Carnegie Mellon University, USA. Her focus is on the design and implementation of creative advanced technological solutions that will benefit developing communities around the world. She is the founding director of the TechBridgeWorld initiative and a founding member of Women@SCS.

Stella Y. Erinosho, Professor of Science Education. She had her university education at Ibadan, Nigeria graduating with an honors degree in B.Ed. (Physics), M.Ed and Ph.D (Educational Evaluation). Her scholarship addresses the issues of gender equity and systemic reform of science education in secondary school in Nigeria.

Carol Frieze, School of Computer Science, Carnegie Mellon University, USA. She is the Director of Women@SCS, and Co-Director of Women@IT. She works closely with the Women@SCS Advisory Committee and the Women@SCS web site team. She helps to organize and oversee the wide-ranging program of professional, academic and social activities that Women@SCS develops for the benefit of the greater community of women in the School of Computer Science at Carnegie Mellon.

Orit Hazzan, Associate Professor, Department of Education in Technology and Science, Technion—Israel Institute of Technology, Haifa, Israel. She is particularly interested in information technologies as agents of cultural and educational changes. Her research focuses on human aspects (cognitive and social) of computer science and software engineering. She is a co-author of the book *Human Aspects of Software Engineering*.

Ann C. Howe, University of Maryland, Emeritus, Consultant, Raleigh NC, USA. Retired as Head of the Department of Curriculum and Instruction at the University of Maryland after serving on the faculties of Syracuse University and North Carolina State University. Her research in science and mathematics education has been widely published in leading journals.

Jane Butler Kahle, Condit Endowed Professor, Department of Teacher Education, Miami University, USA, invited advisor to the volume. Her professional career includes: high school biology teacher in rural Indiana, Professor of Biological Sciences and Education and Associate Dean of the Graduate School at Purdue University, and Director, Division of Elementary, Secondary, and Informal Science at the National Science Foundation. Dr. Kahle's scholarship focuses on gender equity and systemic reform of science and mathematics education.

Sarah Kuhn, Professor, Department of Regional Economic and Social Development, and Center for Women and Work, University of Massachusetts Lowell. She was a member of the National Research Council Committee on Workforce Needs in Information Technology and a Fellow at the Radcliffe Institute for Advanced Study.

Anne Laughlin, PhD candidate, Department of Educational Leadership and Policy Studies, Virginia Tech, USA. Past roles include: Assistant Director for Virginia Tech's Career Services Office, and Applications Analyst for Virginia Tech's Web Application Research and Development group. Currently, she is a research assistant on two NSF funded projects examining gender equity issues in the science and technology fields. She has co-authored several presentations and papers related to women's career decision making and women's under representation in IT.

Soyoung Lee, PhD candidate, Department of Human Development, Virginia Tech, USA. She has written and presented 13 papers and over 10 posters about Korean immigrants, women in information technology, decision making, community capacity, family life education, and parent-child relationships at national- and international- level conferences and symposiums. She is a research assistant on the NSF funded research project, "Women in Information Technology: Pivotal Transitions from School to Careers."

Paula Leventman, PhD, Diversity Coordinator, NSF Engineering Research Center, Northeastern University, USA. She was Principal Investigator, Multiple Pathways toward Gender Equity in the Information Technology Workforce (2001-2005) and 4 Schools for Women in Engineering (2001-2005). Leventman was Director of Women's Programs at NU College of Engineering for 20 years.

Holly Lord, PhD candidate, Department of Sociology, and research assistant, Department of Science, Technology, and Society, University of Virginia, USA. Her research interests include gender, organizations, and social capital.

Miranda Marcus, Welding Engineer, Dukane Ultrasonics. She received her BSWE in 2005, graduating cum laude and with honors, subsequently achieving her MSWE in 2006. Miranda has co-authored three papers for, and presented twice at, the Society of Plastics Engineers Annual Technical Conference (ANTEC).

Cecille Marsh, School of Information Technology, Walter Sisulu University, South Africa.

Peggy S. Meszaros, William E. Lavery Professor of Human Development and Director, Center for Information Technology Impacts on Children, Youth and Families, Virginia Tech, USA. She has extensive teaching, research, and administrative experience including middle school and high school teaching of science and has been a faculty member and administrator for 28 years at private and public higher education research institutions. She has published over 80 scholarly articles and book chapters on topics such as academic benchmarking, mother and daughter communication, adolescent decision-making, and technology applications including e-health, cell phone use, and parent education.

Joan J. Michael, Professor, Department of Psychology, Dean Emeritus, North Carolina State University, USA. Her current interests in Industrial, Organizational and Vocational Psychology include tests, measurement, and evaluation, especially Internet testing for selection and placement.

Lesley Parker, Personal Chair in Higher Education, Curtin University of Technology, Australia, Invited advisor to the volume. Her research interests span all sectors of education, focused in particular on educational reform, professional development of educators and policy and practice in the area of gender equity. She is currently a member of the Western Australian Premier's Science Council.

Paula M. Rayman, Professor, Economics and Social Development, University of Massachusetts Lowell, USA. She is a nationally recognized scholar on issues of women and work and labor diversity issues in science and technology. Currently she is Principal Investigator of a National Science Foundation project on social science research on women in science, technology, engineering and math workplaces.

Mladen Vouk, Department Head and Professor, Computer Science, and Associate Vice Provost for Information Technology, North Carolina State University, USA. He has extensive experience in both commercial software production and academic computing. His research and development interests include software engineering, scientific computing, IT-assisted education, and high-performance networks.

Lesley Warner, Emeritus Professor, School of Biological and Environmental Sciences; former Director, Women Into Science & Technology (WIST), Central Queensland University, Australia. Professor Warner is now working as an Honorary Research Associate in Parasitology at the South Australian Museum, Adelaide.

Laurie Williams, Associate Professor, Computer Science Department, North Carolina State University, USA. She leads the Software Engineering Realsearch group and is the Director of the North Carolina State University Laboratory for Collaborative System Development and the co-director of the NC State eCommerce education initiative.

Judith Wooller, Faculty of Arts, Health and Sciences, Central Queensland University, Australia. She is the former Coordinator of the Women Into Science & Technology (WIST) program. She has lectured, tutored, and marked in Literature, Drama, Sociology, History, and Communication and Media Studies during which time she has become increasingly interested in women's issues and the barriers which are in place to discourage women from studying in non-traditional areas.

Index

A

Abu-Hanna Nahhas, I., 126
access to technology, 6–7. *See also* computer use
Adams, J. C., 110, 115
Adler, P., & Adler, P., 44, 80, 91
Advanced Placement courses, 51, 60, 68, 125
advisors, recommendations for, 256
affirmative action/equal opportunity, 196, 240
Ahuja, M., 185
Al-Jabri, L. M., 29
Al-Khaldi, M. A., 29
Allen, M., 241, 245
Allen, M. W., 81
Almstrum, V. L., 15
Altman, J. H., 26
Ambrose, S., 200, 207
American Association of University Women (AAUW), 44, 51, 52, 60, 65, 172
Armsden, G. C., 15
Aspray, W., 4, 9, 100, 105, 159, 181
Association for Computing Machinery (ACM), 182
Astin, A. W., 7
attitudes about IT and IT workers, 30, 55, 59, 85, 88, 169, 170
Australia, 245

B

Babco, E. L., 200
Baichoo, S., 110, 115
Bailey, K., 195
Bailyn, L., 195, 196
Bandura, A., 15, 135

Bardhan, A. D., 231, 232
Barling, J., 74
Barnett, R., 113
Baroudi, J. J., 81
barriers, 42–43
Bartol, K. M., 181
Bastalich, W., 241, 245
Bauer, V., 110, 115
Baxter Magolda, M. B., 8, 16, 19, 20, 35, 78, 79, 83, 90, 99
Baylor, K. M., 7, 154
Becker, A., 54
Bell, N. E., 200
Berenson, S., 43, 54, 66, 68, 70, 73, 74, 172
Bernstein, D., 139, 140
Bernt, P. W., 184
Betz, N. E., 15, 135
Bleak, J. L., 242, 245, 247
Bluestone, B., 200
Blum, L., 110, 111, 116, 117, 119, 121, 123
Blustein, D. L., 26, 27
Boaler, J., 42
Bookman, A., 200
Borders, D., 15, 27
Bradley, K., 158
Bravo, M., 52
Brett, B., 200
Broihier, M., 81
Brown, C. D., 225
Brown, S. D., 27
Browne, J., 246
Brubaker, L., 43
Bunderson, E. D., 28
Bureau of Labor Statistics (BLS), 171, 212
Burger, C. J., 30, 81
Burton, C., 247

Byrd, T., 47
Byrne, E. M., 240, 247

C

Camp, T., 7, 185
Campbell, L. A., 200
Campbell, P., 183
Caravalho, G., 225
career information and advice, 31, 44, 92, 106
career interests
  in post-secondary school, 163–165
  in secondary school, 58–59, 59, 92
Career Interest and Choice Questionnaire, 22, 82
careers in IT
  job security, 198–201, 207
  nature of work, 46, 59
  pathways into, 183–186, 201–203, 213–219
  pathways within, 245–246
Carnegie Mellon University (CMU), 116
Castleman, T., 241, 245
Catalyst, Inc., 225
Cennamo, K. S., 139, 140
Center for Women and Information Technology (CWIT), 173
Chang, B., 122
Charles, M., 158
Chen, L.-Y., 7
Chen, M., 81
Chesterman, C., 247
Chi, M. T. H., 81
Christensen, M. E., 28
CIO Magazine, 231
Cockburn, A., 111, 123
Cohoon, J. M., 7, 100, 105, 148, 154, 159
collaborative development methods, 68–69, 114, 123–125, 172. *See also* programming
  and time savings, 68
Collaborative Software Laboratory at Georgia Institute of Technology, 172
Commission on Professionals in Science and Technology, 212
computer use, 28–29, 85, 88, 92, 139, 143–144
conferences about women in IT, 3–4, 100
confidence, 7, 116, 119, 141–143, 143–144, 144, 181
Cook, E. P., 43, 77
Cook, J. M., 147
Cooper, J., 28, 184

Costa, G., 75
Creamer, E. G., 20, 30, 81
Cross University Research in Engineering and Science Group, 241
cultural perspective, 101–102, 106, 110, 111–116, 125–126, 245–248, 253–254
culture, institutional, 150, 196, 245–246, 248
culture of IT, 52, 75, 185–186
Cumpston, A., 79–80
Cuny, J. E., 159

D

D'Agostino, D., 6
Davis, J., 204
De Leon, B., 79, 92
decision-making, 20, 31–32, 79, 90
decision orientation, 31, 85
demand for IT workers, 186, 202–203, 212, 234–235, 242. *See also* internet boom and bust
  and layoffs, 226–233
Department of Commerce, US, 212
Department of Labor, US, 180
DiDio, L., 163
discrimination, 243, 245–246, 246
Dobson, I. R., 241, 242
Downs, B., 197
Dryburgh, H., 6, 28
Dubinsky, Y., 111, 124
Dunkle, K., 200, 207
Durham, P. H., 80

E

Eastern cultures, 114, 128
Eaton, S.C., 195, 196
Eccles, J., 41, 172
Educational Testing Service, 166
Eidelman, L., 110, 125, 126
Elder, V. B., 81
Ellen, D., 185
Ellis, R., 227, 231, 232
Engineering Projects in Community Service program at Purdue University, 172
Epstein, C. F., 113
Ergon-Polak, E., 247
Ertl, H., 6
Ertmer, P. A., 139, 140
European Commission, 242, 245
Everbeck, E., 139, 140
evidence, need for, 257

F

Facer, K., 81
factors that influence IT interest and
    choice, 17–19, 33, 71–73, 85–90
    availability of part-time work, 73
    challenge, 203
    enjoyment of computing, 57, 150, 158
    flexibility, 71–72
    fun, 103, 162–163, 163–165, 171
    gender differences, 33
    independence, 71
    pay/income, 204
    race, 26
faculty, recommendations for, 256
Fan, C., 122
Fassinger, R. E., 7, 15, 27, 106
Felsman, D. E., 27
female-friendly, 41, 110
female head of household, 139
Fennema, E., 54
Ferguson, K., 246
Filipczak, R., 74
Finley, M., 180, 184
Fisher, A., 52, 53, 65, 74, 116, 122, 143,
    161, 171, 172, 184, 191, 202, 208
Fisher, H., 124
Fisher, T. A., 26
fitting in, 122–123
Fleetwood, C., 81
flexibility
    in academic programs, 102, 151, 159
    in work roles, 71–72, 195–196, 206
Flowers, L. A., 26
Foley, C., 246
Fox, M. F., 147
Friedman, S. M., 15
Frieze, C., 110, 111, 116, 117, 119, 121, 122,
    123
Funk, S. A., 196

G

games, video/computer, 28, 52
Gardner, E. P., 81
Garner, S. N., 225
Gaskel, J., 47
Gavin, R., 227
Geekman, 173
Gender Advisory Board, 180
Gender and Science and Technology Asso-
    ciation, 3
gender, cultural vs. biological construc-
    tion, 100–101, 111–116, 122–123

gender differences, 81–82, 85–90,
    141–143, 151
    and attitudes toward IT workers, 29,
    141
    in experience and skill, 219–221
gender equity, 136–137, 157, 196, 236,
    246
Georgia Institute of Technology, 172
Gibson, S., 6
Gilbert, L., 52
Girls on Track (GOT), 53, 66
Glasscock, J. M., 27
globalization, 186, 232
Gonsoulin, M., 159
Gorman, E. H., 147, 159
graduate education, 148
Greenberg, M. T., 15
Greenfield, B. S., 242, 245
Greenspon, P., 68, 70, 74
Griggs, M. B., 26
Gupta, U., 81
Gurer, D., 7

H

Hackbarth, S., 26
hacker/geek stereotypes and culture, 123,
    173–174
Hackett, G., 135
Hafkin, N., 6
Halpern, D., 114
Hanks, B., 172
Harkus, D., 200, 207
Harrington, P. E., 227
Harrison, A. W., 81, 135
Harrison, B. C., 26
Hazzan, O., 111, 124, 125, 126
Henwood, F., 81
Herman, C., 185
Herring, S. C., 185
Hesketh, B., 135
Hewitt, N. M., 31
high-achieving girls, 51, 68
Highsmith, J., 123
historically black colleges and universities
    (HBCUs), 115
Ho, C. W., 43, 68, 73, 172
Hofer, B. K., 20
Holohan, M., 161
Hoppel, C., 81
Houtz, L., 81
Howe, A., 54, 66
Howe, N., 43, 45, 74
Howie, S. J., 139

Huyer, S., 6
Hyde, J. S., 114

I

Igbaria, M., 81
information and communications technol-
    ogy (ICT), 5
information credibility, 31, 32
information orientation, 30–31
information processing, 90–92
information sources, 32, 85, 92
information technology (IT), 5, 16, 111,
    179–180
Information Technology Association of
    America, 6, 77, 180
Information Technology Association of
    Canada, 161
Internet boom and bust, 192, 227–234,
    234–235. *See also* demand for IT
    workers
Isaacs, E., 81
Israel, 125

J

Jamieson, L. H., 173
Jenkins, H., 52
Jesse, J. K., 200
Jingelski, J., 43
job satisfaction, 221–222, 224–227, 235
Joy, B., 211
Julien, H., 79

K

Kahle, J. B., 4, 9, 41, 99, 253, 254
Kanter, R. M., 113, 122
Kaplan, R., 81
Kearney, L., 52
Kegan, R., 19
Kelly, A., 41
Kennedy, K., 211
Kent, N., 81
Ketterson, T. U., 26
King, P. M., 20
Klein, S., 181
Klingman, A., 126
Kmec, J. A., 147
Koch, J., 61
Koch-Miramond, L., 242
Korn, W. S., 7
Kotrlik, J. W., 26
Krendl, K., 81
Kress, H. M., 27
Kroll, C. A., 231, 232

Kuhn, S., 194, 203, 204
Kvale, S., 244

L

Labor Law Talk, 179
Lakes, M. K., 41
Lancaster, H., 161
Lancaster, L., 74
Lapan, R. T., 43
Latih, R., 115
Laughlin, A., 20, 30, 92
Laughlin, C., 74
Laurel, B., 51, 52
Layman, J., 159
Lazarus, B., 200, 207
Lazonick, W., 206
Lee, A. C. K., 7
Lee, P., 110
Lee, S., 20
Lee, V. E., 47
Lehman, J. D., 139, 140
Leventman, P. G., 180, 184, 225
Lim, V. K. G., 81, 92
Lindholm, J. A., 7
Linn, S. G., 15
Lopez, A. M., 115
Lowell, L., 227, 231, 232
Lowry, D. W., 26

M

Maccoby, M., 206
MacCready, R., 227
Mackie, D., 28
Mahoney, K. M., 7
Malcom, S., 200
Manzi, A. J., 27
Marcoulides, G. A., 24, 85
Margolis, J., 52, 53, 65, 74, 116, 122, 143,
    161, 171, 172, 184, 191, 202, 208
Marks, H. M., 47
Marsh, C., 135, 138
Maruyama, G. M., 24, 85
Massachusetts Institute of Technology
    (MIT), 247
Massachusetts Software & Internet Coun-
    cil (MSIC), 192
Maus, T., 225
McBrier, D. B., 147
McDowell, C., 172
McLean, E. R., 81
McPherson, M., 147
McWhirter, E. H., 27

mentors/mentoring, 181, 199–200,
    225–226, 240
Meszaros, P. S., 30, 81, 92
Michael, J., 68, 70, 74
microculture, 116, 122, 127, 254
millennial generation, 73–74
minorities, 26
misconceptions about IT, 161, 170–171,
    207–208
Miura, I. T., 28, 135
Morris, J. H., 110
Morse, J. M., 244
Mounfield, L., 183

N

Nair, I., 200, 207
National Research Council, 183, 194
National Science Board, 6, 212
National Science Foundation, 6, 35, 62,
    66, 75, 93, 104, 160, 202, 208, 212,
    236
Nelson, D. J., 242, 247
Nelson, L. J., 184
Nespor, J., 74
networks for IT professionals, 207, 226
Newmarch, E., 79–80
Niederman, F., 180
Noble, G., 29
North Carolina State University, 65
Northeastern University IT Workforce
    Study, 211, 213
Northeastern University Master of Science
    in Information Systems, 213

O

O'Brien, K. M., 7, 15, 27, 106
O'Connor, S., 29
O'Neill, L., 75
Office of Immigration Statistics, US, 232
Office of Status of Women, Australia, 246
Ogan, C., 185
Ohio State University, 173
Open University, UK, 185
Othman, M., 115
outsourcing, 186, 207, 226–233

P

Paa, H. K., 27
Pajares, F., 181
parents
    educating, 44, 128, 255
    education level, 27–28

influencing career interests and choice,
    60, 81
    providing support, 26–28, 28
Parker, L., 4, 9, 104
participation rates for females in IT, 6, 51,
    77, 114–115, 161, 180–181, 211–212
Pasearella, E. T., 26
Patterson, D., 186
pay/income, 221–223, 235
Pecora, N., 184
pedagogy, 105
Pedro, J., 54
peers/peer influence, 80
Peleg-Popko, O., 126
Pennsylvania State University School of
    Information Sciences and Technol-
    ogy, 21, 180
Perlman, L., 183
Perlow, L., 208
Perry, W. G., 19
Person, A., 68, 70, 74
perspectives
    on females under representation in IT,
        7, 42, 99, 254, 258
    on gender differences, 42, 100–101,
        141–143, 253–254
Peters, H., 124
Peters, M., 247
Pierson, C. T., 26
Pintrich, P. R., 20
pipeline metaphor, 185, 203
Podd, J., 135
policies, 105, 136–137
political climate, 137, 144, 247
Post, P., 43
Pritchard, A., 44, 80, 91
problem solving, 123, 204
professionals in IT, recommendations for,
    256
programming
    agile methods, 68, 114, 123–125. See
        also collaborative development
        methods
    experience, 119–120, 120–121, 128
Project TechForce, 194
Purdue University, 172

Q

Qatar, 126
Qureshi, S., 81

R

Radcliffe Public Policy Institute, 195, 198

Rainer, R. J. Jr., 81, 135
Raines, C., 74
Rainey, L. M., 15, 27
Raykov, T., 24, 85
Rayman, P., 194, 200, 201
receptivity to information and advice, 32, 85
recommendations for increasing female participation in IT, 92–93, 105, 171–174, 254–256
recruiting
   in post-secondary education, 34–35, 102–103, 104, 151–157, 159–160
   in secondary education, 46–47, 92–93
   to IT Careers, 187
Reid, M., 81
research, suggestions for future work, 34, 47–48, 62, 105, 187–188, 257–258
Reskin, B. F., 147
retention, 105, 187
Richards, L., 244
Riemenschneider, C., 81
Rivers, C., 113
Robinson, J., 185
Rogers, D. C., 242, 247
Rogers, J., 185
Roldon, M., 179, 180, 183
role models, 139–141, 143, 144, 240
Ross-Smith, A., 247
Rossmann, M. M., 26
Roy, M., 81
Ruth, S. R., 81
Ryan, N. E., 27

S

Sadker, D., 181
Sadker, M., 181
Sánchez-Franco, M. J., 81
Sanders, J., 52, 61, 100, 103
Sargent, J., 171
Sawyer, S., 185
Sax, L. J., 7
Schinzel, B., 110, 115
Schulte, L. J., 115
Schultheiss, D. E. P., 27
secondary education
   curriculum, 44, 60
segregation by gender, 105, 125
self-authorship, 19–20, 32, 78–79
self-efficacy, 135. See also confidence
Seymour, E., 31
Shashaani, L., 28
Shauman, K. A., 183

Silverman, S., 44, 80, 91
Slaten, K., 43, 68, 73, 172
Smith, C., 225
Smith-Lovin, L., 147
Smits, S. J., 81
social and community benefits of IT, 173
socioeconomic context, 136
socioeconomic status, 136–137
Soe, L., 179, 180, 183
Solberg, V. S., 27
Sonnert, G., 183
South Africa, 135
Statistics South Africa, 136
STEM (science, technology, engineering and math), 78, 147, 257
stereotypes, 29–30
   dispelling, 61, 173–174
Stillman, D., 74
Strauss, B., 43, 45, 74
Sum, A. M., 227
Sumner, M., 180
Systers, 184

T

Tang, M., 77
Tanner, J. R., 81
Tapscott, D., 74
Taylor, H. G., 183
Taylor, K. M., 15
Taylor-Steele, S., 79–80
teachers, 61
   recommendations for, 254–255
Teague, J., 180
technical degrees, 198–199
Teich, A. H., 200
Teo, T. S. H., 81, 92
theoretical frameworks, 257. See also perspectives, on females under representation in IT
Thibodeau, P., 161
Third International Mathematics and Science Study, 139
Thorne, B., 100, 113, 115
Tillberg, H. K., 148
time
   and working hours in IT careers, 194–195
   as a factor in IT success, 74
   as a value, 43
Tipton, L. C., 15
Trauth, E. M., 99, 100, 184
Treat, E., 110
Trower, A., 242, 245, 247
Turner, S. V., 184

U

UCLA Higher Education Research Institute, 136
Ullman, E., 180
Urso, J., 61

V

Vallone, T. J., 225
van Eck, E., 26, 28, 81, 92
Vashti, G., 110
Vasil, L., 135
Vegso, J., 161
Volman, M., 26, 28, 81, 92
Vouk, M., 66, 68, 70, 74

W

Wadia-Fascetti, S., 225
Walker, E., 75
Wardell, M., 185
Warner, L., 241, 243
Way, W. L., 26
Weise, G. M., 184
Wenneras, C., 159
Werner, L., 172
Wilder, G., 28
Williams, L., 43, 68, 73, 172
Williams, M., 43

Wold, A., 159
Wolleat, P., 54
Women@SCS, 117, 174
women-CS fit, 116, 125
Women in Computer Engineering
     (TWICE) program at Ohio State
     Univeristy, 173
Women in IT project at North Carolina
     State University, 66–67
Women in IT project at Virginia Tech, 82
Women In Technology International
     (WITI), 192
work/life balance, 45, 73, 182–183, 186,
     194–195, 206, 235, 244–245
     working mothers, 196–198, 206, 235
Wright, P., 241, 245

X

Xie, Y., 183

Y

Yakura, E. K., 179, 180, 183

Z

Zeldin, A. L., 181
Zemke, R., 74
Zhang, Y., 26